Haroldo de Campos

Haroldo de Campos
A Dialogue with the Brazilian Concrete Poet

Edited by
K. David Jackson

Centre for Brazilian Studies
University of Oxford

K. David Jackson is Professor of Portuguese at Yale University.

The Oxford Centre for Brazilian Studies is grateful to the Brazilian Ministry of Culture for providing the financial support that made possible the publication of this book.

© Centre for Brazilian Studies, University of Oxford, 2005

Published by
Centre for Brazilian Studies
University of Oxford
92 Woodstock Road
Oxford OX2 7ND

ISBN 09544070-5-9

Front cover photograph: Haroldo de Campos lecturing at Stuttgart University, 1964 (courtesy of Elizabeth Walther-Bense)
Back cover photograph: Haroldo de Campos, 1980s (courtesy of Carmen de Arruda Campos)
Cover design by Andrew Chapman, Chapman Design,
Typeset by Koinonia, Manchester
Printed by Lightning Source

Contents

Preface vii

Notes on Contributors xi

PART I Haroldo de Campos

The Ex-centric's Viewpoint: Tradition, Transcreation,
Transculturation *Haroldo de Campos* 3

PART II On Haroldo de Campos: Poet, Critic, Translator

Haroldo de Campos and the Poetics of Invention
  K. David Jackson 17

The Origins of Haroldo de Campos *Gonzalo Aguilar* 27

Haroldo de Campos: the Theorist and the Critic
  Leyla Perrone-Moisés 39

Haroldo de Campos's Work: Story-telling and Wit
  Nelson Ascher 49

A Long Hold: Haroldo de Campos, Brazilian Avant-Garde
Tradition, and Spanish-American Literature *Horácio Costa* 59

Lifting the Great Ball of Crystal: Haroldo de Campos and
  the Crystallographic Tradition *Craig Dworkin* 71

A Half-Century of Haroldo de Campos
  João Alexandre Barbosa 81

PART III Concrete Prose: *Galáxias* and After

Facing *Galáxias* *Wladimir Krysinski* 99

Translation as Creation and Criticism: *Galáxias* as Text and
  Theory of Translation *Inês Oseki-Dépré* 107

Music of the Spheres in *Galáxias* *K. David Jackson* 119

Arabesques in *Galáxias* *Luiz Costa Lima* 129

Concrete Prose in the Nineties: *Galáxias* and After
  Marjorie Perloff 139

PART IV Concrete Poetry from Noigandres to Finismundo

Brazilian Concrete Poetry: How it Looks Today. An interview
with Augusto and Haroldo de Campos *Marjorie Perloff* 165

Concrete Poetry at the Crossroads *Willard Bohn* 181

Semiotic Conditions of Originality in Concrete Poetry
  Elizabeth Walther-Bense 205

The Last Voyage *Piero Boitani* 217

PART V Haroldo de Campos: a Selected Anthology

PART VI Postcript: Homages to Haroldo de Campos (1929–2003)

On the Death of Haroldo de Campos
  Andrés Sánchez Robayna 243

The Death of a Poet *Umberto Eco* 245

The Inexhaustible Astonishment of Haroldo de Campos
  Jorge Schwartz 249

Salutation from the Wise Poet *Gonzalo Aguilar* 253

Galaxy of Thousands of Stars *Guillermo Cabrera Infante* 257

Usura Blunteth the Needle in the Maid's Hand *Regina Vater* ... 259

Haroldo de Campos, a Great Brazilian Poet *Lello Voce* 263

Bibliography 267

Preface

IN 1999 THE Universities of Oxford and Yale co-sponsored two integrated conferences in honor of the Brazilian author Haroldo de Campos on his seventieth birthday. The conference at Oxford held at Wadham College on the 13th and 14th October was immediately followed by the Yale symposium held at the Whitney Humanities Center on the 17th, 18th, and 19th October. This joint initiative of the Centre for Brazilian Studies, University of Oxford and the Council on Latin American & Iberian Studies, Yale University paid tribute to a distinguished Brazilian poet, essayist, translator and theorist, bringing together internationally renowned literary scholars and poets to discuss and debate the work of Haroldo de Campos.

Sadly, Haroldo died in São Paulo on 16 August 2003. The joint Oxford/Yale conferences were the last major international events dedicated to his literary achievements in which he participated.

Haroldo de Campos (1929–2003) graduated in law and later completed a doctorate in literature from the Universidade de São Paulo. One of the founders of the movement of "concrete poetry" in São Paulo in the 1950s, Haroldo de Campos was also an essayist, translator, and theorist whose works are internationally known. He was one of the most active figures in world movements of experimental and visual poetry for over three decades, corresponding and collaborating with poets in Japan, Europe, and the Americas. In 1996 he was awarded an honorary doctorate from the Université de Montréal and subsequently won several important prizes, among which are the Lumière UNUPADEC (Italy, 1998), the Octavio Paz Foundation prize (Mexico, 1999), and the Roger Caillois prize (France, 1999). In Brazil, his works have been awarded the Jabuti prize five times (1991, 1992, 1993, 1994, 1999). An emeritus professor of semiotics at the Catholic University of São Paulo, Campos's academic career includes a visiting professorship at Yale University (1978) at the invitation of the eminent hispanist Emir Rodríguez Monegal; an Edward Laroque Tinker visiting professorship at the University of Texas at Austin (1981); as well as teaching and lecture tours in Germany, Spain, France, Italy, Canada and elsewhere.

Nicknamed by German semiotician Max Bense "the locomotive of São Paulo," Haroldo de Campos's prolific career includes some 12 books of poetry, 18 of literary studies, 14 of "transcreations," as well as projects for the theater, cinema and plastic arts. In 1996 the Catholic University produced the video "Diálogo das Artes" ("Dialogue of the Arts") in his honor, with addresses from a constellation of intellectuals including Jacques Derrida, Octavio Paz, Cuban novelist Guillermo Cabrera Infante, and the Brazilian poet João Cabral de Melo Neto. Campos was the focus of the 1995 "Yale Symphosophia on Experimental, Visual, and Concrete Poetics," the proceedings of which were published in *Experimental-Visual-Concrete: Avant-garde Poetry Since 1960* (Amsterdam: Rodopi, 1996). Special issues of the Italian journal *Baldus* (1996), edited by Lello Voce, and the Spanish/Portuguese journal *Espacio/Espaço Escritos* (2002), edited by Andrés Sánchez Robayna, were dedicated to Haroldo and his work. *Nova*, edited by Sérgio Bessa and Odile Cisneros (Northwestern University Press, 2005), is the first major collection of his poetry and essays in English translation.

Concrete poetry

In the 1950s, Haroldo and his brother Augusto de Campos, together with Décio Pignatari, launched the controversial concrete poetry movement in Brazil. Departing from an early correspondence with Ezra Pound, the Campos brothers refined their concept of a synchronic universal tradition, from the Chinese ideogram to contemporary Brazilian prose, as well as a practice of translation as criticism and invention. Attempting to unite the verbal, vocal, and visual dimensions of poetry in a poem-object, the São Paulo poets exhibited their works in galleries and published a *Theory of Concrete Poetry* (1964) describing their isomorphic "word-objects in space time." The Campos brothers published the journals *Invenção* and *Noigandres*, now rarities, working in contact with composers of new music, plastic artists, and the vocalists who were forming the *Tropicália* movement in the mid 1960s. Schools of twentieth-century musical composition, from Webern to Stockhausen to

Cage, were an important influence on their poetry, as were the geometrical and abstract painters. One of Haroldo's best-known poems, "Nasce/Morre" ("Live/Die"), became the text of a choral composition by the contemporary Brazilian composer Gilberto Mendes. His visual poetry was featured in anthologies of world concrete poetry (Solt, Williams), and he continued extensive travels, lectures, and exhibits. *Xadrez de Estrelas* (1976) brought together the collected poetry representing twenty years of the concrete poetry movement. An elegant Spanish language edition spanning all of Brazilian concrete poetry, *Galaxia Concreta*, was published in Mexico by Gonzálo Aguilar (México D.F.: Universidad Ibero-americana, Artes de México, 1999).

Novel of fragments

Throughout the 1960s and 1970s, Haroldo de Campos was composing his great novel of prose in poetry, the *Galáxias* (*Galaxies*), which was finally published as a book of 50 full-page prose fragments in 1984 (2nd ed., 2004). Reflecting the epic and oral sagas of the pre-classical world, the *Galáxias* recount the wanderings and adventures of the poet through lands, texts, and language in a mosaic consisting of torrential verbal forms and inventions. The complete French translation was published in 1998 in the translation by Inês Oseki-Dépré.

Transcreation: translation as reinvention

Translation was the concretists's literary and cultural project, devoted to inventive authors little translated into Portuguese: Pound, cummings, Dickenson, Williams, Dante and Joyce, Japanese haikus, Maiakovsky and Mallarmé. Conceiving of his role as that of a transformer or transcreator, Campos drew on creative Brazilian language in order to "re-imagine" the texts of Western tradition. At the same time, the concretists "rediscovered" forgotten or neglected Brazilian poets of the past, from the baroque poet Gregório de Mattos to the bizarre romantic Sousândrade, the symbolist Kilkerry, and the modernist Oswald de Andrade. Turning increasingly to translation in the 1990s, Haroldo published new Portuguese versions of the Biblical books of *Genesis* and *Ecclesiastes*, and classical Chinese poetry. His final translation was a two-volume bilingual Greek/Portuguese edition of Homer's *Iliad* (2002–3).

Critical essays

Haroldo de Campos is also well known as a major contributor in the press to the critical discourse on Latin American nationality, identity, and cultural autonomy through his essays focusing on the school of *Antropofagia* ("Cannibalism"), drawn from Oswald de Andrade's 1928 "Cannibal Manifesto." Brazil as a center of cultural and literary production, rather than a periphery of passive receptors, is a central tenet of Campos's influential essay, "Europe under the Sign of Devoration." He also wrote numerous essays on concretist aesthetics, the theory of translation as criticism, the production of poetry in underdeveloped societies, creative and experimental writers in Brazilian and Spanish American literatures (Murilo Mendes, João Guimarães Rosa, Octavio Paz, and others), and comparative literature.

The national literary and cultural influence of the "Campos brothers," as they are known in Brazil, has been enormous, perhaps incalculable. Caetano Veloso alludes to them in his songs, the *Tropicália* movement circulated their works to an entire new generation of young people, and the writing of poetry in Brazil universally reflects concrete techniques and materials which they promoted. Haroldo de Campos's essays, published in literary supplements of large circulation newspapers, played an important role in shaping public critical debate on literary and cultural themes. At the same time, much of his poetry and many of the essays have been translated into the major Western languages and published internationally.

The present homage to Haroldo de Campos, which brings together Haroldo's own opening address at the conference in Oxford and many of the papers presented at the Oxford/Yale conferences, recognizes his multilingual work uniting many national literatures, his influence as a teacher, and his devotion over fifty years as a writer to the international and comparative dimensions of Brazilian literature and Portuguese language poetry.

Leslie Bethell
Director, Centre for Brazilian Studies, University of Oxford
K. David Jackson
Council on Latin American and Iberian Studies, Yale University

Notes on Contributors

Gonzalo Aguilar is a researcher at Conicet (Consejo Nacional de Investigaciones Científicas y Técnicas) in Buenos Aires. He is the author of *La poesía concreta brasileña: las vanguardias en la encrucijada modernista* (2003), which was published in Portuguese in 2005. As well as numerous essays on Latin American literatures, Aguilar has published anthologies of concrete poetry in Spanish: *Poemas de Augusto de Campos* (1994); *Galaxia concreta* (1999), with texts by Haroldo, Augusto and Décio Pigntari; and *El angel izquierdo de la poesía*, an anthology of political poems by Haroldo de Campos (2003).

Nelson Ascher is a poet, critic, and journalist in São Paulo who collaborated with, and wrote articles and reviews on the work of, Haroldo de Campos. Ascher's poetry includes *Sonho da Razão* (1993) and *Algo de Sol* (1996). Translations of his poetry into English are included in the anthology *Nothing the Sun could not Explain* (1997).

João Alexandre Barbosa is emeritus professor of literature at the University of São Paulo and one of Brazil's most distinguished literary essayists. He has been a visiting scholar and professor in the United States, including at Yale and at the University of Texas at Austin. His books of literary interpretation and theory include *Mistérios do Dicionário* (2004); *Alguma Crítica* (2002); *Entre Livros* (1999); *Biblioteca Imaginária* (1996); *Leitura do Intervalo* (1990); *Ilusões da Modernidade* (1986); *Opus 60* (1980); *Imitação da Forma* (1975); A *Metáfora Crítica* (1974); and *Tradição do Impasse* (1974). Barbosa coined the phrase "Cosmonaut of the Signifier" to describe Haroldo de Campos.

Willard Bohn teaches at Illinois State University, where he is Distinguished Professor of French and Comparative Literature. He is the author of one hundred articles and twelve books, including *The Aesthetics of Visual Poetry* (1986, 1993), *Modern Visual Poetry* (2001), *The Rise of Surrealism* (2001), *The Other Futurism* (2004), and *Marvelous Encounters: Surrealist Responses to Art, Film, Poetry, and Architecture* (2005).

Piero Boitani is professor of comparative literature at the University of Rome "La Sapienza." He has been visiting professor at universities in the United States, Canada, Japan, and England. Among Boitani's many publications are *Chaucer and Boccaccio* (1977), *English Medieval Narrative of the 13th and 14th Centuries* (1982), *Chaucer and the Imaginary World of Fame* (1984), *The Tragic and the Sublime in Medieval Literature* (1989), *The Shadow of Ulysses: Figures of a Myth* (1994), *The Bible and its Rewritings* (1999), *Parole Alate: Voli nella Poesia e nella Storia da Omero all'11 Settembre* (2004), and *Esodi e Odissee* (2004).

Guillermo Cabrera Infante (1929–2005) participated in the "boom" of Latin American fiction with *Así en la paz como en la guerra* (1964) and *Tres tristes tigres* (*Three Trapped Tigers*, 1968). In exile in London, the celebrated Cuban novelist's work became noted for its humor and linguistic play. Cabrera Infante's books include *Cuentos de humor* (2001); *Infantería* (1999); *Ella canta boleros* (1996); *Delito por bailar el chachachá* (1995); *Mea Cuba* (1992); *Diablesas e diosas* (1990); *Próxima Luna* (1990); *Vista del amanecer en el trópico* (1981); and *Habana por un infante defunto* (1979).

Horácio Costa is a poet, essayist, translator and professor at the University of São Paulo. His most recent book of poetry, *Fracta* (2004), is an anthology of his oeuvre selected by Haroldo de Campos. In 1968, at age 13, Horácio Costa was introduced to modern poetry when he bought, in a book fair at Praça da República, the first edition of *Poesia Russa Moderna*, an anthology edited and translated by Haroldo and Augusto de Campos and Boris Schnaiderman. Set against the grim days of Brazil's military government, he regards that particular reading as having opened a window that never closed to world poetics.

Luiz Costa Lima is a professor of comparative literature at the Universidade do Estado do Rio de Janeiro and Pontifícia Universidade Católica, Rio de Janeiro. Three of his books have been translated into English as *Control of the Imaginary: Reason and Imagination in Modern*

Times (1988); *The Dark Side of Reason: Fictionality and Power* (1992); and *The Limits of Voice: Montaigne, Schlegel, Kafka* (1996). Recently, he collaborated on *A New History of German Literature* (2004). Costa Lima first worked with Haroldo de Campos on essays concerning the Brazilian poet Joaquim de Sousândrade, published in *ReVisão de Sousândrade* (1964) edited by Augusto and Haroldo de Campos.

Craig Dworkin is associate professor of English at the University of Utah. He is the author of *Reading the Illegible* (2003) and co-editor of *Architectures of Poetry* (2004). His books of poetry include *Signature-Effects* (1997), *Smokes* (2004), *Strand* (2005), and the forthcoming "Parse." Dworkin also curates two on-line archives – "Eclipse" (Princeton) and "The UbuWeb Anthology of Conceptual Writing" – and is currently preparing a critical collection on misreading and a book on the early writings of Vito Acconci.

Umberto Eco is a celebrated Italian humanist, semiotician, novelist, and specialist in medieval literature and aesthetics. He is a professor at the University of Bologna and has been a visiting professor at universities in the United States, Canada, and France. He is the author of the best-selling books *The Name of the Rose* (1983) and *Foucault's Pendulum* (1989). Eco has acknowledged that Haroldo de Campos's essay "The Open Work of Art" preceded his own book *The Open Work* (*Opera Aperta*, 1962) on the same concept.

K. David Jackson is professor of Portuguese at Yale University. He met Haroldo and Augusto de Campos in 1968 during their first tour of the United States and in 1971–2 he worked under their guidance in São Paulo on a dissertation on modernist Oswald de Andrade. Jackson visited Haroldo at Yale in 1978 and invited him as Visiting Tinker Professor at the University of Texas at Austin in 1981. At Yale, he coordinated the 1995 "Symphosophia" on experimental, visual, and concrete poetry, with Haroldo and Augusto in attendance, and in 1999 he organized the Oxford and Yale University symposia in honor of Haroldo's seventieth year. Jackson translated Haroldo's poem "Visão do Paraíso," composed in 1978 and published in a limited edition in Spain.

Wladimir Krysinski is professor of comparative literature at the Université de Montréal. He has taught, lectured, and written on many national literatures, including the Brazilian, and on experimentation and concretism in contemporary letters and arts. His books include *Carrefours de signes: essais sur le roman moderne* (1981); *Romans et intertextes* (1984); *Paradigma inquieto : Pirandello e lo spazio comparativo della modernità* (1988); and *Novela en sus modernidades: a favor y en contra de Bajtin* (1998). At the 1995 Yale "Symphosophia" he spoke on "The Endless Ends of Languages of Poetry: Between Experiments and Cognitive Quests."

Inês Oseki-Dépré was born in São Paulo where she studied at the Dramatic Conservatory and the University of São Paulo. In France, she completed a doctorate on the work of Michel Butor at Aix-en-Provence in 1971. An author and translator, she is professor of general and comparative literature at the University of Provence. Editor of a book on Fernando Pessoa, *Le Spleen du poète* (1997), her many literary translations into French include the Brazilian novel *Iracema* by José de Alencar and Haroldo de Campos's *Galáxias* (1998). She published a prize-winning selection of Haroldo's poetry in Brazil (1992) and is currently preparing an anthology in French.

Marjorie Perloff is a prolific essayist, scholar of modernism, and Sadie Dernham Patek Professor of Humanities, Emerita, at Stanford University. She dialogued with Haroldo de Campos at Yale in 1995 and 1999, after being in Brazil for the publication of her book, *The Futurist Moment*, in Portuguese (1993). Her many books on art, philosophy, and literature include *Vienna Paradox* (2004); *Differentials: Poetry, Poetics, Pedagogy* (2004); *21st Century Modernism* (2002); *Luca: Discourse on Life and Death* (2001); *Dance of the Intellect* (1996); *Strangeness of the Ordinary* (1996); *Wittgenstein's Ladder* (1996); *John Cage: Composed in America* (1994); *Radical Artifice* (1991); *Poetic License* (1990); *Postmodern Genres* (1989); and *Poetics of Indeterminacy* (1981).

Leyla Perrone-Moisés is a professor of literature at the University of São Paulo and a leading figure in literary studies in Brazil. She directs the Brazil-France project at the Institute of Advanced Studies, while teaching and lecturing widely, in both France and Brazil. Her books include *Inútil Poesia e Outros Ensaios Breves* (2000); *Vinte Luas: Viagem de Paulmier De Gonneville ao Brasil, 1503-1505* (1992); *Flores da Escrivaninha: Ensaios* (1990); *Fernando Pessoa: Aquém do Eu, Além do Outro* (1982); and *Falência da Crítica; um Caso Limite: Lautréamont* (1973).

Andrés Sánchez Robayna is a professor of Spanish literature at the University of La Laguna in Tenerife, in the Canary Islands. He was a longtime collaborator with Haroldo de Campos on poetic translation and in 2002 edited a special number of the journal *Espacio / Espaço* dedicated to Haroldo with articles, interviews, translations, poems, and memoirs. Sánchez Robayna has translated many of Haroldo's poetic works into Spanish, including *La educación de los cinco sentidos* (1990), *Finismundo: el ultimo viaje* (1992), and *Yúgen, cuaderno japonés* (1993).

Jorge Schwartz is a professor of Spanish-American literature at the University of São Paulo. He is has organized major international expositions including "Brazil, 1920–1950" in Valencia, Spain, which transferred to São Paulo where the catalogue *Brasil, 1920-1950: da Antropofagia a Brasília* (2002) was published. His production of a *Caixa Modernista* (modernist box) contained multiple genres and cultural objects from the 1920s (2003), while he explored Brazilian cultural identity in *Brasil: o Trânsito da Memória* (1994). Schwartz is editor of an essential anthology on the Latin American vanguard, *Vanguardas Latino-americanas* (1995), which had a prior edition in Spanish.

Regina Vater represented Brazil at the *Biennale des Jeunes* in Paris in the early 1960s. Coming from a family of poets, poetry has been an important source of inspiration for her work, as has been installation, photography, video, and graphic design. In 1972, she won the most prestigious award for art in Brazil, the prize taking her to New York. Vater represented Brazil at the 1976 Venice Biennale and has shown her work in museums and galleries around the world. With a Guggenheim fellowship, she lived, worked, and showed in New York after 1980. In 1982, she was a co-editor of FLUE, the first North American art magazine totally dedicated to the experimental art of Latin America. Since 1985, she has lived and worked in Austin, Texas.

Lello Voce is a poet, novelist (*Eroina: Romanzo*, 1998), and performer living in Treviso, Italy. His six books of poetry, with audio CDs, include *Fast Blood* (Antonio Delfini prize, 2004) and *Farfalle da cambattimento* (2003). His latest novel, *Cucarachas*, was written completely on line and published on the net. Voce has performed in many international poetry festivals and is one of the art directors of The International Rome Poetry Festival. In 2002 he was the EmCee in the *First European Poetry Slam –*

Big Torino 2002, Turin. With Giacomo Verde he created the net art opera *QWERTYU* on the Italian website of the international architectural magazine DOMUS. Voce performed poetry at the 1995 Yale Symphosophia.

Elisabeth Walther-Bense is professor of semiotics in the Institut für Philosophie at the University of Stuttgart. She first met Haroldo de Campos, who had written about the works of Max Bense, when he went to Stuttgart in 1959, meeting many more times over subsequent decades. In the early 1960s she accompanied Max Bense to Brazil for lectures on aesthetics in the Museu de Arte Moderna and the Escola Superior de Desenho Industrial in Rio and met with intellectuals in Rio, São Paulo, and Brasília. Haroldo returned to Stuttgart in 1964 to lecture on Brazilian literature, leading to the publication by Bense of his "versuchsbuch – galaxien" in their edition "rot" (1966). Haroldo published Walther-Bense's *Teoria Geral dos Signos*, translated by Pérola de Carvalho (2000). Walther-Bense went to the United States for the Yale "Symphosophia" in 1995 and published a detailed memoir of her contacts with Haroldo in *Experimental – Visual – Concrete* (1996).

PART I
Haroldo de Campos

The Ex-centric's Viewpoint: Tradition, Transcreation, Transculturation

Haroldo de Campos

BRAZILIAN LITERATURE – AND this may also be true for other Latin-American literatures (leaving aside the problem of the great pre-Columbian cultures, to be considered from a special angle) – was "born" under the sign of baroque. The idea of "birth" here is just metaphorical. It cannot be understood from an ontological, substantialist, metaphysical point of view. It should not be understood in the sense of an idealistic quest for "identity" or "national character." As a quest for a "national spirit" or "soul" envisaged as a total presence, *terminus ad quem* to be reached after an evolutionary linear process of a biological type based on an "immanent teleology," according to the model proposed by the last century's "patriarchs" of romantic, "organicist" historiography. Baroque, paradoxically, means non-infancy. The concept of "origin" here will only fit if it does not imply the idea of "genesis," of a generative process with beginning, middle-phase and maturity (or "climax"). If it is conceived with the double meaning of "leap"/"spring" and "transformation," as Walter Benjamin does in his book on the German *Trauerspiel* from the same baroque period, when he emphasizes the word *Ursprung* in its etymological sense, explaining: "Origin, although an entirely historical category, has, nevertheless, nothing to do with genesis (*Entstehung*)... Origin is a whirlpool in the stream of becoming." In my opinion, another possible illuminating analogy is with the chemical term *precipitation* (from Lat. *caput*/head, meaning "throw down headlong"). Likewise Brazilian literature has had no origin, in the genetic, embryonic, evolutionary sense of the term; as it has had no *infancy*. The word *infans* (child) means: "one who does not speak."

Baroque is, therefore, a non-origin. A non-infancy. Our literature, springing up from the baroque vortex, was never aphasic; it has never developed from a speechless, aphasic-infantile limbo, into the fullness of discourse. It was already "born" as an adult (like certain mythological heroes) and speaking an extremely elaborate universal code – the baroque rhetorical one – in a quite self-assured manner. (In the Brazilian case, that code was already pre-formed by the mannerism of Camões, a poet who, in turn, had influenced Góngora and Quevedo, the two great names of the Spanish baroque period.)

The matter of Brazil's literary "nationalism" cannot be considered from a closed, monologic point of view. It cannot be explained as the projection or emanation of a national "spirit" that would gradually be unveiling and revealing itself as such, until embodying itself in a full presence in a moment of "logophanic" completeness, which would coincide with a kind of national "classicism" (Machado de Assis, at the end of our "formative" period – "romanticism" – would be, by definition, the exponent of this moment of apogee.) Hence, rather than in terms of *formation* ("formative" instances), it would be more exact to think in terms of *transformation* ("transformative" moments) in order to describe the main process working throughout Brazilian literary history, a non-lineal intertwining principle.

Ever since the baroque, that is, since always, we cannot think of ourselves as a closed and finished identity, but rather as *difference*, as *overtness*, as a dialogic movement of difference against the background of the universal. (It was not by sheer coincidence that Macunaíma, the "hero of our race" celebrated by Modernist Mário de Andrade, is a hero without a precisely definite character....) Our entrance on the literary stage is right away a vertiginous leap onto the scene of the baroque, that is, a differential articulation with an extremely sophisticated universal code. Gregório de Matos (1636–95), nicknamed "Hell's Mouth," the first great Brazilian poet, recombines Camões, Góngora and Quevedo; at the same time, he incorporates Africanisms and Indianisms into his language, a "trans-ethnical language" (in the words of Portuguese critic Alfredo Margarido). Gregório resorts also to parody and satire in a "carnivalized" intertextual game, where local elements mingle with universal "stylemes" according to a continuous hybridization process (moreover, the hybrid Portuguese in which Gregório de Matos wrote is actually sprinkled with Spanish loan words...). Like Mexican 10th Muse Sor Juana Inés de la Cruz, Peruvian Juan del Valle Caviedes, Colombian Hernando Domínguez Camargo, Brazilian Gregório de Matos develops a differential baroque, one that cannot be reduced to its European model.

The Ex-centric's Viewpoint: Tradition, Transcreation, Transculturation

After mastering the rules of the game, he exploits, in a personal and even subversive way, the combining possibilities of that common code: an ever-mobile and changing code, apt to be "mongrelized," susceptible of new, critical, and even contesting individual reconfigurations. Thus, Lezama Lima is right in speaking of the Latin-American baroque as the art of "counter-quest," "a great creative leprosy." An opinion which can be compared to the one held by the Brazilian modernist Oswald de Andrade, who sees in the baroque the style "of the discoveries," which rescued Europe from a kind of "Ptolemaic egocentricity." The "sub-altern" colonial condition to which Matos reacted by converting baroque polite court witticism into ferocious satire against metropolitan representatives. The *alternating* under-current of the *sub-altern's* language *ad*-ulterates (mongrelized) the *over-altern's* rhetorical master code, by committing incestuous intercourse (ad-*ulterium*) with the colonizer's imposing mother's speech....

This differential practice articulated with a universal code is also, by definition, a *translation practice*. Gregório de Matos has been accused of "plagiarism" for having recombined and synthesized two famous sonnets by Góngora ("Mientras por competir con tu cabello" and "Ilustre y hermosísima María") into a third "miscellaneous" one ("Discreta e formosíssima María"). The critics who made this indictment did not realize that Gregório de Matos acted toward Góngora as a creative translator (like Ungaretti in our century); at the same time, the Brazilian "Baiano" poet was carrying out the ironical "deconstruction" of the baroque rhetorical machine, metalinguistically uncovering the combinatory devices that made it work. (And we should not forget that Góngora, to draw up his sonnets, the ones worked over by Gregório de Matos, had in turn extracted elements from Garcilaso de la Vega, Camões and from the *carpe diem* Latin poetry, in accordance with the general practice of "imitatio," typical of the period.)

Therefore baroque, in Brazilian and in several Latin-American literatures, means at the same time hybridism and creative translation: translation as transgressive appropriation and cross-breeding, as the dialogic practice of telling the other and telling oneself through the other, under the sign of difference. In this sense, Walter Benjamin's thoughts on "allegory" have a special meaning for the Ibero-American baroque: "allegory" in its etymological sense of an "alternate saying," a "saying something else;" a style in which, at its extreme limits, anything can be expropriated in order to symbolize anything else. (Or, in Benjamin's own terms: "Jede Person, jedwedes Ding, jedes Verhaltniss kann ein beliebiges anders bedeutet"/ "Any person, any object, any relationship can mean absolutely anything else.")

The writer who best stated this view of an "ex-centric" (that is, out of center, de-centered) Latin-American literature – or more exactly, Brazilian literature, my subject here – as a transformational process of creative and transgressive translation was, I believe, Oswald de Andrade, in his "Manifesto Antropófago" ("Antropophagous Manifesto," 1928). His "cannibalistic" proclaiming of independence – resumed by the author at the end of his life in the 1950s in a polemic essay, "The Crisis of Messianic Philosophy" (1952), written against Marxist totalizing dogmatism by a former member of the Brazilian Communist Party – that libertarian proclamation was nothing but the expression of the need for a dialogic and dialectic relationship between the national and the universal. Andrade's motto, not by accident, is a phonic usurpation, a mistranslation by homophony, of Shakespeare's famous dilemmatic verse: "To be or not to be, that is the question." Andrade reformulated this verse impinging upon the verb "to be" the noun "Tupi" (name of the general language of the Brazilian Indians at the time of the conquest) and proclaimed: "Tupi or not tupi, that is the question..." Anthropophagy, the answer to this ironic equation of the "problem of the origin," is a kind of brutal *deconstructionism:* the critical devouring of the universal cultural legacy, carried out not from the submissive and reconciled perspective of the "good savage," but from the challenging, aggressive point of view of the "bad savage," devourer of foreign white people, cannibal. "I am only interested in what is not mine," states Oswald de Andrade in his "Manifesto," proposing to change "the taboo into a totem." This process of anthropophagic swallowing up does not involve submission (catechizing), but a "trans-culturation" (an expression I first used in my 1975 prologue to *A Operação do Texto*, alluding to the translation of the "cultural series" of Lotman's so-called "extratext"); it is, rather, a "transvaluation," a critical reconsidering of history as a "negative function" (in Nietzsche's sense). The whole past that is alien to us deserves to be denied. It deserves to be eaten up, devoured, Andrade would say. This is a non-reverential attitude toward tradition: it implies expropriation, reversion, de-hierarchization. It is not by sheer coincidence that once more one can remember here the Cuban Lezama Lima, who tried to read the past (its history) somehow from a "devouring" perspective, as a "succession of imaginary eras," liable to be thought over by a "spermatic memory," an erratic one, capable of replacing the logical links by surprising analogical connections. For Oswald de Andrade, by the way, the first celebrating date of the cannibal's calendar was the year of the "deglutition" of the Portuguese missionary Bishop Sardinha (a family name that premonitorily means "sardine") by the ferocious Brazilian Indians....

It seems to me that the remarks made by Czech structuralist Jan Mukarovsk, in an essay dated 1946, "On Structuralism" (reformulated and confirmed by the same theoretician in 1963, during his Marxist period), a critical reflection on the subject of the influence of "preferential" literatures upon so-called "minor" ones, also apply both to Brazilian and to the remaining Latin-American literatures. This problem had been put in an aprioristic and one-sided way by traditional literary science. For Mukarovsk, this traditional comparative view – responsible for the "small people complex" in Czech literature – would be a non-dialectic, mechanistic view. The image of a "passive literature" whose evolution would be guided by the alleatory, "casual intervention of external influences," looks false to him. Influences do not act on their own in the environment in which they intervene without presuppositions; they combine with the local context, to whose needs they become subordinate; furthermore, several different influences work simultaneously, at times operating reciprocally. As a result they are submitted to a selection and to a re-articulation: they change their inflection. Hence, Mukarovsk's conclusion: "Influxes are not expressions of the essential superiority and subordination of one culture in relation to another; their fundamental aspect is reciprocity" (in the sense of a "mutually fruitful dialectic tension"). Present-day thinkers of "postcolonial" literatures, as for instance Maria Tymockzo or the Kenyan writer Ngâugâi Thiong'o, seem to sustain an analogous criterium: "Languages should meet as equals;" "Through translations, the different languages of the world can speak to one another;" "Interlanguage communication through translation is crucial."

Machado de Assis (1839–1908) in Brazilian literature is not simply the harmonious culmination of a gradual literary "formative" evolution, which had been supposedly unfolding since our nativist-oriented preromanticism. His appearance can neither be explained nor foreseen as a fully mature result of a homogeneous process of almost "genealogical construction," a "rectilinear process of Brazilianization." Machado de Assis does not represent a moment of "aboutissement," but rather a moment of "transformative" rupture. His nationalism is no longer the naive nationalism of certain romantics with ontological aspirations, but a "critical" nationalism "in crisis," torn to pieces, in constant dialogue with the universal. He is national because he is not exactly national, like Ulysses, the mythological founder of Lisbon, in Fernando Pessoa's poem, who "was, for not having existed," and, only in this sense, has he "created us...." It was Machado de Assis (as critic Augusto Meyer pointed out) who created the metaphor of the head as a "ruminant's stomach," where "all suggestions, after being mixed and ground up, get ready for a new mastication, a complicated chemistry in which it is no longer possible to distinguish the assimilating organism from the stuff assimilated." As a consequence, by his uncharacteristic character, by his atypicalness, Machado de Assis, "devourer" of Laurence Sterne and countless other influences, was regarded as not very Brazilian, as an "Anglophile," by the most important literary critic of his time, Sílvio Romero, who depreciatively baptized his elliptically interrupted, fragmentary way of writing as "the style of a stutterer"; who despised Assis's late phase major novels (*Dom Casmurro, Quincas Borba*) as being "abortive products of a powerless imagination;" "monkey-like" counterfeits of a pretentious "mulatto" trying to paraphrase Sterne's humor. Nevertheless, it is Machado de Assis, for his universalist features, for his non-aprioristically typified Brazilian character, i.e., for his selective and critical reading of the universal literary code from within a Brazilian context, but also from an extremely personal standpoint within this very context, who is the most representative of our writers of the past. He is already, in a certain sense, for Brazilian literature, with all the implications of the idea, our nineteenth-century Borges.... It is not by sheer accident that contemporary writers like John Barth, Susan Sontag, Carlos Fuentes, John Updike or Cabrera Infante are readers and admirers of his anticipating works. And why not think of Macedonio Fernández, the master of the "unfinished," as the "missing link" between Machado and Borges?

To finish, I would like to offer a personal testimony. I belong to the *Noigandres* group of Brazilian poets who, in the fifties, launched the national and international movement of concrete poetry (along with the

Swiss-Bolivian Eugen Gomringer), a movement that, in the Brazilian context, took its own peculiar course. It resumed the dialogue with our neglected modernism of the twenties (especially with the polemical pioneer Oswald de Andrade). While sustaining proposals of a radical avant-garde on the level of language, in an attempt to develop an anti-discursive, synthetic-ideogrammic poetry, the Brazilian *Noigandres* group never put aside its concern with social commitment (political *engagé* poems), as well as with the polemical revision of tradition, from a critical and creative viewpoint. In this sense, we rethought the baroque: Gregório de Matos was defined by Augusto de Campos as "the first experimental cannibal in our poetry;" my own book *Galáxias* (*Galaxies*) is an essay on the abolition of the boundaries between poetry and prose, which tries to combine constructivist rigor and neo-baroque proliferation. In our romantic period, we discovered the forgotten poet Sousândrade (1832–1902), author of "O Inferno de Wall Street" (The Wall Street Inferno). This vertiginous composition was part of a longer poem, *Guesa Errante* (The Wandering Guesa), a kind of anti-colonialist "Walpurgisnacht," having as its setting the New York Stock Exchange around 1870, and written in a kaleidoscopic and polylingual style, anticipating the film montage techniques of contemporary poetry. The fact that this same group of poets programmatically converted "creative translation" (or "transcreation") into a constant practice, taking their inspiration from Ezra Pound's example ("make it new") and from Walter Benjamin's and Roman Jakobson's theories on the task of the translator, is something extremely coherent. We have endeavored to "transcreate" into Portuguese an anthology of Ezra Pound's *Cantos*; visual poems by e. e. cummings; fragments from James Joyce's *Finnegans Wake;* Mallarmé's constellation-poem "Un coup de dés"; Goethe, Hoelderlin and Brecht, as well as Dadaists and German avant-garde poets; Dante and Guido Cavancanti, as well as Ungaretti; the Provençal poets, Arnaut Daniel in particular; Bashô and Japanese "haikaiists"; Russian poets since Blok's and Biely's symbolism, through Khlebnikov, Maiakovski, Pasternak, Mandelstam, up to the little known at the time (1968), abstract-metaphysical Guenadi Aigui, and so forth. My last works in the field were: the recreation of "Blanco," the great reflexive and erotic poem by Octavio Paz, in 1986 (*Transblanco*); texts from the Hebrew Bible (the two histories of creation; *Qohéleth* / Ecclesiastes; *Shir ha Shirim* / "Song of Songs"; excerpts from *Job*). To translate fragments from the Bible, I tried to employ the most advanced techniques offered by the repertoire of modern poetry (in German, there is the example of Rosenzweig and Buber; in French, of Henri Meschonnic). Having as a paradigm my biblical "transcreations," Antonio Risério, poet and anthropologist from Bahia, "recreated" into Brazilian Portuguese some ritual songs belonging to the African (*Yorubá*) language; I published Risério's *Oriki Orixá* (1996) in my collection SIGNOS (São Paulo: Perpectiva).

As can be seen, this is a broad process of critical "devouring" of universal poetry, the aim of which has been to install a tradition of invention and to create, in this way, a treasury of "significant forms" for the creative stimulus of the new generations. Translation, from this point of view, is an active pedagogical form. Mainly when one translates that which is regarded as untranslatable: "Sólo lo difícil es estimulante" ("Only difficult things are stimulating:" Lezama Lima).

"*Écrire quoi que ce soit (...) est un travail de traduction exactement comparable à celui qui opère la transmutation d'un texte d'une langue dans une autre*," observes Paul Valéry. Writing today in the Americas as well as in Europe will mean, more and more, as far as I can see it, rewriting, remasticating. Writers of a monological, "logocentric" mentality – if they still exist and persist in that mentality – must realize that it will become more and more impossible to write the "prose of the world" without considering, at least as a reference point, the differences of these "ex-centrics," at the same time Barbarians (for belonging to a peripheral so-called "underdeveloped world") and Alexandrians (for making "guerrilla" incursions into the very heart of the Library of Babel). Ex-centrics who are called Borges, Lezama Lima, Guimarães Rosa, Clarice Lispector, and so on, to give just a few meaningful examples of non-negligible, fundamental contemporary authors. On the other hand, it will also be impossible to assume the tradition of the modern poem – or already "post-modern," since Mallarmé's pioneering "coup de dés" – without taking into consideration the inter-textual hypotheses of Vallejo's *Trilce*, Huidobro's *Altazor*, Girondo's *Enlamasmédula* or Octavio Paz's *Blanco*. Failing to realize, for example, that there is a system of poetic communicant vessels linking William Carlos Williams' "objectivism," Francis Ponge's "parti pris des choses," and the constructivism of the geometry-poet João Cabral de Melo Neto (an obligatory reference point for Brazilian concrete poetry). The problem of "major" and "minor" literatures, as seen from a semiological point of view, may be a pseudo-problem, as Mukarovsk managed to demonstrate. If each literature is an articulation of differences throughout the infinite text – "signs in rotation" – of universal literature, each innovative contribution is supposed to be measured as such; it is a kind of "monadological," irreducible moment, at the same time singular and interdependent in this combinatory game. Góngora's glowing *Soledades* do not abolish the splendid difference of Sor Juana's *Primero sueño*, a critical and meditative poem that leaps over diachrony to fraternize with Mallarmé's *coup de dés*, as Octavio Paz pointed out in his striking book on the Mexican poetess. Laurence Sterne's *Tristram Shandy* does not cancel out the differential features of Machado de Assis's *Dom Casmurro*, a work which, in turn, pre-figures Borges's elusive-ironical style (Borges who, apparently, had never read Machado de Assis...).

The polytopical polyphonic planetary civilization is, I believe, under the devouring sign of translation *lato sensu*. Creative translation – "transcreation" – is the most fruitful manner of rethinking Aristotelian *mimeses* which has marked Western poetics so profoundly; of rethinking this concept not as a passive-oriented theory of copy or reflex, but as a usurping impulse in the sense of a dialectic production of differences out of sameness. Old Goethe (whose idea of a *Weltliteratur* resounds in Marx's "Communist Manifesto" of 1848, in the passage proclaiming the overcoming of "local narrowness and exclusiveness") already warned: "Each and every literature, locked up in itself, will eventually languish into tedium, if it does not allow itself, again and again, to liven up by means of foreign contribution." To face alterity is, above all, a necessary exercise in self-criticism, as well as a vertiginous experience of breaking the limits.

Translated by Stella E. O. Tagnin and Haroldo de Campos.

Second thoughts: the dialectics of *sub*altern and *over*altern literary models

What I definitely cannot accept is the act of imposing a "normative paradigm" upon the third-world writers and their literatures, as a "cognitive model" apt to rescue them from the dangers of super-developed cultural post-modernism.

When facing poets like Octavio Paz and João Cabral de Melo Neto, and prose-writers like Machado de Assis, Borges or Lezama Lima – to mention only a few Latin-American examples – it seems an arrogant nonsensical exercise of dogmatic wishful thinking to sketch a presumptive "theory of the cognitive aesthetics of the third-world literature," prescribing, for instance that third-world novels, having as a necessary goal the achievement of a "national allegory," will not offer "the satisfaction of Proust or Joyce;" that, on the contrary, they will tend to remind first-world readers "of outmoded stages of their own cultural development," causing the impression of "novels written by Dreyer or Sherwood Anderson." This is the supercilious alternative given by *over*altern first-world critic Frederic Jameson to *sub*altern writers of the underdeveloped peripheral world. (When I use here the adjective *subaltern*, I am doing it in a broad sense, not as the specialized category proposed by Gayatri Spivak and other essayists; moreover, I am playing with the etymological meaning of this pivot word.) Jameson refers to Guimarães Rosa's novel *Grande Sertão: Veredas* as "that curious Brazilian *high literary* variant of the Western." The first thing that occurs to me, before a somewhat deprecating label like this one, is that the author of *The Political Unconscious* ignores the Brazilian Portuguese language and has built a fake, oversimplified image of the complex Faustian, metaphysical struggle between God and Devil embedded in the deep structure of Rosa's masterpiece (Max Bense named it an "epic theodicy" in his *Brasilianische Intelligenz,* 1965). My forceful conclusion is that Jameson read *Grande Sertão* in the American rendering of it (*Devil to Pay in the Backlands*), a most defective version. In fact, by suppressing most of the fascinating invention of language and by watering down the corresponding semantic density, the main distinctive features of Rosa's prose, that version converts *Grande Sertão* into a trivial "banana Western." The anglophone master's discourse of the *over*altern "salvationist" critic works as a rhetorical by-product of unconscious imperialism, by effacing the *sub*altern "minor" languages and by underrating their creative verbal power.

The Jamesonian "pseudo-cognitive," prescriptive model – as is notorious by now – was the subject of a vigorous refutation by the Urdu Indian writer Ajaz Ahmad. Among other impressive arguments, Ahmad pointed out that the reductionist "oppositive binarism" of Jameson's formula "capitalist first-world / pre-or-non-capitalist third world" was "empirically ungrounded." He argued that "the ideological conditions of text production are never singular but always several," that there is no "homogeneous" third-world literature. "Outmoded realism" – I would like to stress – is not a fit standard for the contemporary literature of *Nuestra América*, where the Cuban Lezama Lima, with his labyrinthian neobaroque *Paradiso*, has been called a kind of *criollo* Proust; where the Brazilian Guimarães Rosa, with his multifaceted *Grande Sertão* and his gift for word-playing, has been compared to Joyce, being both – the Cuban and the Brazilian – utterly distinct from their "first-world" counterparts, since they are profoundly anchored in their own literary and linguistic tradition and persistent in their singular way of decrying (or rather defrauding) the universal code, by deviating from its resulting European products.

PART II

On Haroldo de Campos: Poet, Critic, Translator

Haroldo de Campos and the Poetics of Invention*

K. David Jackson

"O Poema ilustra a teoria do seu vôo"
Teoria e Prática do Poema

"THE LOCOMOTIVE OF São Paulo," to quote Max Bense's lightning portrait of Haroldo de Campos, has redefined what it means to be a Brazilian poet in the last half of the twentieth century. His innovations in language and form have brought the world of literature into a dialogue with contemporary plastic arts, music, and semiotics, while his role as essayist, theorist, and "agitator of ideas" has informed and prolonged a public debate on the role of experimental aesthetics in "developing" societies. Perhaps it would have been more appropriate for Bense to have called Haroldo the "Boeing" of Brazilian poetry, in light of his aeronautical *ars poetica*: "The Poem illustrates the theory of its flight," a proposition that carries João Cabral de Melo Neto's poem "Engineer" (1945) into the space age. The works of Brazil's "jet locomotive" were celebrated at the Yale Symphosophia on experimental, visual, and concrete poetry in April 1995, where Haroldo dialogued with poets across a spectrum of languages and cultures and was recognized as one of the most significant and influential contemporary experimental poets.

The collected poetry published in São Paulo in 1976, *Xadrex de Estrelas*, whose title plays on the baroque questioning of universal design in Antônio Vieira's sermons, has been superseded by 20 more years of writing. In the 1992 anthology *Os Melhores Poemas de Haroldo de Campos*, the concrete and visual poetry of *Fome de Forma* and *Lacunae* (*poemandala, serigrafias, excrituras, tatibitexto*) and the "transcreated" prose of *Galáxias* – works written prior to 1976 – foreground a poetic

---

* First published in Italian in *Baldus* (1996) and in Spanish in *Espacio Escrito* (2002).

odyssey continuing into the 1990s: *Signância, Entrefiguras, A Educação dos Cinco Sentidos, Transluminuras, Metapinturas e Meta-Retratos, Novos Poemas,* and *Finismundo: A Última Viagem.*

The theory of Haroldo de Campos's poetic voyage can be illustrated critically through key aesthetic schools that have shaped his philosophical and linguistic expression over time: concretism, neo-baroque, and transcreation (creative translation). Within these modes, Haroldo carried out a project founded on radical vanguardism (whose techniques include permutation, chance, fragmentation, inversion, systematic linguistic variation, paronomasia), classical and literary referentiality, musicality, the blurring of genre boundaries, knowledge of many languages, and the post-utopian distancing of the text as remains or ruins separated from its origins both as fable and as symbolic form.

Invenção / Invention

Pensar o texto num espaço inpensável /
To think the text in an unthinkable space

Beginning with the journals *Noigandres* and *Invenção*, Haroldo and his companion poets practice, on the one hand, a sharply focused poetry of graphic representation and visual information that is integrated, on the other, with Brazil's radical architectural project and with a public cultural debate in influential literary supplements on the nature and social role of literature. Illustrating the encounter of art and culture, the high concrete ("tension of word-objects in space-time," *Teoria da Poesia Concreta*) was a major influence and co-existed with Brazil's cultural movement of resistance in the 1960s, *Tropicália*. Guided by theory and research, Haroldo's poly-faceted production across genres includes poetry, theory, translation, criticism, the essay, conferences, interviews, and university courses. As if he were an anthropologist of letters, Haroldo's wide-ranging production finds its theoretical basis in the interplay among diverse linguistic, cultural, and poetic concepts. The multiplicity of his interests is highly synthesized in the concision and economy of his poetic language, which is sparse but extremely dense in meaning. Formal experimentation comes about as the consequence of his synchronic reading of an innovative tradition across Western poetry, grounded in the practices of the early twentieth-century avant-garde movements. His first experimental works are introduced in 1956 in the Brazilian concrete poetry exhibit at the first Bienal of São Paulo. *Poesia Concreta* sets about to modernize and even revolutionize Brazilian poetics, consonant with the pilot plan for Brasília and the national utopian architectonic and urbanistic schemes of Neimeyer, Costa, and Burle Marx. Through intimate acquaintance with experimental poetics and comparative critical theory, Haroldo de Campos became a virtuoso in applying the techniques of contemporary arts to Brazilian language and reality.

The concrete aesthetic brought Haroldo into early contact with such international innovators as Ezra Pound, Roman Jakobson, Francis Ponge, Max Bense, and Octavio Paz. In 1968 I met Haroldo for the first time in his role as articulate spokesman and ardent defender of concretist poetics during a tour of American universities, at the time when Mary Ellen Solt and Emmett Williams were preparing their celebrated anthologies of world concrete poetry. With extraordinary energy over four decades, Haroldo has continued to represent innovative Brazilian poetics on the international scene. His contemporary poetic contacts include not only Europeans such as Eugene Gomringer, Heissenbüttel, Pierre Garnier, Jacques Roubaud, Ana Hatherly, E. M. de Melo e Castro, and Andrés Sánchez Robayna, but also dialogue with Hispanic American intellectual and literary culture through Octavio Paz and extend to Japanese poets Kitasono Katsue and Seiichi Niikui. Haroldo's international activism continues a line of development seen previously in the aesthetic universality of Brazilian poets Murilo Mendes and João Cabral de Melo Neto, who lived and wrote in Europe in contact with artists, writers, and musicians.

Sincronia / Synchrony

devoração crítica do legado cultural universal /
critical devouring of the universal cultural legacy

Haroldo de Campos's poetry recapitulates and synthesizes the principal radical currents of modernity. It exemplifies the fragmentary, permutational, visual, and semiotic techniques and structures of contemporary experimental arts as prepared by the historical avant-gardes and their predecessors across time and space. His poetics is intellectually constituted by the confrontation of contemporary critical theory with aesthetics and is marked by attention to and control of the materials of composition and their aesthetic effects, promoting a pervasive consciousness and reflexivity of and within the works. Within the Brazilian modernist tradition, Haroldo draws on the "Manifesto Antropófago" of Oswald de Andrade (1928) to take up a comparable position as indigenous or nationalist devourer of literary goods arriving from abroad, converting foreign influences into native raw material through the metaphor of cannibal assimilation in the guise of Oswald's *Abaporu*: "o ponto de vista do 'mau selvagem', devorador de brancos." Brazil's concrete poetry movement, a consequence on one level of Haroldo's voracious reading, was exported as a product of Oswaldian cultural devouring. Haroldo also draws upon the rediscovered nineteenth-century Brazilian poet Sousândrade (Joaquim de Sousa Andrade), a professor of Greek from Maranhão whose epic poem celebrating indigenous mythology, *O Guesa*, was written on three continents and contains a highly inventive final canto, "O Inferno de Wall Street," a precursor of avant-garde experimentation.

Another formative influence on his poetics is the synchronic reading of literary innovation as a tradition in authors selected from a wide range of languages and periods of world literature: "de Homero a Dante, de Goethe a Pessoa." Such a universal, selective view of literature has given rise to his own "Western canon" of formative writers and precursors, beginning with "classical" masters representing diverse cultures (Homer, Dante, Camões, Li-Tai-Po, Bashô), leading to the recovery of forgotten or neglected writers in Brazil (Gregório de Mattos, Sousândrade, Kilkerry, Oswald de Andrade) and the chosen, assembled formative masters of modernity (Mallarmé, cummings, Apollinaire, Joyce, Pessoa, Maiakovsky, Cage). Part of his literary project is such a radical reordering of literary history, marked by his thorough knowledge of Greek, Latin, Classical civilization and mythology, as well as the classics of Western and non-Western literatures.

Although known primarily as a member of the Brazilian movement *poesia concreta* that he founded with Augusto de Campos and Décio Pignatari, Haroldo's poetry and imaginary have since far outpaced concretism. The broad scope of his information, for example, incorporates music composition (Webern, Boulez, Stockhausen, Cage), Calder's mobiles, and experimental plastic arts as well as literature. A literary cardsharp who recasts Mallarmé's dice while keeping score with the calligraphy of Chinese ideograms learned in Pound, Haroldo represents an apotheosis of the modern. He "makes it new" by placing his own peculiar stamp on traditions of literary, verbal, and visual experimentation received from masters of the art. While reconstituting his ties with experimental modernism and its innovative contributions to poetry since Mallarmé, Haroldo's poetic project constantly reinvents and rewrites this legacy in his own poetic language.

Concretist: *â mago do ô mega*

ágil atleta da palavra nos trapézios da aventura /
agile athlete of the word on the trapezes of adventure

Two prominent directions in Haroldo de Campos's early concrete poetry are experimentation for social and aesthetic purposes. "Proêmio," from the 1961 *Servidão de Passagem*, treats the role of poetry in denouncing hunger and its accompanying ills of poverty and disease. In a landscape of "pouca poesia," Haroldo creates a poetry to serve a time of hunger, in which the ritual of naming becomes the poet's denunciation of social injustice: "nomeio a fome." Sonorous and semantic variations based on rhyme and alliteration are exploited in a way that could be compared to an operatic dialogue and chorus, or to a verse and refrain form. Throughout *Servidão*, alliterative sequences explore morphological and lexical paronomasias, producing collages and inventing Joycean portmanteau words and neologisms that provoke shock and estrangement: "homemmoendahomemmoagem."

The poem "nascemorre" from *Fome de Forma* (1958) is one of the most formally perfect and expressive of the concrete works and was employed as the text for one of the most well-known compositions of Brazilian composer Gilberto Mendes for a capella chorus. "Nascemorre" is structured in four right triangles placed in two groups. The triangles are bounded by the key thematic word "se", indicating the chance operation reflective (and reflexive) of life and death. The inner links of the triangles are based on the inversion of the "se" theme, which is "re," standing for repetition and reinvention or rebirth. The second triangle, for example, is born from a repetition of the final letters "re" of the word "morre" (to die), which thus change their condition and meaning in order to begin a literal and literary rebirth of the poem, "renasce." The second triangle ends with the theme of "re" or reinvention standing along. This particle carries over to the second group (third triangle) as an initial fragment, placed on the page under the "re" of another "morre" above it. In this case, however, the "re" introduces a sequence defined by the prefix "des" (to be de-born, to undie) to form the neologism "re-de-born" or "re-undie," thus carrying the thematic sequence to a further temporal level, defying normal semantic logic through retrograde inversion. In the final triangle, the theme words "nascemorrenasce" are reintroduced as in a strict recapitulation, whereby one term is removed or deconstructed (or dies) from the extended word with each of three fatal repetitions, until only the final closing interrogative "se" remains. The flux of life and the poetic epic of its rebirths remains as the core of a structural variation on a theme, which is also the birth and life of the poem itself.

Neo-baroque stylist

Um código universal extremamente elaborado /
An extremely elaborate universal code

A major contribution of Haroldo de Campos to Brazilian poetics, along with the recovery of Oswald de Andrade's "cannibalist" theory, is the revaluing of the Brazilian baroque as a national poetic corpus and stylistic forerunner of contemporary experimentation. Implanted as a mature and formative style in territories extending from Brazil to Macao throughout the sixteenth century, the baroque style is explored in one of Haroldo's essays as one of the elements constituting the "dialogue and difference" that characterizes Brazilian letters in contrast to Europe and Spanish America in terms of its ties with world culture: "um código extremamente elaborado – o código retórico barroco" (an extremely elaborate code – the baroque rhetorical code). The poetry of Gregório de Mattos, with its vision of the sacred and corrupt colonial world of Bahia, and the sermons of Antônio Vieira, with their ornate rhetoric and conceits, are cited by Haroldo as the origin of a style of fusion of opposites in texts of semantic and syntactical effects.

The *Galáxias*, composed over more than a decade in 50 fragments of poetic prose, is the major example of neo-baroque composition and aesthetics in Haroldo's work. Universality dominates all levels of theme, technique, and form: *Galáxias* is every book and no book; it is all styles and the erasure of style; it is eternal myth and today's story, fable and speech; it is paradise and inferno of the archetypes of the human archive of experience. The fragments also refer to the wandering poet's remembrance of things past in certain cities of the world. *Galáxias*, above all, is a never-ending sound, an all-encompassing single word that synthesizes, yet in a story without end, the All and the Nothing. Pessoa explains: "O mito é o tudo que é nada" (Myth is the everything that is nothing). The baroque aesthetic also extends to the Orientalism of Haroldo's pan-global and trans-temporal vision: it is our age's *Thousand and One Nights* told in order to save language, story, and poet from extinction. *Galáxias* is a remarkable act of invention by Brazil's "prodigious physicist."

Finismundo: A Última Viagem returns to the Ulysses theme, recasting the story of his Odyssey in post-Utopian urban society. Modern myth recapitulates the classical in the negative. The everyday Ulysses is trapped by traffic signals, computer glitches, and sirens in a voyage through seas without mermaids. The mail brings postcards from Eden. Haroldo's eschatological vision carries social criticism to profound and enigmatic depths through the reenactment of ritual.

Transcreator

dança interna das línguas /
internal dance of languages

The union of translation, theory, and criticism is illustrated in the earliest concretist poetic translations, published in journals. Beginning with Pound and e.e. cummings, the talents of Haroldo and his brother Augusto de Campos as translators would lead them to Joyce, Ungaretti, Maiakovsky, Wallace Stevens, Reverdy, William Carlos Williams, Poe, Mallarmé, William Blake, Dante and other major writers. The Brazilian poets selected each of these authors because of a perceived innovative position or experimentation with literary themes and forms. I participated in a bilingual reading from the *Panaroma de Finnegans Wake*, one of the most successful and creative translations of Joyce that takes advantage of the poetic qualities and flexibility of the Portuguese language. The many innovative volumes of translations by Haroldo and

Augusto range from early twentieth-century Russian poets to late medieval Provençal troubadours, Mallarmé's "Un coup de dés," Octavio Paz's radical poem *Blanco*, Goethe's *Faust*, Pound's *Cantos* to the classical Chinese poet Li-Tai-Po.

In Haroldo's poetry, "transcreation" is the radical operation of the translation of form with the added intention of rescuing and enhancing the poetic function in order to create, in Jakobson's terms, a renewed isomorphic version of the original. The translator is, for Haroldo, a choreographer of a mobile and multidimensional semantic and visual rhythmic interchange of languages. Transcreation replaces the literary work within an international context of validity and interchangeability. To renew a poetic form through another inventive language is to rewrite it and to renew it through "transcreation."

Transcreation also seeks to recover the significant meanings of texts that have been lost through time. Haroldo has undertaken the re-translation of Biblical texts, *Genesis* and *Qohélet*, for which purpose he has studied Hebrew. His commitment to the universal heritage of literature has at the same time led him to the Japanese *Nô* theater (Hagoromo) and to Bashô.

Transcreation is moreover a kind of immediate poetic experience for Haroldo. During his stay in Austin as Visiting Professor in 1981, he accompanied me to the local lumberyard to select a new front door. The resulting poem from "Austinéia Desvairada" (in *A Educação dos Cinco Sentidos*), titled "The Front Door" and dedicated to me, is an oral *poème trouvé* based on the regional, popular wisdom of an old Texan who warned us, as we selected a wooden door, that without ten coats of varnish it would dry up under the Texas sun like the scales of a fish. Haroldo captured the aesthetic significance of this advice and transcreated it into a poem with the qualities of haiku. The "Mad Austin" poems illustrate the invention inherent in the discovery and enhancement of the poetic function in an oral text.

For Haroldo, all experience can be transcreated into poetry and contributes to a craftsmanship unlimited by school or theme. On another Austin occasion, when I received a new violoncello from the local luthier, Charles Ervin, Haroldo transcreated the vibrant yellow tones of the instrument into the song of the "melro de ouro" (Oriole). During Brazil's recent presidential elections, Haroldo composed a poem for the populist campaign of the candidate of the Worker's Party, Lula, illustrating the civic contribution of poetry to political society, a concept present in Haroldo's earliest essays on the social function and responsibility of poetry.

Multiharoldian metalanguages and epic-logue

Haroldo de Campos is the exponent of contemporary experimental literature in Brazil who, like the baroque Vieira, acts on a universal scale. A poet of the *Paulicéia* (city of São Paulo), Haroldo is multiple. More than Mário de Andrade's 350 modernist selves, Haroldo is three thousand, three thousand and five hundred. With Caetano, he is the *circuladô* of "Sampa." From *Noigandres* and *Invenção* to *Galáxias* and *Finismundo*, the Haroldian titles confirm his commitment to the modern tradition and constitute a tele-grammatic dialogue of the present across space and time with earlier masters of poetic experimentation. Through his multi-writings ("multiescrituras"), we gain a vision of Haroldo's literary mephistofaustian paradise.

In place of a traditional epilogue, Haroldo's farewell came in the form of an epic-logue, which is his masterful translation of Homer's *Iliad*, sixteen thousand verses in XXIV Cantos or Rhapsodies, trans-created in dialogue with Trajano Vieira, a scholar of classical Greek. For Vieira, Haroldo's transcreation assures us of the originality and power of the first of all epics. By completing his final epic task, which lasted almost five years, Haroldo shares in the title of "polypansábio," the universal, creative wisdom described by Pythia in her answer to Emperor Hadrian's query about the birthplace and lineage of Homer. Haroldo's trans-Helenized "Brazilian *Iliad*" – a crowning synthesis of his poetics, invention, and scholarship – is the epic-logue through which his creative work will be re-evaluated in its totality.

The Origins of Haroldo de Campos

Gonzalo Aguilar

IN HIS TRANSCREATIONS from the Bible in the 1990s, Haroldo de Campos translated the first verses of the Genesis:

    1. No começar § Deus criando   §§§
        O fogoágua § e a terra

    1. At begin § God creating   §§§
        Firewater § and the Earth

The scene of the origin is thus replaced by a scene of the beginning; that which cannot be repeated (the origin) and appears as concluded from the very start is unlocked in its translation into Portuguese. The gap opened by creation – as it is suggested by the use of the infinitive "começar" (to begin) and the gerund "criando" (creating) – can only occur, paradoxically, in a time with no beginning or end. In Western culture, we can conceive of no single act more closely related to a completed, intransitive, and absolute origin than that of divine creation. The Bible is not only placed at the origin but, furthermore, narrates it once and forever: the beginning of the *Book of Genesis* stands for the casual genesis of the world. Whereas Mallarmé writes that the world exists for the purpose of becoming a book, in the Bible the world exists in order to be derived from The Book. In his transcreational act, Haroldo de Campos repeats the text of the origin and, through repetition, transforms it retrospectively. He looks on the origin from the perspective of the beginning, transforming it into a process, a leap, and a transitivity. This strategic, constructive, and systematic use of "origin" all throughout Haroldo de Campos's lifetime poetic and intellectual production helped him develop a non-substantialist approach to the concept of "origin" in the last decade.

The scene of the origin that opens the translation is a way to give form to the past. As an artifact, the beginning sets up not only possible or desired scenes, but also a series of devices that work between an act and its environment, as well as a series of discursive figures that are the self-consciousness of this speech about its own possibilities.

Biblical transcreation highlights the question of origin and beginnings, which I consider of extreme importance to understanding Haroldo de Campos's writing, be it regarded from poetic, historic, literary, or even religious angles. Written in 1989, Campos's essay *O Seqüestro do Barroco na Formação da Literatura Brasileira: O Caso Gregório de Mattos* (*The Abduction of the Baroque in the Formation of Brazilian Literature: the Case of Gregório de Mattos*) puts this question in the very core of his discussion with Antonio Candido about the latter's theses in *A Formação da Literatura Brasileira* (*The Formation of Brazilian Literature*, 1957). One and the same question guides both texts: what to do with the past?

Haroldo de Campos's objections to Candido's book focus mainly on two aspects: Candido's belief in the objectiveness of historical reconstruction of the past, and his assumption of a closed process, which runs towards an ending, and its resulting sense of wholeness. In other words, Haroldo de Campos disagrees with Candido's idea of the formation of a Brazilian literature as the unfolding and fulfillment of a national spirit. Undoubtedly, Candido solves several problems common to literary histories, especially by converting works into active – and not merely passive – factors of history. However, in the methodological and aesthetic choice of neoclassicism and romanticism he makes to outline this literary formation, Candido decides on a national representative frame that leads him to exclude the baroque (since it is previous to this "wish" for nationality) and devalue, as minor figures, writers such as Sousândrade, who are elusive to this proposed canon. Critically, Haroldo de Campos identifies the conception of an axiological canon under the presumption of objectiveness, as well as he detects, under the description of this formative process, the model of a representative and organic literature which is doomed to be built on the basis of abduction and organic exclusion. In his book, Haroldo de Campos does not intend only a positive appreciation of the baroque and the outbreak of modernism. I think there is a political and ideological criticism as well: by assuming literary history as representative and homogeneous, Candido's *A Formação* ends up describing the vision of a social group which emerged as dominant and, consequently, was able to make an organic reading of the past.[1] The "mouths of hell" of Gregório de Mattos and the "clandestine" earthquakes of Sousândrade are a very powerful counter-history but, being themselves disperse and incidental, they can seldom be included in the process of national canon formation. Their exclusion can be explained by a time restriction that is a characteristic feature of the system itself – that is the case of Gregório de Mattos – or because these texts themselves are reluctant to be identified with that ideological representation – as is most evident in the case of Sousândrade.

To rescue the "kidnapped" Gregório de Mattos, Haroldo de Campos's essay considers that the formation is not concluded in the past and suggests that we should view the past itself as a construction and regard literary history as "a constant and ever-renewed inquiry of diachrony by synchrony," a method the author designates "a synchronic-retrospective view." In a complementary movement, in order to reinsert the excluded Sousândrade, Haroldo de Campos reads the symptoms of the singular subverting the general and of margins rejecting centrality. As Flora Süssekind has accurately observed, stabilizing scenes of the formation of literature are substituted by the scenes of instability that appear in *O Seqüestro do Barroco*. Whereas Candido imagines a beginning (dated in 1750), which is the onset of the teleological unfolding of the origin, Haroldo de Campos puts forward a constellar beginning – built up from the present – that commences an open, non-accumulative, and episodic series.

Although Haroldo de Campos's book was written thirty years after Candido's, the basic principles of their diverging conceptions of beginnings stir up exactly at the same moment. In December 1956, while the Exposição Nacional de Arte Concreta is inaugurated in the Museu de Arte de São Paulo, Candido is finishing the first volume of his book. In its introduction, he presents the concept of "estilo do tempo" (style of its

---

[1] In "Dialética da Malandragem" Candido himself admits that: "*Memórias de um Sargento de Milícias* does not fit in any of the then dominant ideological rationalizations of Brazilian literature: Indianism, nationalism, greatness of suffering, redemption by pain, pompous style, etc.... (*Memórias*) may be the only text in Brazilian XIXth century literature which does not express a vision of the dominant class." In *O Discurso e a Cidade*, op. cit., 51. In this essay Candido revises his previous work and suggests that the formation could be understood as the history of the literature of a dominant class. Of most interest is that concepts such as "factor," "nationality," and "continuity" are now related to power rather than desire, thus opening up the way to the consideration of subaltern literatures.

time), which, in his opinion, allows for "as generalizações críticas" (critical generalizations).² Concretists, instead, approach the literary past through the concept of *paideuma* that, since its early use, contests that of the "spirit of time."³ In the same way this idea is employed by Pound in his *Guide to Kulchur* or by the Paulista poets in their manifestoes, a difference in the present is established to separate living and exhausted traditions. *Paideuma*, a concept that operates by contrast and differentiation, rejects the valuation of literary tradition according to its dominant representative and stabilizing lines. Instead, in the modernist way, the concept of *paideuma* intends to trace *evolution lines*, which are not to be found in the "atmosphere" or in the habits of a period, but in the margins, in the non-representative, in the ordeal of the inorganic and unstable.

The notion of *paideuma* conceives of beginning as the construction of a lineage. This device does not seem to match the conventional idea of newness of the avant-gardists or their well-known trait of promoting scandals and iconoclasm. However, there is only incongruity as long as we understand the mid-century avant-garde as a derivative of the historical avant-garde. To grasp the movement of concrete poetry, we must go not to the historical avant-garde but to the peculiar inflections of Brazilian high modernism in the 1950s.

The device of building up a lineage can be linked, on one hand, to the language of modernism. As Adrián Gorelik observes about the urban designer Lúcio Costa, this language brings about "in each artistic object, simultaneously, a future and a tradition."⁴ On the other hand, the making of a lineage is closely related to some spatial patterns, chiefly that of the museum, which play a configuring role. Indeed, the national exposition of 1956 takes place in a museum. Although the rise of an avant-garde movement in a museum may seem a paradox, it is not so: the struggle for the setting up of a new programme does not occur *against* but *within* the frame of institutions.

Since the beginning of concretism, the mediating space of the museum provided a bearing for the practices of the group. It was in the

---

2   *Formação da Literatura Brasileira*, vol. I, 39. Candido began writing this book in 1945 and then "resumed his work on it in 1955 for a revision, the first volume of which was finished in 1956 and the second in 1957."
3   Ezra Pound, *Guide to Kulchur* (New York: New Directions, 1939), 58.
4   Adrián Gorelik, "Tentativas de comprender una ciudad moderna" in *Block* (*Revista de cultura de la arquitectura, la ciudad y el territorio*), no. 4 (número dedicado a Brasil), Buenos Aires, Universidad Torcuato di Tella, Dec., 1999.

museums founded in São Paulo around those years (Museu de Arte de São Paulo in 1957, Museu de Arte Moderna in 1948), where a modernist tradition was first recognized, made explicit and revised thoroughly. Among the several exhibits that were organized, the retrospective of Brazilian modernist artists and two key expositions, that of Alexander Calder and that of Max Bill – both around 1950 – loom large. The exhibit of concrete art in the Museu de Arte Moderna, mentioned above, gathered plastic artists, designers, and poets.

In 1951, from an initiative of this museum, the Bienals of art and architecture of São Paulo were inaugurated. With their periodic exhibits, they helped stress the idea of temporality as evolution: each exposition was to be renovating compared to the previous one.[5] In the formation of what Raymond Williams has called the "structure of feeling" of a group or a generation, the museum played a very different role in the 1950s from the one it had played at the beginning of the century.[6] Living museum instead of mausoleum, in its rooms, spectators – and among them, the young poets who would form concretism – were able to

---

5   The Bienals of São Paulo in the 1950s were the best school for the knowledge of the avant-gardes. The first Bienal (October through December 1951) congregated nineteen countries and artists as important as Picasso, Max Ernst (representing the US), Giacometti, De Koonig, Pollock, Torres García, Portocarrero, Lucio Fontana, Léger, Tanguy, Magritte, Delvaux, Edward Hopper, and André Masson. The first prize for architecture was awarded to Le Corbusier. The second and fourth prizes went to Niemeyer and Lúcio Costa, designers of the Brasília Project a few years later. However, the most resounding artist was the sculptor Max Bill with his work "Tripartite Unity," which was outstanding among the other paintings and sculptures shown in the Bienal. Among Brazilians, it is worth noting the participation of special guest artists such as Lasar Segall, Cândido Portinari, and Emilio Di Cavalcanti. Source: I Bienal do Museu de Arte Moderna de São Paulo (outubro a dezembro de 1951), catalogue, São Paulo, MAM, 1951.

The second Bienal ran from November 1953 through February 1954. Forty countries were represented and sixteen retrospectives were organized. It turned out to be a much larger event than the first Bienal, differing also in that the restriction by which only retrospectives on living artists were allowed was suppressed. Among the works that were exhibited, we can note down those of Pablo Picasso (51 of his paintings including *Guernica*, besides ten more works exhibited in the retrospective of Cubism), Henry Moore (29 works), Pietr Mondrian (20), Calder (45), Paul Klee (65), and Torres García (4). Gropius was the central figure of the second Bienial, as Le Corbusier had been the focus of the first. Special notice deserve the notable retrospectives on futurism and the works of Rufino Tamayo, who won the international prize for painting (the Great Prize went to Henri Laurens). The award for best national painter was shared by Volpi and Di Cavalcanti. The absence of surrealism (a synonym of the avant-garde in many countries at those times) and the broad range and variety of aesthetic proposals were two significant characteristics of the second Bienial.

6   For this concept, see Raymond Williams, "Estructuras del Sentir" in *Marxismo y literatura*, (Barcelona: Península, 1980), 150–8.

experience the transformation of the avant-garde movements and also incorporate the paradigm of modernism.[7] It was there within the frame of those museums and biennials where another decisive mechanism was generated: the attitude of research. Although this was certainly a characteristic feature of the avant-garde at those times, it reached a particular slant and a stronger persistence in the Brazilian group.

With the arts of the Bienals – painting, sculpture, architecture – poets created a space for dialogue and performance. By drifting poetry away from its conventional place, they coined a third device: the concept of beginning as dislocation. Visual poems borrowed the format of plastic arts and, hung on the walls of the museums, contested the place of traditional expositions and their conventions. Manifestoes were published in *ad*, a magazine of architecture and decoration. Poetry was promoted as "planning," "design," and "construction," all categories which clearly linked it to the visual arts and to the poetics of João Cabral de Melo Neto and, above all, to the discipline that had become an emblem of modernist tradition in Brazil: architecture – the title of the 1958 manifesto being "plano piloto" (pilot blueprint).

These three devices (making of a lineage, systematic research, discursive dislocation) that work in the textuality of concrete poets are still a key feature in the most recent writings of Haroldo de Campos. I am conscious that I would be driven to a paradox if I pretended that the key nuclei of his work were already condensed, once and forever, at the very beginnings of concretism. How should we then read the initial baroque of his early books of poems? How could we give account of the strong evolutionary – albeit constructive and not organic – element of modernist tradition, which is left aside gradually during the 1960s? And, finally, how could we understand the existence – though theoretical – of an open process in which discontinuities and displacements are so remarkable? There is not just one single beginning in the work of Haroldo de Campos but, instead, a plurality of them: different programmatic conditions signal, each time, new starting points. Beginning must not be regarded

---

7 "MASP was located until 1968 in the Diários Associados building on 230, rua Sete de Abril. The MAM settled in the same building in 1949. I remember going to both museums on rua 7 de Abril and, especially, to Cinemateca Brasileira (film library of the MAM), where we saw great retrospectives of avant-garde films: Eisenstein, Dziga Vertov, German expressionist films, the surrealist films of Artaud and Buñuel, the abstract adventures of Fischinger and others, some of them younger, like Norman MacLaren, a whole cyclopedia of experimental filming." Testimony by Augusto de Campos.

simply as the manifestation of a change or transformation; it is rather to be grasped as the explicit figure through which variations and displacements, links to traditions, and their revision are processed.

Galáxias, begun in 1963, reopens the scene of the origin:

> E começo aqui e meço aqui este começo e recomeço e remeço e arremesso
> (…) quando se vive sob a espécie da viagem o que importa não é a viagem mas o começo da[8]
>
> and I begin here and here I cradle this beginning and re-begin and re-cradle and assail
> (…) when one lives under the species of travel what is important is not the trip but the beginning of

In *Galáxias*, Haroldo employs the first person for the first time after concretism. In a peculiar way, he also lays the poem within the space and time of history. In this *mise en scène* of the subject and the referent, the poem is based on postulates that noticeably differ from those of concretism. The elocutionary presence of *I* reveals a discontinuity: the poem breaks and puts under new conditions the collective strategy of concretism, which had rebuffed the notion of the subject and questioned the idea of authority as beginning. In their search for a common writing and a plural voice, the poets themselves had suspended their styles to join a collective and anonymous practice from the viewpoint of the lyrical voice. In *Galáxias*, concrete asceticism becomes devouring and exuberant, and this creates the setting for the return of the subject, not as sign of an expression or an authority external to the text, but rather as an effect of language and "fiction."[9] However, as the subject emerges as a rupture from the first line of the poem, the relation to history is modified as the writing of *Galáxias* proceeds. A text open to historical contingency, *Galáxias* was written between 1963 and 1976, and as the author points out "imagined at the extreme of the limits of prose and poetry." What happens in this interval is a passage from the evolutionary paradigm, which used to organize the materials of concretism, to the ever-increasing

---

8 As in his early but also foundational "Cirópedia ou a educação do Príncipe" (1951), the poem begins by pondering its own conditions to get started: "A Educação do Príncipe em Agedor começa por un cálculo ao coração."

9 See the epigraph of *Galáxias*: "fiction will blossom and dart off, fast."

presence of a synchronic-retrospective paradigm that is displayed in constellations.

This passage is possible because *Galáxias* is written under the sign of experimentation, regarded – as Walter Moser suggests – not as a proof of instrumental rationality but as a self-reflexive activity that experiments with language.[10] *Galáxias* is an experiment in the most rigorous sense of this word: they set up conditions for writing, produce texts at different moments following these conditions, and attain different results. In the presentation of the first series, which was published in *Invenção*, Haroldo writes a brief preface (titled "dois dedos de prosa sobre uma nova prosa" and then suppressed in the final version of the book), in which he puts forward the guiding points of his project:

> preveer un libro. de cien páginas. o cerca de. no más. la primera y la última fijas: formantes. las demas sueltas y permutables. la primera y la última hablando sobre el escribir: el comienzo y el fin. el fincomienzo de. por lo tanto ni comenzando ni terminando (...) el fluir de los singos (...) todos los materiales. no jerarquizados. o una nueva fabulación. un nuevo realismo. clivaje: mente de guimarães rosa y mente industrial de oswald.[11]

> foresee a book. of a hundred pages. or so. no more. the first and the last, fixed: forming. the remaining permutable and loose. the first and the last on writing: the beginning and the end of. the endbeginning of. therefore not beginning nor ending (...) the flow of signs (...) all the materials, under no hierarchy, or a new fabulation. a new realism. cleavage: guimarães rosa's craftsman's mind and oswald's industrial mind.

A flow of signs, *Galáxias* push the poetic sign to the limits: they get mixed up in orality, wander around the world and its languages, search for social and artistic events. A structure open to contingency and to

---

10 Walter Moser, "Haroldo de Campos' Literary Experimentation of the Second Kind" in *Experimental – Visual – Concrete: Avant-garde Poetry Since the 1960s*, ed. by K. David Jackson, Eric Vos, and Johanna Druker (Amsterdam and Atlanta, 1996).
11 This programmatic texts, which bears the title "dois dedos de prosa sobre uma nova prosa" was published in the magazine *Invenção* (number 4, December 1964). Once this project was finished, this text was suppressed from the final edition of *Galáxias* (São Paulo: Ex Libris, 1984). An oral version recited by Haroldo de Campos is available on CD: *Isto Não é um Livro de Viagem* (16 fragments from *Galáxias*), (Rio de Janeiro: Editora 34, 1992); the CD is also included in the second edition of *Galáxias* in 2004.

political and personal changes: the text is imagined in the flow of history and foreshadows what this history might turn out to be. As a legacy of both Haroldo's concrete phase and the paradigm of high modernism, this programme is integrated, at its first stage, in an evolution line. We must read the beginning of *Galáxias* keeping in mind the editorial notes of the magazine *Invenção* and in relation to an *evolutive linearity*, an epic hope in the potentially revolutionary scope of 1963. In its third issue of June that year, the prospectus of the magazine avows: "new poetry – of *Invenção* – is addressed to the people-producers. Of revolution. Against the pragmatism and the empiricism of art consumption, and against all forms of revolution intended through the competent channels of bureaucratic-formalist poetry." These programmatic proposals are to be contrasted against the description of the process of composition that Haroldo de Campos makes at the end of *Galáxias*, thirteen years later: "today, retrospectively, I would see it as an epic insinuation that resulted in an epiphany."

From the start of the project, there is an oscillation between history (epic) and a "restricted – though epiphanic – action" which will be resolved by swaying towards the latter. Whereas *Galáxias* begin with a perspective of utopia, they end up being written in a post-utopian era. At first, the autonomy of poetic writing is taken to its limits, but finally a movement back to the epiphany of poetic writing prevails. This can be interpreted as a Mallarmean programme of restricted action and negative politics, or as a creative response to the historical impossibility of modernism, or even as the cultural outburst, which is announced by *Galáxias* themselves, of the parodic, the burlesque, and the corporal. While utopia is the historical possibility of the avant-gardes, epiphany is the transhistorical potential of poetic materiality. This materiality is transformed into the basic criterion of the synchronic-retrospective view: I believe, says Haroldo de Campos, that today, all poetry which deserves this name is concrete. From Homer to Dante. From Goethe to Fernando Pessoa. For the poet is the one who configures the materiality of language.[12]

Through this constructive matrix, which is a key feature of Haroldo de Campos's stances, beginning, as was seen, in the fragment I quoted from *Galáxias*, is converted into a figure of speech. In the poems of his

---

12 "Minha Relação como a Tradição é Musical," *Metalinguagem & Outras Metas* (São Paulo: Perspectiva, 1992), 264.

concretist period, this figure had already appeared: in *O â mago do ô mega*, on a linguistic plane, with the initial letter "alpha"; and in "nascemorre" (isborndies), on a vital plane, with the verb "nascer" (to be born), which will come out again in the title of his last book of poems, *Crisantempo: No Espaço Curvo Nasce Um*. Signs of beginning, their insertion on the space of the page call for their antonyms and, defying the principle of identity, form an ideogramme: alpha and omega, "Zero/Zenith," be born and die, *nascemorre*. In *Galáxias*, this crucial sign is repeated until it meets its opposites: from "começo" (I begin) to "recomeço" (I begin over again), to "descomeço" (I unbegin), to "acabarcomeçar" (to endbegin), to "fimcomeço" (endstart). Syntheses in tension, conciliation of contraries, tiny Möebius strips. What shall we do with these ideogrammes? Shall we submit them to a conceptual reading or let them shine as they sparkle? The reason why I have chosen to go for a conceptual reading is that, in this play of antitheses ("morrenascemorre," "acabarcomeçar," "fimcomeço"), we can see a double attribute of beginnings. In their immanence, they invert the hierarchical relation of cause-effect and antecedence, proposing, in its place, constellar relations of contiguity and juxtaposition. As namings of limits, these ideogrammes link what stands as separate out of the text, place each sign (be born and die, end and beginning) within the space of a relationship, as if only such a relation (antithesis, contradiction or adjacency) could account for their dynamics. Beginnings do not bear an unlocked and complete identity; they produce meaning along their transit.

In *Galáxias* we find a micro-archeology of beginnings: they repeat and, in each of their repetitions, while modifying – retrospectively – their antecedence, produce a translation to the future ("or what will become of it"). A writing, as defined by Severo Sarduy, "the functional support of which is difference and the motor of which is repetition." In "nascemorre," the recurrence of the terms is unfolded following two vectors, "se" and "re": a repetition ("re") without a subject ("se," i.e. the impersonal form of the verb), brought about by the display of verbal material itself. In *Galáxias*, the subject assumes repetitions and transforms them under its own law: "e aqui me meço e começo e me projeto eco do começo eco do eco de um começo em eco" (and here I cradle myself and begin and project myself echo of beginning echo of an echo of a beginning in echo). Words gravitate one upon the other, each one being a center of repetition and each repetition being itself singular. In lyrical language, says Deleuze, "each term cannot be replaced, it can only be repeated."[13]

Repetition, "vertical" (Deleuze) and anomalous, crawls back to the interior of words. In the language of the planetary music of *Crisantempo*: "os ecos dos teus ecos" (the echoes of your echoes). As a figure, beginning procures its energy from this semiotic space (constellation of signs), in which each term is an echo of another in a kind of generalized parallelism. As a device, beginning is a constructive act that always occurs, in Valéry's words, "between a particular vision and the selected materials." As a scene, each beginning stands for the outbreak of instability. We could even think of a fourth dimension of beginnings: that of desire, the wish to start over again, the desire of "keeping entelechy active," of facing – in ethical as well as aesthetic terms – the task of doing new things.

Plurality of origins and beginnings, Haroldo's writing and reading trace diagonal lines between the eccentric and the disperse, for it is there where desire is rooted as the simultaneous transformation of present and past. Between alpha and omega, zero and zenith, be born and die, between "começo recomeço" in *Galáxias* and "começar" in his transcreation of the *Genesis*, between the "polyphonic origin" and the placentary poetry of *Crisantempo*:[14] at each beginning, Haroldo de Campos keeps poetry alive.

Translated by Nicolás Lucero.

---

13 In this paragraph, I owe several concepts to the essay "Repetición y diferencia," in *Theatrum Philosophicum Seguido de Repetición y Diferencia*, ed. by Michel Foucault and Gilles Deleuze (Barcelona: Anagrama, 1995, 51).

14 *Crisantempo: No Espaço Curvo Nasce Um* (São Paulo: Perspectiva, 1998), 329.

Haroldo de Campos: the Theorist and the Critic

Leyla Perrone-Moisés

To REREAD THE theoretical and critical work of Haroldo de Campos is to go on a trip through time and space. It is to travel a long way in the company of a traveler who is not only alert to what happens around him, but who reacts to everything and participates in all things, with an enthusiasm which is constantly being renewed.[1]

The collection of H.C.'s essays, according to a list provided by the author himself in a recent publication (*Crisantempo*, 1998), is made up of 18 books. In *A Arte no Horizonte do Provável*, which consisted of articles dating from 1956 to 1969, he summarized his field of reflection: "the problem of creation and criticism *today*, the problems of an avant-garde text production and of the metalinguistic discourse which is capable of focusing them" (*Preface*). His last book of essays, *O Arco-Íris Branco* (1997), shows not only a great fidelity to those matters, but also a remarkable ability to review them while taking into consideration the time elapsed, the new theories available, and the perplexities of the last two decades.

The concrete poetry movement, led by H.C. in the 1950s together with his brother Augusto de Campos, Décio Pignatari and others, was a movement founded in a theory, characterized by large international information and a great internal coherence. Their project implied the contact among artists from several forms of art and from a variety of countries, under the sign of the invention of new forms and the patronage of some tutelary names of high modernism: Mallarmé, Pound, Joyce, cummings. The strongest theoretical influence came from Ezra Pound,

---

1 Works by Haroldo de Campos quoted in this paper:
 (AHP): *A Arte no Horizonte do Provável* (São Paulo: Perspectiva, 1969)
 (OT): *A Operação do Texto* (São Paulo: Perspectiva, 1976)
 (MTL): *Metalinguagem e Outras Metas* (São Paulo: Perspectiva, 1992)
 (AIB): *O Arco-Íris Branco* (São Paulo: Imago, 1997)

from whom the Brazilian poets adopted the motto *make it new*, the maxim of updating tradition, the criticism through demonstration and ideogrammic sampling, the search for a universal standard of poetic quality, the systematic exercise of translation. The practice of concrete poetry would therefore suppose a theoretical foundation and a critical attitude. Invention and translation, theory and criticism would feed each other mutually and have a pedagogical aim.

Until the mid-1960s, the texts signed by H.C. did not substantially distinguish themselves from those signed by his companions; many of these texts were jointly signed. These were pragmatic texts, which divulged the project of concrete poetry. However, with the end of the heroic phase of concretism, H.C. became the author of the largest and most varied theoretical and critical work: a work that includes the manifesto, the critical poem, the commented translation, the critical monograph, the essay covering propositions of language theory and literary historiography, apart from general aesthetic and political considerations. In this way, H.C. enrolls himself in the tradition of the critic-poets introduced by the romantic German poets and since then followed by a whole lineage of modern poets: Poe, Baudelaire, Mallarmé, Pound, Eliot, Valéry, Pessoa, Borges, Octavio Paz and others.

At the end of the 1960s, H.C. also became a university professor of literature, an activity that would result in the writing of a doctoral thesis: *Morfologia do Macunaíma* (1972). The transformation of the poet into a scholar did not at all mean his withdrawing into an academic posture of good stylistic behavior and adhering to established values. H.C. could carry out his job as a professor without giving into or become accommodated, not only thanks to the conditions offered to him at the institutions in which he taught, but also to the circumstances of time in which this fusion of activities took place. The moment was that of French structuralism, of the new linguistic trends and semiotics, tendencies that were favorable for the continuation of the concrete project, whose greatest objective was what then became known as "the work of the significant."

It was, for H.C., a moment of euphoria, in which he produced some of his best creative texts, such as *Galáxias*, and some of his most instigating essays. During this phase his conceptual repertoire grew considerably. The Russian formalists and semiologists became strong inspirers, especially Bakhtine and Roman Jakobson, who apart from being an inspirer became an interlocutor. He was also aware of the

Frankfurt thinkers, above all Walter Benjamin, and of the then recent aesthetic of reception.

In the 1980s, always alert to the new directions in literary studies, H.C. sensed the possibilities of returning to some of the topics which he had been interested in for a long time: the artistic and cultural relationship between the center and the periphery, the conditions for having an avant-garde poetry in a derived culture, the dialectic of the old and the new, the universal and the particular. The winds of post-modernism were also detected by H.C., who wrote an essay in 1984 about the "post-utopian poem," whose text was dedicated to the celebration of the 70 years of his friend and collaborator Octavio Paz.

Having laid out in general terms the very rich theoretical way of H.C., I will make some incursions into his essays, through some topics. These topics will act as privileged places in a vast territory that is worthwhile exploring. As Pound would say, this is a periplus, not a map.

Avant-garde

The concrete movement, according to H.C. himself in the retrospective assessment carried out in 1984, "was the last collective and international avant-garde movement" (AIB, 263). Conceived in the 1950s to fight the formal retrocession that was then taking place in Brazilian poetry, the project of concrete poetry took back the courageous and provocative attitudes of the historical avant-gardes of the twenties.

Though relevant and necessary at that moment, the word "avant-garde" was later slowly abandoned by H.C. The project it stood for though was not. The avant-garde work became to him a synonym of *obra aberta* (which he named before it was done by Umberto Eco), of "radical work" (in the daring of its project and in the rigor of its execution), of the "text" in the strong sense of this term, in short, of "modern work." The avant-garde in the discourse of H.C. is a trans-historical qualitative concept, which can only be understood in relation to the practice of "synchronic poetics."

Synchronic poetics

Since his first book of essays, H.C. restated what was in the concrete poetry manifestoes: "Every present of creation proposes a synchronic reading of the past of culture. The seizure of the new represents the continuity and the extension of our experience of what has already been done" (AHP, 154). The project of re-reading the literary tradition according to the creative needs of the present and of the immediate future was collected in Pound's work, and to a smaller degree in Eliot's. The Poundian concept of *paideuma* was redefined by H.C. an infinite number of times. One of the most concise formulas is the following: "selective approximation carried out by creative imagination for the 'nourishment of the impulse'" (AHP, 80).

In the 1960s, the linguistic concepts of diachrony and synchrony helped him to deal with the problems of a literary history that was not simply a catalogue but a significant and inspiring selection. At the same time, Bakhtine's considerations on the anachronisms that complicate the historico-literary process came to reinforce his arguments against a linear historiography, evolutional and finalist. So, the incisive proposals of Ezra Pound were being developed and enlarged by H.C. with the support of the most recent subjects.

Despite the interest he took in linguistics and semiotics, H.C. never suffered the temptation of being scientific. The theories engaged his attention as *ad hoc* arguments to enjoy literature, as intellectual games in tune with poetical games. He related the precepts of Pound with the suggestions of other more recent critic-poets: Jorge Luis Borges (*Kafka y sus precursores*), Michel Butor reading Balzac in the light of Mallarmé, and Octavio Paz reading Sor Juana in the light of Lezama Lima.

The language in which he discussed these theories has always had the taste of poetical texts, in which we find formulations such as "the stellar reception," or the "planetarium of signs" in which only the "luminous points" would be focused. Meanwhile, the international *paideuma* proposed by Pound was being enlarged by H.C. in commented translations of works belonging to many different languages and cultural traditions, but always submitted to the principles of a rigorous selection.

Rigorous selection

Rigor and radicality are constant words in the theoretical texts of H.C. Ever since its first phase, his poetical and critical production could be put under the maxim of Valéry: "The greatest freedom comes from the greatest rigor." He then recognized the "programming of hazard" as "one of the main concerns of the international avant-garde of the constructive artists" (AHP, 25). Therefore his critical choice always achieved the "drastic separation" recommended by Pound. His preference went to the authors who showed the greatest formal rigor. On the other hand, he always showed his suspicions related to the experiences that trusted more to "inspiration," like the surrealists, who believed in the creative power of the psychic automatism (AHP, 41). He likewise distinguished the "intrinsic romantics" (Hölderlin, Leopardi), from the "extrinsic romantics," who remained tied to emotion "without reaching an aesthetic configuration" (AHP, 185).

Everything which is halfway, conciliatory, tepid, always displeased him and of this we can give some examples. The experience of Raymond Queneau in *Cent mille milliard de poèmes*, an apparently daring work for its proposal of an open combination of verses, was judged limited as it stuck to the form of a traditional sonnet in Alexandrine verses (AHP, 27–8). In another work, about the *kitsch* and its complex relations to *pop art*, this is finally rejected, in literature, as a *mid-cult* and belletristic version of that which had one day been avant-garde (AHP, 201). These considerations of the 1960s would be subscribed today by H.C., whom the years have made wiser but not more conciliatory. Recently he rejected the translations made by "little daring translators," who are "explicit, mediating, satisfied with being halfway" (AIB, 50).

H.C.'s rigor borders on being intolerant. However, one can argue that his adventure in poetry, criticism, and translation could only be of some value if it was radical. Concrete poetry as a typical avant-garde movement would not have been so important in literary history if its poets had not been so intransigent with the principles they wished to implant. As Pound used to say: "gli indifferenti non hanno mai fatto la storia."

It was with this selective rigor that H.C. proposed, from the beginning of his journey, to carry out a critical revision of the history of Brazilian literature. Since 1963, he has proposed a "creative history of Brazilian poetry" (MTL, 18). In 1967, having fed this project with more recent reflections, he outlined the index of an "Anthology of the Brazilian Poetry of Invention" (AHP, 208), retaken in 1969 (OT, 18). He then distinguished a "textual history," selective and synchronic, of a "literary history," cumulative and diachronic. The project of the "anthology" was not carried out as such, but was explored in the form of monographic essays. And the wondering about literary history led him to think, in an original and stimulating way, of the old dichotomy "national-international."

National-international

Once the concrete movement had passed, internationalism became for H.C. less a group project and more a question of valuation. Just as the synchronic evaluation of tradition should be done according to a trans-historical standard, likewise the evaluation of national literatures should take into account an international standard. Though concerned about the literature of his country, H.C. refused to adopt a nationalistic, complaisant posture, which would put Brazilian artistic production in a straight dependence on the economic, social and political conditions. Quoting Engels's statement that "countries which are economically latecomers may nevertheless play the first violin in Philosophy" (in a letter of 27 October, 1890), he continued to pursue a standard of *weltliteratur*, the only one, according to him, capable of tearing the national literatures from provincial conditions, and the emergent literatures from the position of being derivative and minor. "I can only conceive nationalism from a modal point of view, non-ontological: the Brazilian way of talking with the universal, articulating in a different way its combinations and data, specifying choices, renovating and also innovating" (AIB, 9).

Thinking about the literary phenomena from the ex-centric angle of Brazilian literature, H.C. undertook an exciting theoretical alliance of the principles of Jacques Derrida's deconstruction with the proposal of "cultural anthropophagy" of the Brazilian writer Oswald de Andrade. The *décentrement*, as deconstruction of metaphysical essentiality, and "the devouring of the Other," as an antidote to the anxieties of nationalism, were laid out in the essay "Da Razão Antropofágica: Diálogo e Diferença na Literatura Brasileira" (1980), which was translated into several languages and published in various countries. The practical demonstration of this theoretical posture was a critical retaking of the Brazilian literary historiography. His concept of literary history as a space in which a morphological evolution takes place, but not an axiological progression, led him to criticize romantic-nationalistic literary histories and to revalue a period which would have been "kidnapped" in Brazil by this type of history: the baroque.

Baroque

The aesthetic, axiological, and historical questions put forward by the baroque have always been present in H.C.'s essays. To evaluate just how much the question of the baroque is fundamental in his work, one needs only to remember that this is one of the few points in which he disagrees with Pound, who did not hold this tendency in great esteem. Nevertheless following Pound's own method, H.C. pointed out a trans-historical and transnational "architexture" of the baroque, in a lineage that would include the Greek Licofron, the Chinese Lin Shang-Yin, the Spaniard Góngora (naturally), the French Mallarmé and the modern Latin-American writers (OT, 139).

Considering the baroque as "one of the formal constants of Brazilian sensitivity," present since the beginning of its history up to now, even in concrete poetry, H.C. refuses the concept of the baroque being the "childhood" of this literature. He considers that the baroque offers many advantages: "Already in the baroque a possible 'rule of anthropophagy' develops; it deconstructs the logocentrism we inherited from the West. Differential within the universal, it began in the baroque the distortions and contortions of a discourse which could disentangle us from the same" (MTL, 243).[2]

Parallel to these reflections on the baroque, the poet went on further spilling the baroque of his own work, in long, cunning and lexically over-refined poems. The baroque is in this way one of the touchstones of the work of H.C., and we could even say this of his psychological and intellectual personality. When commenting on the two versants of Roland Barthes' work, the "science of the signs" and the "pleasure of the text," he saw the former as being classical and the latter "baroque." This last one, he says, "contains the ignition, the best of Barthes, the Barthes of the body" (MTL, 126). This valuation of the baroque as "a playful and liberating practice of the sign" can also be used to describe H.C. himself. In fact, not only did his poetical work present clear baroque features, but also his essays underwent a formal evolution in the same direction. The "manifesto" style of the articles of the first phase and the didactic style of those of the second were progressively substituted by a dense writing of

---

2 "The Rule of Anthropophagy: Europe under the Sign of Devoration" (translated by María Tai Wolff), in *Latin American Literary Review*, no. 27, Special Issue: Brazilian Literature (ed. by K. David Jackson and Yvette Miller), Vol. XIV, Jan–June 1986.

a complex syntax and rare vocabulary, in texts abounding with references and suggestions, exploding constellations.

The essays of H.C. are never neutral texts, because they are born, according to his own words, from "a never ending passion, poetry," because it comes from a "beaming vein" that gives them an "(almost) dance step" (AIB, 9). In fact, what connects the multiple facets of the poet-critic and gives them its flavor is their quality of products of an *intelletto d'amore*.

Intelletto d'amore

If one carefully examines H.C.'s motivations, one can see that in the origin of his proposals and refusals there is always an affective disposition that stimulates him in the defense of the new against the old, of the live against the dead, of the ardent against the lukewarm. For example, literary criticism only interests him when engaged in "the life of literary experience" (MTL, 21), and not when it is a "by the grave discourse" (AHP, 52), "a neutral watchmaker's shop of concepts" (MTL, 17) or "an occupational therapy" (MTL, 142).

Like criticism, translation is for him a vivifying operation. When dealing with an old text such as Pindar or Homer, to translate it is to keep it alive: "This translation is not for philologists who are engrossed in their specialties, like lead tombs, not willing to trade with those who are alive" (AHP, 109). The good teaching of literature is considered the same way: "a pedagogy which is not dead or obsolete, in a pose of contrition and immobility, but fruitful and stimulating" (MTL, 44).

For H. C. poetry and translation, theory and criticism are activities of "devotion and love" (MTL, 43), ways of generosity. More than a generation of young Brazilian poets and critics have shaped their taste and critical judgment, widened their repertoire thanks to his generous and obstinate activity. An activity which has flowed over national frontiers and which made him known and appreciated wherever poetry is cultivated.

Conclusion

The present moment is no longer one of avant-gardes, old or new, neither of scientific metalanguages, neither of the great projects directed to the future, where politics and art would jointly contribute to an ideal world. The last essay of *O Arco-Íris Branco* is representative of the posture adopted by the poet in these post-utopian times. Considering the crisis of the political and ideological utopias, he decided to dedicate himself to a "translating operation" and to a "poetry of presentness": "The present only knows provisional synthesis. The only utopian residuum that could and even should remain in it is the critical and dialogical dimension that is inherent in utopia. That poetry of presentness, from my point of view, is not allowed to promote a poetics of renunciation, is not aimed to serve as an alibi for regressive eclecticism and facility. On the contrary, the acknowledgement of a plurality in history stimulates us to a critical appropriation of the past, envisaged as an analogous plurality, without indulging in a previous exclusivist determining of the future" (AIB, 269). As a post-modern Mallarmé would (and did) say: "Sans présumer de l'avenir qui sortira d'ici, rien ou presque un art".

Maintaining nevertheless the critical and dialogical dimensions, keeping the ethical demand of not giving in to eclecticism and complaisance, H.C. is faithful to his own self and to his story as a poet and theorist of high modernism. When he says he is "anchored in the present" and subject to the "reality principle," he seems to adopt a dysphoric attitude. But being anchored does not mean being immobilized. Lifting the sails of Achilles for a new and resumed voyage, in a bold translation of the *Iliad* like the one he dedicated himself to, is a clear gesture of his trust in the future of poetry and its readers.

Haroldo de Campos: Story-telling and Wit

Nelson Ascher

I

HAROLDO DE CAMPOS is known by many people in his country and elsewhere basically as a concrete poet. That means that he is identified as an avant-gardist and a founding member of a postwar movement in the arts that, specifically in poetry, is recognizable by a kind of short poem, the more or less geometrical pattern of which on the page is as important as the text itself. This misconception, or rather somewhat narrow conception, of Haroldo's work is the result not so much of a bad reading of it as of a too credulous reading of the manifestoes that he, his brother Augusto, and Décio Pignatari wrote in the 1950s and early 1960s. And what happened both to Haroldo and to the two other poets is not exactly new, for it has happened before to most avant-garde movements. Namely: friend and foe alike used to read the controversial and polemical utterances of artists even more literally than they do read, for instance, the bill of intentions of a political party.

With this initial observation I do not want to imply that those manifestoes should be discarded, but only that they can be more interestingly understood as part of a larger whole. They are not something outside or above Haroldo's, Augusto's, or Décio's poetry, criticism, and translations. If they are taken as a key, or even worse, as the only key to interpreting what they wrote, that will turn their accomplishment into something poor indeed. If, on the other hand, they are considered as one of the parts of their work, as a product not of the theoretical mind, but of the literary imagination, and thus, as something that beyond the literal level has many others, even contradictory ones, which may be reached through careful interpretation, then even the meaning of those multi-layered manifestoes will be enriched.

That is perhaps the main irony in Haroldo's career: the success of his early polemics became an actual obstacle, not so much between him and his readers as between his work and his critics. One example will be enough, though many more could be given. Some forty years ago, he and the two other concrete poets tended to stress all that in their work was or, at the time, seemed different from what the older generation were doing. As a consequence, their work came to be seen as a rupture with the poetry of a Carlos Drummond de Andrade or a Vinícius de Morais. It is not difficult at all to prove that anybody coming to the concrete poets' work without the foreknowledge of those old discussions would find so many affinities between them and their forerunners that for him or her these would constitute hard evidence of a strong and basically harmonious continuity.

What is more interesting is that even that apparent rupture is a curious proof of that very continuity because a similar misunderstanding had already taken place between the concrete poets' forerunners and an earlier generation of writers. In other words, even in staging their polemical rupture they were following the tradition to which they belonged. It may be fairly obvious by now that the tradition I am talking about is that which Octavio Paz has called "the tradition of rupture." Thus, whoever opens a book by Haroldo in search of some narrowly defined avant-gardist writing will not be exactly disappointed, for what he or she is looking for is also there, but there will be many other different and unexpected things facing and many questions waiting for him or her.

II

A central point that should be made about Haroldo is that he is not a poet who happens to translate, a translator who once in a while spends time on criticism, or a scholar who also writes his own poetry. None of these activities can be considered more important than the other two. Any of his poems, translations, or essays may, of course, be read independently of the rest of his work. For the critic who is trying to understand him in a more comprehensive way, however, that would be a serious mistake, first because the poet himself has not only not established a hierarchy between the three main branches of his work, but stressed insistently that all of them are literature and should, in their own ways, be creative, and second because those three branches interpenetrate all the time in several levels.

In Haroldo's hands, the starting point of an essay is frequently to be found in the problems stemming from the translation of a poem. After the publication of the essay, if it has aroused some kind of discussion, the poet may feel tempted to answer his critics and drive his point home writing, for instance, a satirical poem. The same verbal material will sometimes be used in Haroldo's poems, translations, and essays, but in ways so different from each other, so skillfully modulated or filtered through the prisms of stylistic, rhetorical, and poetical devices as to be recognizable only by the trained eye. As much as there is in his work an interplay between tradition and rupture, there is another one between uniformity and variety.

It would, nevertheless, be simplistic to suppose that his translations are but his own poems in disguise, his poems just veiled translations, or any of his essays only a kind of prose poem. It is true that they all bear his unique stamp, but this does not mean that they merge into each other. Finding similar terms and expressions, similar rhetorical devices disseminated through the distinct branches of his work generates in the reader both amazement and a peculiar kind of pleasure.

The amazement comes from the unexpectedness of discovering, for instance, that something normally associated with the rigorous prose of literary criticism may be effectively used in a poem and then, as effectively, re-used in a translation without in the least betraying the original. The pleasure, in its turn, is a consequence of realizing with how much skill it has all been done. Thus, the hyperbaton – the changing of the natural or usual order of the words in a sentence, a typically baroque technique – may serve the poet to give a certain reasoning in one of his essays a somewhat satirical touch; then it will be used in a poem not as something archaic but to underline its very modernity and, finally, in a translation, it will become the exact way of reproducing in Portuguese what was already present in the original.

The complexity involved in all this has given Haroldo a reputation as a difficult poet. But what is difficult in his work has more to do with the processes he uses than with their end-product, because something that has never been sufficiently underlined by the critics, but is well-known to the reading public and to the younger poets, is that Haroldo's, and also Augusto's and Décio's, activity has always been marked by a healthy strain of didacticism. Translation, after all, is a way of bringing people closer to things hidden in another language. And making opaque things somewhat transparent by showing them from another angle is, or should be, one of literary criticism's main tasks.

Haroldo's repetitions and variations are not there merely to show his skill, nor is their sole function to give his work a unity that, anyhow, is there from the beginning. They operate as a way of making explicit the process of creation. The methodological explanation of any of Haroldo's writings is in another of his writings, or in the writings of a writer he has translated or written about, or rather, and more precisely, in the way he has translated that poet, or in what he found in him or her to write about. This constant need to allow readers to see by themselves his creative processes at work is what we may properly call Haroldo's modernity.

III

Behind the image of a writer undeservedly considered difficult, other characteristics are concealed. Who, in any case, would look in the poetry of a serious scholar for a strong and powerful comic strain? Who would imagine that an avant-garde and concrete poet may be also, or first and foremost, a true storyteller? Instead of examining the poet through his early polemics, it may easily be more profitable to try to see him through the lens of his more recent work.

Haroldo has been working for some time on a new verse translation of Homer's *Iliad*. He is translating it in a regular but rhymeless twelve-syllable verse, which, prosodically, would be in our language the equivalent of the English blank verse, though it has rarely been used in this way by Brazilian or Portuguese poets. The main model to which he is more or less responding is the nineteenth-century translation by Manoel Odorico Mendes.

This version, though discarded then as barely intelligible and disdained to this day by most Brazilian critics, is one of the glories of our literature because in it the translator managed not only to reproduce accurately the sense of the Greek poem, but also to create for that purpose a different kind of Portuguese, a hieratic language in which new words may be coined to convey Homer's formulaic epithets, and where, contrary to normal usage, word order is as free as in a fully inflected language. To give an idea of what something similar would sound like in

English one would have to imagine John Milton and Gerard Manley Hopkins working together on a joint version of Homer.

Haroldo was one of the rediscoverers of Odorico's translations and has been arguing in defense of them against hostile critics since the early 1960s. Not coincidentally, that was the time when both he and his brother began to work on the re-evaluation of Joaquim de Sousândrade, an epic poet born in the same place as Odorico Mendes whom he considered his own forerunner, and who flourished in the second half of the last century. Haroldo's and Augusto's study of his work and the anthology of it they organized established him as the main romantic poet in the Portuguese language.

In any language, the classics have to be translated anew after some generations, but, besides his affinities both with Odorico and Sousândrade, what made him take up this specific task was his interest in narrative and the important role it plays in his poetry. Many of his poems, notably those collected under the name of *Galáxias* (Galaxies), tell stories. They are not, however, fictional in a simple sense, for they are at the same time about history, about retelling older stories, and about the theory, the practice, and sometimes even the impossibility of storytelling.

Haroldo's longer work in literary criticism has as its subject not, as one would suppose, a poem, but a novel. The book he wrote is the *Morfologia do Macunaíma* and deals with Mário de Andrade's modernist novel. To analyze it, he used as his theoretical basis Vladimir Propp's categories developed for the study of Russian folktales. His interest in Propp was itself a consequence of his study of Russian formalist criticism of the 1920s and of his friendship with Roman Jakobson, and both, in their turn, were a result of his work as a translator of Russian poetry.

The first Russian poet he translated, almost forty years ago, was Vladimir Mayakovsky, and what moved him to do it was the fact that his and his colleagues' poetry was then being criticized by the fashionable Lukacsian Marxists as too "formalist" and non-political. Formalism, according to those critics, was the worst sin, because no politically correct poet could as well spend time becoming a serious craftsman. Translating Mayakovsky, Haroldo set off to prove the thesis that "there cannot be a revolutionary poetry without a revolutionary form." Finally, when already in the 1990s Haroldo wrote some highly explicit political poems, it was Mayakovsky, the superb craftsman, whom he took as his own model.

This may illustrate some of the interplay that is continually taking place between his several activities, but it also shows that, despite being quite a prolific writer, he is equally a very economic one, for once he has mastered a subject or a form, he will do his best to exhaust it, using it in every possible way before turning to the next one to be mastered. Thus, through these many interplays, Haroldo's translation of Homer, if we read it in the context of all his activities, is a work of scholarship and imagination, a way of further refining his own skills, one more chapter in his re-evaluation of both Odorico Mendes and Sousândrade, a homage to both, a dialogue with Ezra Pound, whom he has translated, a defense and vindication of the art of translating and, above all, pure and simple storytelling.

Similar kinds of complex interplay may be found at any point of his career. In the 1960s a famous Czech Kafka scholar visited Brazil. Haroldo commented on his lecture in a newspaper article, ending with a poem called "O 'K' da Questão," an homage both to the scholar and to the author of *The Trial*. The expression "o 'X' da questão" – roughly translatable as "the 'X' of the matter" – means in Portuguese something like "the heart of the matter." Changing, in the title, the X for a K, the poet was obviously also talking about Kafka's character Joseph K. and, less obviously, about the writer's original homeland, the Austro-Hungarian empire, which was known for its double K standing for Kaiserlich und Königlich (Imperial and Royal), the origin of Robert Musil Kakania. The poem, from beginning to end, uses this letter playfully – which does not exist in the Portuguese alphabet – and it is also related, rather unexpectedly, to one of Haroldo's most brilliant translations.

The Russian futurist Velimir Khlebnikov wrote a strange poem called "In Praise of the L." He was referring to the letter L, and his poem, at one and the same time an incarnation of the symbolist idea according to which there are correspondences between everything in the world, and a negation of Saussurean linguistics that postulate the arbitrariness of the correlation between sound and meaning in language, is a tour de force in which the Russian's thesis is that both the words that use the letter L and the things they designate owe their secret strength to it. Of course, in Khlebnikov's poem these words are Russian ones, and there is no reason to imagine that in another, non-Slavic tongue they would be similar. Haroldo, however, overcame this difficulty, making a text in which the "hidden powers of the letter L," as the futurist poet said, resonate perfectly in Portuguese. And he repeated his own tour de force in another translation from the Russian: Andrei Voznesenky's poem about the Spanish painter Goya and about World War II, a poem which takes its emphasis from endless repetitions of the hard letter G. It would be hard to tell which came first, the poem on Kafka or his acquaintance with the Russian ones, but their correlation and interplay seem clear enough.

But Kafka for Haroldo was more than a double K. His reading of this writer may be considered one of the starting points for his interest in the Hebrew Bible. Differently from what happened in English or German, the literature written in Portuguese was never really influenced by the Book of Books and neither in Portugal nor in Brazil is there anything resembling the authorized version or Martin Luther's Bible. This almost scandalous absence also moved the poet to study ancient Hebrew and translate the *Song of Songs*, the *Qohelet* and parts of the *Book of Job* and *Genesis*. A by-product or rather a true consequence of this have been some of his finest recent poems, the "Qoheletic Poems," and his rediscovery and critical re-evaluation of a nineteenth-century Brazilian translation of the *Book of Job* done in Dantesque "terza rima," a text which in spirit and method is close to the Spanish poet Fray Luis de León's poetical versions of some biblical books.

Haroldo's translation, along with those of Augusto and Décio, of some of Ezra Pound's *Cantos*, itself a way of marking a distance between the concrete group and the self-styled "Geração de 45" ("Generation of 45"), an anti-modernist and poetically conservative group of poets who were very influential in the 1950s and who were staunch defenders of T. S. Eliot, led him to the poetry of Guido Cavalcanti, which, besides some translations, resulted in a poem called "Baladetta à Moda Toscana" (*Baladetta* in the Tuscan Way), and then to Dante himself.

He translated part of the Italian poet's *Paradise*, some of his shorter poems and, many years later, wrote his own Inferno under the influence of Mallarmé's "Un coup de dés" (A Throw of the Dice), which he translated into Portuguese; starting from what Dante says about Ulysses's old age and his last trip, he wrote a poem in two parts called "Finismundo: A Última Viagem" (The Ends of the Earth: The Last Trip). In the first part of this poem Haroldo blends Dante's peculiar style with that of Odorico Mendes to describe what would have been the Greek hero's final journey, while in the second, suddenly placing Ulysses in a contemporary traffic jam, he achieves effects strongly reminiscent of those that T.S. Eliot had achieved when, in "The Waste Land," he made of the blind Greek seer Tiresias a witness to twentieth-century sexual sordidness.

IV

As I have said earlier, these brief examples could be multiplied and developed, but the aforementioned poem is as good a place as any for showing how the poet's deep and essential, though quite personal brand of humor works.

In the first part of his *Finismundo*, Haroldo, trying to figure out what Ulysses' last trip would have been like and concomitantly paying homage to his own masters, creates, through his recourse to violent inversions of phrasing and the accumulation of Greek, Latin and Italian terms both untranslated or strangely adapted into Portuguese as explicit neologisms, a style so extremely elevated that no reader could doubt that he or she is facing an epic poem or fragment. In the second part he calls this impression off, turning to a dryly elegiac mood, a kind of telegraphic dirge in which what is lamented is the death of the very possibility of singing in an epic way. This is the poem's second part:

> City-dwelling Ulysses
> who has survived the myth
> (me and you my hypo-
> chondriacally critical
> reader) – urbane
> factotum (polymethis)
> of computerized chance. Your
> epitaph? The margin of error: a minimal
> trace written on the keyboard
> and written hurriedly off
> from the greenishflowing liquid crystal.
> Periplus?
> There is none. The traffic lights watch you.
> Your Promethean fire is but
> a match's phosphorescent head – Portable
> Lucifer and/or
> an inflammable trifle.

> Cool headedly
> your hybris
> capitulates. There is no sign
> of singing sirens.
> Last but one – That is the most to which
> your pauperized lack of a Last
> Thule can aspire. A postcard from Eden
> that is enough to make you happy.
> Alarming sounds of sirens
> tear your everyday heart.
>
> (Finismundo, Part 2)

Here not only the reference to the mythological sirens that will not sing and become the heart-tearing mechanical ones, but also the quotation from Baudelaire's poem addressed to his hypocritical reader that in this poem becomes a hypochondriac and a critic, can easily be traced back to T. S. Eliot's "The Song of J. Alfred Prufrock." The silent mermaids stem also from two other sources: Franz Kafka's short story about their silence and Theodor Adorno's and Max Horkheimer's analysis of the corresponding Homeric episode in their "Dialektik der Aufklärung." Many other myths and sources are present in this short text, but it is more important to observe how its mournful tone becomes slowly ironic and that, when this is eventually realized, the overall effect is purposefully comical.

This kind of skillful contrast is one of the ways through which in his poems, translations, and essays Haroldo successfully achieves an intended comical effect. But he also does it, for instance, unexpectedly putting side by side archaic words and modern slang, by deforming, step by step, a word until it begins to say the very opposite of its original meaning, by using terms created by the advertising industry to translate an ancient Roman poem, by making poems out of the forbidding jargon of academic criticism, and so on. Making a long story short, one of the points rarely made about his work is that he is a supremely witty writer.

V

What I have been trying to do is to discuss Haroldo de Campos's work with the help of certain critical categories and concepts that have not usually been applied to it. I have also tried to show rather briefly the historical and other circumstances that, making this kind of discussion somewhat rare, have generated around him a large number of misunderstandings that, in their turn, worked as so many obstacles between him and his professional readers. I would only like to add that among authors who are as complex, varied, and amazing as he is that is something to be expected. But, if there are many ways of misunderstanding his poems, his translations, and his essays, fortunately there are many more ways that are interesting and intelligent of understanding and enjoying them.

A Long Hold: Haroldo de Campos, Brazilian Avant-Garde Tradition, and Spanish-American Literature

Horácio Costa

ON A NUMBER of occasions over the last few years, I have addressed Haroldo de Campos's important contribution to contemporary Brazilian literature. Two of my essays on Haroldo's work were published in Mexico in 1998,[1] and another was published in 1994 in an academic journal in the United States, although it was written after these two.[2] As a longtime reader of Haroldo's work and a younger poet, in those essays I tentatively tried to interpret his role in Brazilian letters. Nonetheless, the task of critically assessing Haroldo's position is a rather hazardous one, since he is a tremendously dynamic figure who keeps on pouring out an impressive array of contents in the form of poetry books, translations, and theoretical essays onto the Brazilian scene; this trait alone would keep even the most intrepid, not to say the most punctilious or conservative of the literary critics, at bay. However, without considering myself any of these, I still regard that it is an important critical task, particularly for my generation, to evaluate the extension of his hold, in the light of the five decades of his presence at the forefront of Brazilian letters, for deepening our own understanding of some of its most definitive processes. In this sense, I will summarize my critical *démarches* on Haroldo's increasing legacy to Brazilian letters, before focusing on his interchanges with his Spanish-American counterparts.

I sense that three aspects best define Haroldo's intervention in contemporary Brazilian culture. First, and at odds with what is commonly

---

1 *Mar Abierto – Ensayos de literatura brasileña, portuguesa e hispanoamericana* (México: Fondo de Cultura Económica, 1998). *Cf*. "Re-visión: dinámica de haroldo de campos en la cultura brasileña," 77–92 and "Haroldo de Campos: seguimiento de una irreprochable trayectoria," 93–8. See also: "Panorama de la poesía brasileña en el siglo XX," 15–44 and "Acerca de la poesía visual brasileña," 45–76.
2 See "Contemporary Latin American Poetry: a Brazilian Perspective," *Santa Barbara Portuguese Studies*, vol. I, 1994, 193–201.

attached to his persona, a role of *conciliation* in relation to his generational position in the context of Brazilian poetry after modernism; secondly, a role of *decentering of the critical logos*, particularly in relation to his stand against the nationalist-formative literary historiography which was – and still is nowadays to a lesser extent – pervasive in the Brazilian academic milieu; and thirdly, an outstanding role of *cultural dynamization* in relation to the dialogues he has pursued with non-literary-oriented artistic discourses in his career. I will center my analysis on the two first aspects.

To understand the first aspect properly, it is imperative to consider the successive phases that characterize Brazilian literature during the twentieth century; for this reason, I will try to define a literary-historical scheme in a few strokes. First and foremost, it is necessary to recall the differences between the two modernist generations, those of the 1920s and of the 1930s. The elder one, centered in the São Paulo-based group gravitating around Oswald and Mário de Andrade, follows almost literally the characterization of the breakthrough of any avant-garde movement onto the international scene in its heyday: to fight the previous old, belles-lettres mentality, offering a capable substitution for it, better suited for the new times in artistic and ideological terms. Its intervention was profound, youthful, and violent. Its diction was positive, assertive: feeling a responsibility towards history, they worked under the ægis of change. Somewhat anarchically, carnivalesquely, very much imbued of the most ingrained and popular values of the "classic" Brazilian spirit, the modernists destroyed what remained of the formalist and rigid culture of the nineteenth century, which had survived the crepuscular Empire of Brazil. By doing so, they set a new basis for a closer relationship between the writer and his public, between the cultivated body of the society and its social or political body. Notwithstanding, due to their faith that art could change the world or, to put it in other terms, due to their believing that the Utopia of the avant-garde could ever materialize south of the Equator, for the betterment of Brazil, rather than being literally "modern" they were "modernists", i.e., apostles of modern times.

No wonder that in this sense, shortly after the "heroic" period of their cultural crusade was over, thanks to an abrupt alteration of the objective conditions – namely, the eclosion of the pre-World War II Depression – the tone of both Oswald and Mário de Andrade became rather bitter, as the prologue written by the first to the publication of one of his most daring "anti-novels", *Serafim Ponte Grande* (1933) and the reading of a famous lecture by Mário on the importance of modernism, delivered in 1942, may prove to the present-day reader.[3]

Trapped by the imperatives of grimy history, discerning clearly the difficulty set by the surrounding conditions, their assertiveness, their positiveness are effaced, as the diction of the second modernist generation arises. Its diction was much less marked by an aim to renew the cultural panorama according to any dictums as it was, *mutatis mutandis*, remarkably more imprinted by the notion of relativism. Two of the most important names of the moment, Carlos Drummond de Andrade and Murilo Mendes, have the bulk of their oeuvres, both starting significantly in 1930, built around the idea of subjective uncertainty, of non-identification, in short, of doubt. Of course, this dislocation of the principal discursive *foci* between the two generations is not only rhetorical. In itself, it points to a revision of the modernist project, and by doing so it fully meets one of the conditions of plain modernity, the enforcement of the critical spirit, be it in a self-critical way.

In one of his most celebrated poems, Drummond said "como ficou chato ser moderno, / agora serei eterno" ("it's gotten so dull to be modern, / now I shall be eternal"; from "Hino Nacional," 1934); Mendes, in one of his poems, declares that "Não se trata de ser ou não ser / Trata-se se de ser e não ser" ("It is not a matter of to be or not to be / But rather of to be and not to be," from "Pós-Poema," 1945). This is no affirmative discourse, as the one stated by the "heroic" modernists; it posits rather

---

3 In relation to Oswald de Andrade, see his prologue to *Serafim Ponte Grande* (Rio de Janeiro: Civilização Brasileira, 6th ed., 1980). In it, Oswald wrote on what he senses would have been the fatuity of the modernist movement (my own translation): "The modernist movement, culminating in the anthropophagous smallpox, seemed to indicate a quite advanced phenomenon. São Paulo had a powerful industrial system. Maybe the coffee plantation boom would be able to place the nouveau-riche literature of the semi-colony shoulder to shoulder with the costly imperialist surrealisms?" ("O movimento modernista, culminado no sarampão antropofágico, parecia indicar um fenômeno avançado. São Paulo possuía um poderoso parque industrial. Quem sabe se a alta do café não ia colocar a literatura nova-rica da semi-colônia ao lado dos custosos surrealismos imperialistas?", 132). Mário de Andrade's bitterness is stated several times in his mature poetic output, such as in "Meditação Sobre o Tietê," a poem written shortly before his death in 1945; it surpasses the tonus of the conference cited above, a sort of artistic testament, although in it he objectively defines the legacy of modernism as having guaranteed for posterity "the permanent right to aesthetic research; the actualization of the national artistic intelligence; and the stabilization of a national creative consciousness" (in the original: "o direito permanente à pesquisa estética; a atualização da inteligência artística nacional; e a estabilização de uma consciência criadora nacional." Quoted from Alfredo Bosi's *História Concisa da Literatura Brasileira* [São Paulo: Cultrix, 1981], 431).

that the constant production of poetry in a modern sense necessarily leaves behind all definitions that could limit it in conceptual terms, including the term or the will to "modernity" itself. In this sense, freed from the weight stemming from the exclusive and crusading spirit of modernism, the second modernist generation is already fully modern.

But alas, one remark has to be made. When I say "revision," I refer to the process of simultaneous renewal or overcoming *and* affirmation of what came before. Although conceptually playing with modernity, they knew they were deeply indebted to their immediate forerunners, as they knew they were continuing their fertile project. By acting accordingly, they were putting forth in a particularly fortunate way the foundation of a Brazilian modern tradition in poetry, whose core is given by the avant-garde *ethos*.

That lucidity, or historical responsibility, has not found harbor in the so-called Generation of 1945. With the exception of João Cabral de Melo Neto, whose oeuvre displays a rigorous diction and bold literary purposes, the members of this generation felt a loose relation to the idea mentioned above. Had their self-indulgence in aesthetical and ideological terms been victorious, had their re-shaping of the traditon *in nuce* according to their sentimental proclivities and anemic world view prevailed, most probably a return to a pre-1920 mentality would then have become feasible, at least in the realm of Brazilian poetry.

As Walter Benjamim stated in his "VI Thesis" on the philosophy of history, "to articulate the past historically does not mean to recognize 'the way it really was' (...). It means to seize hold of a memory as it flashes up in the moment of danger."[4] Maybe the young poets Haroldo and Augusto de Campos, and Décio Pignatari, the founding triad of the concrete poetry movement, might not have known of Benjamin's idea by 1949, as they were coming of age as citizens of the republic of Brazilian letters, but precisely this seems to have been their *démarche* in the late forties and the first half of the following decade. The group was formed with the clear idea of articulating a strong revitalizing reaction against the menace of loosing the ties with the liberating and creative cultural and ideological propositions of the modernists such as Oswald and Mário, and of the moderns, such as Drummond and Murilo. In this sense, the operation assisting the foundation of the concrete poetry movement

---

4 See W. Benjamin, *Illuminations*, ed. by Hannah Arendt (New York: Schocken Books, 1969), 235.

exemplifies the avant-gardist thread that shapes the core of the production of poetry in Brazil in the twentieth century.

The reasons for that reaction were declared in a conference delivered in Mexico a few years ago by Haroldo de Campos, when he visited UNAM to occupy the chair "João Guimarães Rosa de Estudios Brasileños," directed by me at the time, in the following terms:

> (...) The ensemble of ideas of the poets of the '45, their anti-experimentalism, their inclination to *decorum* and restraint, their preoccupation for the *atmosphere* of the poem in which everything would be harmony and consonance, was something that didn't appeal to us, *novissimi*, who admired Mallarmé's subversive syntaxis and enigmatic lexicon, who were discovering Ezra Pound's ideogrammatic methods in his *Cantos*, who read with enthusiasm Apollinaire's *Lettre-Océan* and *Caligrammes*, and Lorca's *Poeta en Nueva York* dysonating metaphors.[5]

The upsurge of the concrete poets re-enacted a behavior that had been absent from the Brazilian intelligentsia for three decades. Working as a well-tuned team, displaying their ideas in manifestoes whose style recovered in a lower key the one brandished by Oswald de Andrade in his foundational manifestoes of the 1920s, tempering it with a coolness which fitted their rationalist stand, the concrete poets were soon able to create their own space in the somewhat dormant scenario of Brazilian poetry. As did the modernists, the concrete poets were producing an *aggiornamento* of the Brazilian creative process. But, contrary to them, they were not bringing into the country a nucleus of international information, making it new in order to reshape national culture: they were creating "poetry for export," in this point following Oswald de Andrade's seminal advice. Even so, their standpoint was not narrowly nationalistic, but, as Haroldo de Campos stated in the early eighties, they

---

5   See Haroldo de Campos, "De la Poesía Concreta a *Galáxias* a *Finismundo*: Cuarenta Años de Actividad Poética en el Brasil," in *Estudios Brasileños*, ed. by Horácio Costa (México: Facultad de Filosofía y Letras de la UNAM, 1994). My translation into English. The Spanish original reads: "(...) El ideario de los poetas del '45, su antiexperimentalismo, su inclinación al *decorum* y al comedimiento, su preocupación por el *clima* del poema (donde todo fuese armonía y consonancia) era algo que no nos atraía a nosotros tres, poetas *novissimos*, que admirábamos la sintáxis subversiva y el léxico enigmático de Mallarmé; que estábamos descubriendo el método ideogramático de los *Cantos* de Ezra Pound; que leíamos con entusiasmo al Apollinaire de *Lettre-Océan* y de los *Caligrammes* y al Lorca de las metáforas disonantes de *Poeta en Nueva York*."

were practicing a sort of nationalism which was not ontologically oriented, of the brand which the Brazilian academy is most used to, since it relates to the romantic *eidós*, but rather "modal," i.e. functional or tactical.[6] Further on I will return to this point, when I develop the second aspect I wish to focus on here.

Up to now, just one aspect of Haroldo's conciliatory *facies* has been underlined, the one which he shares with the other participants of the concrete poetry movement, which is related, as I said, to the revitalization of the trails opened during the 1920s and the 1930s. A second and possibly less evident conciliatory bias must be recalled at this point.

It has been said that conservative literary criticism in Brazil has concocted a subtle way of freezing Haroldo de Campos's presence – and, at the same time, that of his generational counterparts – in Brazilian culture, as if his œuvre would have continuously obeyed his intervention during the years of the concrete poetry movement of the 1950s and 1960s, which is only partially true. This counter-criticism is right: by denying the natural transformation of a militant writer *after* the years of his overt, more punching militancy, once – just to recover modernist terminology – his "heroic" period is over, there follows a minimization of the problems which would have been aroused if a more accurate, and obviously more respectful, critical consideration of his later production had been made.

In relation to Haroldo's work, to ignore the most important part of it, which few people would argue comes *after* that period, characterizes a sort of "programmed amputation" which has been repeated *ad nauseam* in many circles in Brazil – recalling, for that matter, how Oswald de Andrade's public profile was frozen as the century evolved. My point is that Haroldo has performed a transition similar to the one that the second modernist generation, the plainly modern one, has in its time known how to perform, in relation to the first. In short, the critique the concrete poets, and he particularly, were able to practice, is what fully conciliates their imprint in the present, with a pattern already existing in Brazil, but which, without their having being able to re-enact in such terms, would *also* have run the risk of disappearing – or, at least, of *not* meaning so much, as an ethical reference, in Brazilian culture today.

Instead of theorizing over this point, I want to recall two poems that exemplify what I have just said. The first one is a much-debated poem

---

6 See Haroldo de Campos: "De la razón antropofágica," *Vuelta* (México) no 68, 1982.

written in the late 1980s by Augusto de Campos, which is significantly called "Pós-Tudo," or "Post-Everything." From this title on, Augusto plays with the idea of a "post-modern" situation in the same way Drummond played with the notion of "modernity" in the passage quoted above, thus affirming and critically relativizing a "new" cultural situation, one in which being "modern" – or, in Augusto's case, "concrete" *and* "post-modern" – had already become tiresome. The second is "Minima Moralia" by Haroldo de Campos, which was included in *A Educação dos Cinco Sentidos* ("The Education of the Five Senses," 1985). "Minima Moralia" alludes not only in parodical, carnivalesque terms to the famous philosophical treatise by Theodor Adorno, it also recovers the spirit of Oswald de Andrade's "poemas-piada" ("pun-poems"). Nonetheless, in its two lines this poem states much about renovating an aesthetical and ideological programme *not* through its betrayal or mere negation, but through its relativization, in accordance with the best spirit of the literary mechanism I tried to sketch in the previous paragraphs. "Minima Moralia" reads: "já fiz de tudo com as palavras / agora quero fazer de nada" ("I've done with words all things / I now want to do no things").

Let's move on to the second topic I want to deal with here. I mentioned that Haroldo's role in Brazil has been a de-centralizing one, towards some of the most important assurances that academic literary criticism has developed in its effort to interpret the *corpus* of Brazilian literature. Against the solid conceptual building of a "national" literature as a simultaneous symptom and forger of a "national" identity, Haroldo's *modus operandi* has been to call to the forefront of the cultural debate some of the most important exceptions such a scheme leaves behind. His starting point was working on the substitution of some of the historio-graphic-aesthetic macro-categories (romanticism, symbolism, and so forth) by the notion and analytical display of "literary series" which are bound up by signs of mutuality and traverse the canon of Brazilian literature. If this is the meaning which supports his studying of nineteenth-century "exceptional" poets such as Sousândrade and Kilkerry, much more so is it the reason for his denunciation of the concealed ignorance dealing with the importance of the baroque in the formativist thinking of Brazilian literary criticism. His book *O Seqüestro do Barroco na Formação da Literatura Brasileira – o Caso Gregório de Mattos* ("The Sequestering of the Baroque in the Formation of Brazilian Literature – the Case of Gregório de Mattos," 1989) illustrates with precision what has just been said. In this book, Haroldo opposes a fundamental treatise written by Antonio Cândido de Melo e Souza, *Formação da Literatura Brasileira* (1959) – whose title, it must be noticed, his own book paraphrastically recovers – duly considered a classic in the realm of literary criticism in Brazil. Cândido, possibly the most influential of the Brazilian critics in the twentieth century, focuses on a period of over one hundred years, 1750–1880, underlying thus, in his "formative" reading, the links between the coming of age of Brazilian literature with the social and political transformations suffered by Brazil in the period from a colony to an independent state, from a monarchy to a republic *in embryo*. Haroldo criticizes Candido's "sustantialist" view of the literary phenomena in Brazil, as he considers the latter's eulogy of the romantics as an "absolutization," all leading to the "quest for an origin" under the ægis of a centralizing literary production.

Evidently, the baroque, which spurred the first literary manifestations in Brazil, offers Haroldo a vantage point to exemplify the values of *serialness, inclusion,* and *dissemination.* The baroque series, less "national," is in his view as Brazilian as any other, including the romantic, nationalist one. Gregório de Mattos, the satirical colonial poet who had a troublesome relation with the colony he lived in, but whose oeuvre is of growing importance in contemporary Brazilian culture, fits the Haroldian open view of Brazilian literature as something preceding "Brazil." The stress here relies on literariness, outside of a fundamentalist vision of a nationalist *ethos*. If it goes without saying that this relates to the principles of the concrete poetry movement, it needs be said that this revision of the baroque, not as a historically-bounded category but as a strong *continuum* permanently influencing Brazilian culture, is exemplarily reflected in Haroldo's poetry writing itself. This would deserve a longer analysis than is possible to do here; however, I want to recall that a baroque bent is present in Haroldo's poetry since its beginnings: in "Teoria e Prática do Poema," written in 1952, for instance, he pays tribute to Padre Antônio Vieira, the Jesuit orator who, since the seventeenth century, has been considered *the* model of baroque writing in the Portuguese language, by transforming a passage of one of Vieira's sermons into a verse. This very line – "xadrez de estrelas" ("chessboard of stars") – became so powerful in Haroldo's imagery that when he set out to collect his poetry for the first time in 1974, this was the title he chose for the entire collection.

Needless to say, this decentralizing vision, Brazilian-based but not necessarily Brazil-oriented, was and is broad enough to enthuse a full array of Latin-American echoes or counterparts. In this sense, Haroldo's problematization of the baroque, of the proper site of the literature written during the centuries that really saw the "formation" of the country, i.e., the three centuries preceding its political independence, is no different from many incursions that numerous Spanish-American intellectuals have made in their own region's literary past. Particularly, Octavio Paz's re-dimensioning of Sor Juana Inés de la Cruz and of colonial Mexico in his monumental biography, *Sor Juana Inés de la Cruz o las trampas de la fe* (1983), went in the same direction. Paz's towering figure possibly stands as the closest to Haroldo in Spanish America, for their relationship goes much deeper from their similar stand in terms of the re-evaluation of each country's literary past, and can be better found on the level of poetry writing and criticism, as has already been studied.[7] However, since the time of the concrete poetry movement, long before Haroldo took notice of Paz's work, he had looked for and identified a good number of Spanish-American writers and critics who shared his literary values and with whom he has since developed strong ties.

Indeed, as a confirmation of some points alluded to here, Haroldo's relationship with his Spanish-American counterparts has evolved from a strictly concrete poetry basis to encompass a wider circle of writers. If during the 1950s and 1960s figures such the Bolivian-German poet Eugene Gömringer played an important role in the international recognition of the concrete poetry movement, Haroldo's later friendship with writers aware of the importance of the avant-garde movements in Latin America, but not particularly oriented towards the æsthetic fundamentals of the movement, such as the Argentinian Julio Cortázar or the Cuban Severo Sarduy, have been far more meaningful. This is also applicable to his unrelenting communication with critics such as the Uruguayan Emír Rodríguez Monegal, who keenly sensed the dialogical possibilities Haroldo's position in Brazil could open up with some of the most distinguished Spanish-American intellectuals and artists of the time.

---

7   I recommend Manuel Ulacia's *El árbol milenario: un recorrido por la obra de Octavio Paz* (Barcelona: Galaxia Gutenberg/Círculo de Lectores, 1999), particularly the chapter "La radicalización del signo: Oriente y la poesía concreta brasileña," 151–64.

The relationship Haroldo established with these writers has basically been oriented literarily, stemming from common aethetical and ideological grounds. The values of artistic experimentalism and cosmopolitanism have always played a dominant role in these interchanges; all that notwithstanding, I want to stress two aspects which I consider fundamental, pointing both to the establishment of an important, if instrumental and wordless, pact between the parts. One has been the nature of their relation with their respective national literatures or languages, of the same sort as Haroldo's, which has already been focused on here. The second is more difficult to explain, albeit I think it is of greater significance as an ideological tool to propitiate the communication level that Haroldo – or that any Brazilian intellectual, for that matter – has attained with some of the most meaningful Spanish-American fellow writers, an aspect that goes far beyond the mutual respect or goodwill, or shared literary or artistic proclivities.

I refer to the partaken consciousness of their quite specific situation of producing self-assumed avant-garde literature in a continent devoid of strong institutions, with phenomenal historical discontinuities and, despite rather sound exceptions, traditionally disinclined to "radical" experiments (or behaviors). This relates, of course, to the quite ponderous debate between two so-called opposites that traverse the whole Latin-American cultural situation in the twentieth century: "vanguarda e subdesenvolvimento," "vanguardia y subdesarrollo" ("avant-garde and underdevelopment").

A few weeks ago I asked Haroldo if this subject was ever important when he met – or when he meets nowadays – his Spanish-American counterparts; he told me it was *never* a topic to be focused upon. Maybe this simply adds importance to it and confirms what I have just said. Maybe that was so outstandingly a shared ground that *ça allait sans dire*; it simply was not worth mentioning because the aura emanating from it, once rationalized by the means of a stronger attention, could have led either to differences or to diffidences, it doesn't matter.

What really matters is that the Haroldian stand in relation to Brazilian literature has represented a guarantee against an ever reappearing isolationist mentality that hounds Brazilian letters under the disguise of open or veiled "identitarian" discourses. His stand has reaffirmed, and carried to previously unattended heights, what can be considered a most auspicious modern tradition of literary avant-garde in Brazil.

In a country whose history is taught to children as being the result of a succession of "cycles" – that of "the gold-mining cycle," "the coffee-plantation cycle," and so forth, including at last a quite deliriously-named "cycle," that of "industrialization and policulture" – the existence of a non-cyclical literary avant-garde tradition, fully identified, seems to me to be of capital importance. As its weight ultimately increases, the figures of its forgers, yesterday's and today's, with Haroldo de Campos on top of the present list, decidedly deserve our recognition.

Lifting the Great Ball of Crystal: Haroldo de Campos and the Crystallographic Tradition

Craig Dworkin

> *Modern art tends towards the crystal.*
> – Le Corbusier

IN THE UNITED States, Haroldo de Campos is still best known for his "concrete" poetry. Although the dramatic geometric layouts and iconic semiotic play of that work seem to mark those poems as the "visual" part of the poet's career, I want to argue that Campos's visual sensibility is in fact far more subtle and pervasive, and that even his post-concrete work requires an appropriately attentive *visual* reading. Such a reading, moreover, both accounts for some of his recurrent thematic imagery and also places him firmly in a literary tradition with which he is not usually associated.

As even the casual reader will recognize, Campos's poetry is replete with references to stones and gems and crystals. Throughout his career, this vocabulary has remained surprisingly consistent; in his most recent work, one both reads and reads about "lapidário de grés e pedra-pomes [and *pedra-poemas*] separando palavras como quem escolhe / minerais de textura" (*Crisantempo* 90), and the "O Possesso" section of *Auto do Possesso* – work from half a century ago – concludes with the body of the lover incorporated in the poem itself like a trophy "no topo dos cristais!" Merely to catalogue all of the mentions of stones and stemware and "ecos de diamante" in the poems of the intervening years would take pages, and – though it also lies beyond the scope of this essay – to explicate all of their particular connotations and references would certainly prove to be productive. In fact, when Campos's works are read through the lens of classical and medieval treatises on the science of crystals and their alchemical lore, many of the poems' most seemingly occult, dispersed, and ostensibly discontinuous terms are seen to be disposed with an astounding precision and erudition. Moreover, the references to gems and crystals are clearly evocative of certain specific moments in that crystallographic tradition. Above all, they point to Dante Alighieri, whose name echoes quite literally behind every appearance of "diamante" in these poems. Dante also put the renaissance science of crystals to poetic use, and his entire *Commedia*, like certain of Campos's own poems, might itself be seen as a crystal.[1] Ezra Pound, for one, seems to have seen it as such, summarizing the entirety of the *Commedia* in "Canto C" with the line "Nel mezzo ... the crystal," and even as he adapts and adopts the image of the crystal for his own modernist uses, the ghost of Dante is never far behind in Pound's own writing. That the crystalline imagery in Campos's poems is paying simultaneous homage to two masters who are repeatedly and openly invoked throughout his writings in even more explicit ways should be no surprise.[2]

When Pound transfers the image of the crystal out of the renaissance and into the twentieth century he gives it a particular valence to which readers of Campos's poems should be attentive, because the crystal retains this association when Campos fulfills all of those challenges posed in the last Canto: taking up the golden thread, copying the palimpsest, and lifting the great ball of crystal that Pound had brought from Dante (cf. 625). Pound's crystal is not merely the figure for purity and light, the lozenge cut from the jungle and the sharp, jagged edges of paradise and the *Paradiso* (though it is certainly all of these as well). For Pound, the crystal is also the tuner in the radio, the "crystal set" on which listeners in the 1940s would have heard his notorious radio broadcasts. In short, I want to suggest that the "crystal waves" that keep breaking through in the *Cantos* are not just the tide returning to the "hyaline glass waves" of Canto II, but are also in fact radio waves. One can see that same radio reappear, borne on those waves, with one of the motifs of the late Cantos: "the boat of Ra-Set." The phrase indicates not just the barge of the Egyptian god, but also – with the unwritten *dios* of that god replaced by the hyphen – the "Radio Set." Lest this reading seem too far-fetched, recall that Pound's nickname as a child was Ray, but also formed by

---

1 Robert Durling and Ronald Martinez, *Time and the Crystal: Studies in Dante's Rime Petrose* (Berkeley: University of California Press, 1990), 254 *et passim*.
2 This lineage has been documented by both João Alexandre Barbosa in essays such as "Um Cosmonauta do Significante: Navegar é Preciso" (introduction to *Signantia Quasi Coelum*) and Leyla Perrone-Moisés in *Atlas Literaturas: Escolha e Valor na Obra Crítica de Escritores Modernos* (São Paulo: Companhia Das Letras, 1998).

truncation and spelled "Ra." Reading or writing "Ra" he would surely have heard "ray," however faintly, in his mind's ear. Pound's "Ra-Set," moreover, appears in lines such as "Ra-Set over crystal / moving" and "the boat of Ra-Set moves with the sun" (626, 298, *et passim*). With early radio, sunspots would have produced significant interference and contributed to all the noise and fade that kept the operator constantly moving the crystal. Pound, as evinced in the transcripts of his radio broadcasts, was acutely aware of such interference effects, and his concern had merit. Remember that the sound over primitive radio was filled with cracks and wavers, as well as whistles and moans that would fade and rise so that you might imagine you were hearing, to quote the *Cantos*: "'Ghosts dip in the crystal,/adorned' that the tone change from elegy" (637). The crystal, in the *Cantos*, is a medium, in every sense of the word: channeling spectral voices, and a figure for other medial technologies and the manipulation of noise.[3]

Campos picks up on this connotation of the crystal as he picks up on other motifs from the late *Cantos*. These transcreative borrowings from Pound's poem are especially manifest in the third section of Campos's 1979 book *Signantia quasi coelum*. Pound's "small lions" return as a "formicaleão" [ant-lion], his "great cloud" as "essa nuvem," and in both poems one finds not only a shared *mise-en-scène* of lacquer, stone, pollen, and insects with their "wings of light" (Pound, 744 *et passim*, cf. 689), but also a strikingly coincident chromaticism of particular colors: azure, russet gold ("ruivo"), and "the green deep of an eye" – or as *Signantia* has it, "um verde de pupila." That eye, moreover, turns out to be none other than the eye of Ra: "o olho de Ra / diante dele / as coisas" ("the eye of Ra before things," 43). The eye, as we learn at the end of the poem, is "diamante," and it is not only in front of things, but also – if one reads across the line break – "radiante" ("radiant"), a word that itself points back to Pound and his famous definition of the image as a "radiant node or cluster." In Campos's poem, the opening image of the crystalline, radiant eye of Ra suggests the pairing of "radio" and "cristal" that the first section of the poem then pairs within a few hermetic lines, as sound and the crystal come together ("coerem") and make sense in a "cúpola radiosa" ("radiant cupola"). In fact, a survey of Campos's oeuvre reveals

---

3 Although he does not address the crystal, or Ra-Set, see Daniel Tiffany's *Radio Corpse: Imagism and the Cryptaesthetic of Ezra Pound* (Cambridge: Harvard University Press, 1995) for a further elaboration on the theme of Pound's interest in a spectral radio.

that he frequently associates crystals not only with the visual connotations one might expect from a refracting and focusing substance but also with sounds; the crystals in his poems are rustling and murmuring and humming, "vibrante de som." They seem to corroborate Fillipo Tomasso Marinetti's claims in his manifesto for a futurist radio: "*La Radia* shall be the reception, amplification, and transfiguration of vibrations emitted by matter." And as we shall see, for Campos those vibrations are emitted by verbal matter and the transfiguring (transcreating) tremblings of the signifier.

Such tremblings, in fact, cement the pervasive conjunction of the radio and the crystal in Campos's writing; the words "cristal" and "quartzo" are repeatedly paired with variations of the word "radio." One reads, for instance of "uma radia / estável / como quem olha pelo cristal." Similarly, in *Teoria e Prática do Poema* the reader finds "cristal" aligned perfectly below the anagrammed *radio* of "raios do." And again, in *Opúsculo*, a piece in which "há poeira radiante [there is radioactive dust]" the crystal-radio ghosts behind the conjunction of "radiosa" and "quartzo."

The radio, in other words (or, quite literally, *as* other words), thus functions as what Michael Riffaterre would call a matrix. In a sophisticated revision of Ferdinand de Saussure's work on anagrams – a topic on which Haroldo de Campos has also written extensively – Riffaterre argues that poetic texts are created when a gap opens between a word and a text. Poems, in his account, are constructed around a *punctum coecum*: a single unwritten word or phrase that does not actually appear in the poem but which nonetheless governs its composition.[4] Riffaterre calls that encoded, unwritten core the "matrix," and with an analogy to the way in which an anagram encodes a word by rearranging its letters he terms the encryption of the repressed matrix a "hypogram" (*hypo*

---

4 In brief, Saussure suspected that classical verse contained the names of otherwise unmentioned dedicatory figures, whose monikers were disseminated through the text in disarticulated phonemes. "Apollo," for instance, might appear distributed as "*ad mea templa portato*." With a chilling meticulousness, Saussure labored to enumerate the intricate and unfailingly consistent rules he saw governing these paragrammes, but faced with the sublime prospect of any text's ability to produce an almost infinite production of names, Saussure abandoned and suppressed his work. For an introduction, see Jean Starobinski, *Les Mots sous les Mots* (Paris: Editions Gallimard, 1971); for Campos's most extended mediation of the literary implications of Saussure's work, see "Diábolos no Texto (Saussure e os Anagramas)," which originally appeared in *Idem*, in two parts (26.7.1969, and 2.8.1969) under the title "O Lance de Dados de Saussure"; it is reprinted in the collection *A Operação do Texto* (São Paulo, Editora Perspectiva, 1976).

Lifting the Great Ball of Crystal

"under" + *gram* "writing"). Quite literally the sub-text of the poem, the hypogram underwrites the text on the page as the rest of the poem presents variations of the matrix, skirting its absent center and offering equivalents to the key word or phrase but never mentioning the specific word or phrase itself. Like matter on the brink of a black hole that cannot itself be seen or recorded, the words that do in fact appear in a poem deform themselves around its gravitational mass. As the language of the poem approximates but avoids the matrix, detouring around it and rewriting it in other words, ungrammatical and awkward phrases result, providing clues to its presence. The poetic text thus "functions something like a neurosis," in Riffaterre's psychoanalytic terms: "as the matrix is repressed, the displacement produces variants all through the text, just as the repressed symptoms break out somewhere else in the body" (19).

So when, in one of Campos's poems, you find "um texto/ *radia*" ("a text radiating"), the synechdocal crystal of the almost written *radio*, is not far behind; the line repeats later in the poem as: "um / texto / pó-diamante" ("a diamond-dust text"). That diamond-dust text, as it happens, is written over what might be a nice description of Riffaterre's matrix:

sobre	(over
sambaquis	a shell-midden
hífen	hyphen
entre	between
esqueletos	skeletons
figuras	figures
de	of
linguagem	language
calci-	calci
ilegível	illegible
-nada	nothing)

Variations of this image of a calcinated (*calci-nada*), crystallized text consistently recur in Campos's poetry. In the final section of *Signantia quasi coelum*, for example, with "crisântemos" not far from "cristais," one finds "crisântemos / escritura solar / na sala / in)/o bloco de cristal/ ex)/ vaso" ("chrysanthemums/ solar scripture in the room in a crystal writing pad from a vase"). One might well read this literal "photography" and "crystallography" as an illustration of how to "escrever/ no vidro/ sentenças de vidro" ("write in glass sentences on glass"), as several earlier lines state. Accordingly, one finds "a palavra/ topázio" ("a topaz word") in another poem, and realizes that with an echo of "pó-diamante," the "poeira radiante" ("radioactive dust") in one work becomes, in another poem, an explicit "pó de letras/ no vento" ("a dust of letters in the wind").

These figurations are perhaps the literalizing effect of the contemporaneous theoretical interest and insistence on the "materiality" of poetic language. Additionally, one might well characterize Campos's poems – especially the rigorously concrete work from the mid- to late 1950s – as "crystalline" in a colloquial sense of the word. Consider, for example, the cut of the angular geometric planes of *se nasce morre* and all of the poems in *Fome de Forma*, with their atomized and abstracted vocabulary cut into a "forma cristal" of distinctly hard, intense, lucid, poetry. Even the most recent work has been described as "uma lírica que é um cristal a vibrar pelas ondas dos signos e dos versos…. rede cristalina de crescimentos" ("a lyric that is a crystal to vibrate through waves of signs and verses…. a crystalline network of expansion").[5] These characterizations are certainly accurate enough, but I want to argue that the particular interest of these references is not just the presence of some hidden matrix, or that they repeatedly open onto figures of communication and writing, but that the particular mode of communication proposed by these poems actually establishes and enacts a model of crystalline language. To begin with, crystals are – appropriately enough – quite literally *concrete*: they grow by concretions, developing through a series of interlocking, formal combinations and exhibiting various precessions of symmetry, as well as shearing and cleaving along certain stress boundaries to produce new forms. All of which is precisely how one might characterize the play and process of language in the poems of Haroldo de Campos.

So, for a few specific examples of this crystallography from just one of Campos's poems, recall how he fractures "radiante" into "Ra diante," productively splits words along the lines of their greatest morphemic strength, just as crystals shear to create new forms. Moreover, he deploys language so that it rotates, like a crystalline structure, along lines of

---

5   Jacó Guinsburg, jacket copy for *Crisantempo*.

symmetry. The portmanteau "coxiaberta" ("passageopen") for instance is easy enough to decipher, but at first glance seems unnecessarily collapsed; when read backwards, however, the compound reveals the word "baixo" [small, lowly, humble], and rhymes nicely with its figurative synonym "formigas" [ants] at the bottom of the page. Similarly, the poetic and literary neologism "colitera," its letters (*letras*) literally (*literalmente*) stuck together (*colaram*), suggests the inverse – both graphically and denotatively – of its learned and literary allusions; when repeated (*itera*) backwards, the collateral word reads: "aretino" ("hack writer").

Indeed, Campos's habit of generating vocabulary through a permutation of letters – moving anagrammatically and paragogically from one word to another with the change of a single letter – itself suggests the way in which the variety of crystal structures are permutations on a set number of possible forms (32 unique types of symmetrical arrangements of 14 types of spatial lattices). In Campos's writing, such rhizomatic chains are often fairly obvious, but they coalesce in more subtle ways as well, linking words in a poem through absent, matrix-like third terms. The first section of *Signantia*, for example, opens with the "glande de cristal/ desoculta" ("gland of crystal unveiled") and ends with ("gomos/ do grande copo de som") ("segments of a large glass of sound"). Those segmented "gomos" suggest the facets of the crystal, which is perhaps cut into a diamond shape ("globo diamantino") that rhymes with the image of the segmented "umbela [umbrella]" that is also mentioned in the poem and which in turn echoes the shape of the "cúpola." In all events, the sound of "copo" suggests *corpo* (the body), which the "glande" ("gland"), now "grande" ("swollen") has grown to become.[6] But "gomos" is also gesturing towards *gonos* (gonads), the spermatic "glande" with its "sêmencia," and from the sexually stimulated *gonos* to *gongos* (gongs): the "campana estimulada" ("stimulated bell") with its "cúpola" radiating sound. At the same time, the conjunction of *gongo* and "campana estimulada" suggests the caffeinated stimulation of wild coffee, *gongo do campo* – and with "campo" hypogrammatically signing the poem, which ends, like Francis Ponge's *Pré*: "assim me assino" ("I sign myself thus"). In fact, the word "hypogram" derives directly from the Greek *hypographein*, which denotes a signature, and the poem is

---

6   In *O â mago do ô mega* (1955–6), one reads of "um corpo cristalino."

actually doubly signed, because *gono* also suggests *gonoptera*, which is, in other words, a Harold moth.⁷

With these crystallizations of language, Campos can be seen as a nature poet. Given the way that "quartzo crescente" (that "quartz proliferates"), "a natureza incuba a metáfora da forma/ e tresnatura: formas em morfose" ("nature itself imagines a metaphor of form, in which, quite naturally, forms morphose").⁸ Not so much describing bucolic scenes as enacting mineral formation, Campos's poems might be read next to those of John Cage, who sought "to imitate nature in the manner of her operation." If the most hermetic of Campos's poems are sounding the "átimo das coisas" in the *átomo das coisas* ("the instant of things in the atom of things"), they also recognize that words are things too, with their own atomized "pó de letras" ("dust of letters") – phrases which recall Lucretius's famous account of the manner of nature's operation. In *De rerum naturam*, his poem on the nature of things, Lucretius explains variations in matter by recourse to the *clinamen*: that slight, chance swerve of atoms from their otherwise linear fall. Moreover, Lucretius illustrates clinanematic deviation with a linguistic analogy: the clinamen, he argues, is like an anagram. Atoms, in this account, recombine so that matter takes on diverse forms and accounts for varied substances, just as a fixed and finite number of letters recombine to form different words with various meanings. By the seventeenth century, atomists such as Pierre Gassen had elaborated Lucretius's metaphor in specifically crystalline terms and developed a material linguistics not just of atomic letters but of molecular words, accreted phrases, and latticed sentences.⁹

Haroldo de Campos, of course, is not alone in developing a modern version of Gassen's crystallography, and he is among a number of writers who simultaneously describe and prosodically enact models of

---

7 These paregogic chains are even more extensive than I have enumerated, and one could continue to unveil the fracture and factures of their branching paths ("deoculta/ ramagem de signos"). With the addition of technical vocabulary drawn from geometry (such as "sub/ tendendo"), the *gono*, from "gomos," also suggests *gonio* (the angle of the jaw) and *gosma* (spittle), which together ghost up *goma* (chewing gum), which in turn recalls the glue (*cola*) of "colitera." And so on.
8 The lines are from "Poema mandala" and "Opúsculo Goetheano – 1" respectively; in the former, the quartz has evolved from the "quarto crescente" (waxing moon), and in the latter it is a "quartzo iridescente."
9 Alfred Jarry, one of the great modern clinanematicians, saw words approach "a crystalline form [that] emerges at intervals out of the random movements of the cosmos" (quoted in Steve McCaffery and Jed Rasula, *Imagining Language*, Cambridge: MIT University Press, 1993) 538, n.4.

crystalline language: from Alfred Jarry to André Breton, Rene Daumal, and Michel Leiris, and then from this surrealist tradition, via J. G. Ballard and Robert Smithson, to Clark Coolidge and Christian Bök, among others. In closing, I want to suggest one reason why the crystal has proven to be such an attractive metaphor for the recombinatory processes of alphabetic language.[10] Crystals, which are said to "grow," capture the natural, generative, and vibrantly animate productivity of linguistic processes: the way in which language can seem to be motivated by its material composition, so that the logic of the pun or the anagram or a similar event suggests new words, which in turn suggest still others. And yet, at the same time, the radically inorganic nature of crystals and their threatening incompatibility with organic processes also suggests the inhumanness of language: the way in which all of those permutations, recombinations, and encryptions generate meanings which proliferate beyond our control, proceed discontinuously with our desires, and signify without regard to our intentions.

The beauty of these crystalline moments – balanced between chance and necessity, perfection and error – can be sublime; they are what lead, in one of Campos's poems, from "esgarças no papel" to "garças no papel" ("tears in paper" to "herons on paper"). "Poetry," as William Carlos Williams wrote, "has to do with the crystallization of the imagination," and poems that take in these aspects of language are a rush, and a terror. They heighten our awareness of language, in all its aspects, and quicken the attention to linguistic detail, bringing single letters into the sharpest focus. But they also leave their readers a little paranoid, and ask them to consider the degree to which they use language, and the degree to which language has adapted them for its dissemination and proliferation, just as the crystalline structures of certain amphetamines, saprophytically, physically restructure the architecture of the brain to make it more receptive to their absorption. Poetry as hallucination, or poetry as revelation? *Esgarças* or *garças*? As Clark Coolidge put it: "Some felicities of salt cause a delirium."[11]

---

10 In general terms, I would extend my speculation to also account for the analogy of the "language virus" proposed by Laurie Anderson and William Burroughs.
11 Clark Coolidge, *Smithsonian Depositions and Subject to a Film* (New York: Vehicle Editions, 1980), p. 43.

A Half-century of Haroldo de Campos

João Alexandre Barbosa

I

THE TEMPORAL LIMITS of the poet Haroldo de Campos are well established: the complete works in *Xadrez de Estrelas* (1976) registered his initial "textual itinerary" since *Auto do Possesso* (1950), collecting texts from the last years of the previous decade. At the twenty-year mark, however, found in the poem-title of that book, the *persona* of the chess player becomes glued to that of the poet, who goes on metamorphosizing in successive experiments and moves, given that, between the lover, his beloved, the possessed and the exorcist, a poetry, or better, "a poet is born / in the August bulbs." He refuses to renounce and opts for the difficulties of the poetic form. ("Difficult dawn" was what Sérgio Buarque de Holanda called the newspaper article in which he discussed Haroldo de Campos's first book).

Fifty years later, as revealed in *Crisantempo: No espaço curvo nasce um* (1998), having definitively banished from his chessboard the immoderate bishop (to which he alludes in the verses spoken by the "chess-player": "Moderate, oh nocturnal bishop/ the fatigue on my chessboard/ and wait: a poet is born/ in the August bulbs"), the chess player renews his moves and once more takes charge of the possessed and the exorcist.

In this long period, there are two books of collected poems by the same author (1976 and 1998), from which other books were excluded, such as *Signantia Quasi Coelum* (1979) and *A Educação dos Cinco Sentidos* (1985) which, in turn, were collected in part in the anthology organized by Inês Oseki Dépré, *Os Melhores Poemas de Haroldo de Campos* (1992). Fragments of *Galáxias* appear, whether in the collections of 1976 or 1992, whose beginning dates from 1963 and whose full edition is from 1984.

On the other hand, fully configuring the mark of his trajectory, there are still the books of criticism and the translations that expound a poetic art, so to speak, since the 1960s, whether in groups of essays or in separate studies of authors, works, or literary movements, from *Metalinguagem* (1967) to *O Arco-Íris Branco: Ensaios de Literatura e Cultura* (1997). There is the case of the essays, extending from the *Cantares* of Ezra Pound, translated together with Augusto de Campos and Décio Pignatari in 1960, to the "Canto II" of the *Iliad*, translated with Trajano Vieira in 1999, in the case of his work as translator.

All this still does not refer to the numerous translations done of other poets as instrumental evidence for arguments in critical or theoretical essays, in which Kurt Schwitters, Gomringer, Palazzeschi, Ungaretti, Bashô, Katsue, Marianne Moore, Arno Holz, Brecht, and Hoelderlin stand out.

If one adds to this list of works his decisive role in the creation of a literary movement of great repercussions for the later history of Brazilian literature – concretism – it will be possible to understand the level of importance that the presence of Haroldo de Campos had, and has, in the contemporary literature of his country. It is a presence that, although shocking given its dimensions, cannot be reduced to a list of published works or of authors and themes treated by the poet-critic.

There is a certain quality in all of his texts that, without a doubt, can only be glimpsed from an angle of critical articulation which, without deprecating its vertiginous content, attempts to capture its basic unity. And that quality is perhaps the one that precisely, without wanting to precipitate a conclusive argument, responds in favor of unity: the prevalence of a feeling for the poetics of language that makes each critical annotation, each critical-historical intervention or each act of translation adhere through the poet's action, as the final stage of creation through language.

For this reason I have already referred to the urgency for an angle of critical articulation: its absence seems responsible for the monotonous affirmation that there are three Haroldos, the poet, the critic, and the translator, each one receiving different critical evaluations, depending on the point of view chosen by the one who judges. What is most suggestive of that kind of viewpoint is that it almost always leaves the poet in last place in the scale of values adopted.

In this fashion, what is most polemical in his critical-historical essays or inventive in his experimental translations seems to pass over his essential quality as a poet, that is, his feeling for the poetic function of language that derives from the literary text as the operation of a reconfiguration of sensibility, as if two of his books of criticism were not thought explicitly as an articulation between text and poetics. In the first, *A Arte no Horizonte do Provável* (1969), all of its six parts designate poetics, whether of the alleatory, the precarious, brevity, translation, vanguard, or synchronism. In the second, *A Operação do Texto* (1976), departing from pages that are, as the poet says, "a 'synchronic' provocation of history" – Poe, Maiakóvski, Hoelderlin, Saussure, Japanese dramatic poetry, the latest Italian poets and an archeological reconstruction of the baroque – all the essays assume the perspective of the prevalence of the textual operation as a matrix of literary invention. And in a pungent way the first works of that book situate the kind of criticism practiced by Haroldo de Campos:

> This book belongs to a critical modality that Baudelaire called *partial*, the only one that truly interested him (as recently remembered, coincidentally, by Octavio Paz in *Los hijos del limo* and Robert Greer Cohn in *Nodes*). Better than anyone, Walter Benjamin defined it in an aphorism (from *A Técnica do Crítico em 13 Teses)*: "Whoever is not capable of taking sides should keep quiet." The operation of the text here is a jubilant exercise. When so many are classifying and schematicizing, it is good that someone, or some, restores to criticism its heuristic dimension.

II

principiava a encadear-se um epos mas onde onde onde sinto-me tão absconso
como aquela sombra tão remoto como aquele ignoto encapelar-se de onda
quantas máscaras até chegar ao papel quantas personae até chegar à
nudez una do papel para a luta nua do branco frente ao branco
o branco é uma linguagem que se estrutura como a linguagem seus signos
acenam com senhas e desígnios são sinas estes signos que se desenham
num fluxo contínuo e de cada pausa serpeia um viés de possíveis em
cada nesga murmura um pleno de prováveis o silabário ilegível formiga
como um quase de onde o livro arrulha a primeira plúmula do livro viável
que por um triz farfalha e despluma e se cala insinuo a certeza de um

João Alexandre Barbosa

signo isca ex-libris para o nada que faísca dessa língua tácita
a tughra de sulaiman o magnífico é um tríplice recinto de pássaros
violeta e ouro sua cauda se abre em lobulados espaços florais
não se saberia por onde ela começa e onde ela termina...

This is a fragment of *Galáxias,* a work that since the beginning of the 1960s, and for ten years afterwards, accompanied the poet and that only twenty years later would be configured as a book. Or, in Haroldo de Campos's own words, in a note written in 1983 for the 1984 publication:

> the formative beginning of *galáxias* (fim/começo: "e começo aqui") is from 1963; the last (fim/começo: "fecho encerro") from 1973. As a text imagined at the extreme limits of poetry and prose, bioscriptural pulse in galactic expansion between those two changeable and changing formative elements (having as a thematic magnet the voyage as a book or the book as a voyage, and for that reason understood as well as a "book of essays") today, retrospectively, I would tend to see it as an epic insinuation that resolved itself in an epiphanic one.

The reading of this selection from the work, at the same time as it confirms our retrospective evaluation of the poet, in which the epic development is taken by surprise from the first sentence (and the surprise comes from the writing whose movement keeps imposing the flowering of epiphanies), serves better to accentuate that quality so often referred to as giving "initiative to words," in the manner of Mallarmé, recovering in the strict space of the text its fundamental dependence on a certain biography and its poetic written form. This quality, meanwhile, brings together elements of metalanguage that are not innocent of the proliferation of language, of a history of language, whose shards are collected in the interstices of biographemes, masks that are named as *personae* of those passages between the *ego* and the *ego scriptor* of Valéry.

In this way, if meditation about the actual movement of language functions as a matrix of meanings, the recurring images of birds and trees cover and activate the calculus of reflection, establishing once and for all a dependence between saying and doing, or its *intention*, in order to recuperate mutely another expression of Valéry. But it is a dependence whose horizon is the nothingness that flashes from that tacit language and which for that reason cannot be resolved in terms of signifieds. Thus, like the "tughra de sulaiman," it opens "em lobulados espaços florais não se saberia por onde ela começa e onde ela termina."

Language being thus between beginning and end assumes its eminent domain among the biographical fragments: that of circularity, which in its poetic form exercises enormous centripetal power, dragging in everything and making it converge. The contrary centrifugal movement is a synonym for everything that ends in critical-theoretical depiction of the force of consciousness represented by the tensions of circularity. Therefore, the work of translation and criticism, synonyms of that depiction when it occurs, is informed by that same centripetal power.

III

While admitting in principle the thesis of the untranslatability of creative texts, it seems to us that the same engenders the corollary of possibility, also in principle, of the recreation of these texts. We will have, as Bense wanted, another esthetic information in another language, autonomous, but both will be linked together by an isomorphic relationship: they will be different as language, but as isomorphic bodies they will crystallize within the same system.

Then, for us, the translation of creative texts will always be a recreation, or parallel creation, autonomous however reciprocal. The more full of difficulties this text, the more recreatable, the more seductive as a possibility for recreation. In a translation of this nature, one does not translate only what is signified, *one translates the sign itself*, that is, its physical and material nature (sonorous properties, with visual imagery, all that according to Charles Morris forms the iconicity of the esthetic sign, understood as iconic sign, which "is in a certain way similar to what it denotes"). The signified, the semantic parameter, will be just and only the demarcating guide post of the place of the recreating enterprise. This is, of course, the other side of so-called literal translation.

In this valuable text written in 1962, pubished in a journal in 1963 and now part of the book *Metalinguagem e Outras Metas* (1992) titled "Da Tradução como Criação e como Crítica," it is possible to confirm our earlier observation. Being an essay that establishes the preeminence of Odorico Mendes, who in the nineteenth century translated Homer and

Virgil, challenging the *fable convenue* of a literary historiography that insisted, and still insists, on seeing translations of that author as "monstrous" exceptions to a pretended literality, Haroldo de Campos on the contrary snares the question of translatability of poetry. On opting for re-creation, or transcreation, as he will later prefer, the poet establishes a strict dependence between reading and poetic creation itself: to read poetry no longer as a process of decyphering meaning but of recyphering structures of language, through which the semantic elements are captured in the highest degree of intensity, which is that of the poetic sign.

But an option of this order could only occur, as it occurs, in the convergence of long experience with the making of poetry and a poetic sense that privileges the materiality of language, exemplified by the products resulting from the most radical phase of experimentation of concrete poetry; from a long and intimate acquaintance with the history of poetry, above all its most intense periods of renovation, whether one refers to poetry in general or to Brazilian poetry in particular; and, moreover, to the wide panorama of modern theories about poetics. One comes to understand, therefore, that on one hand the theoretical supports for his essay come from authors such as Fabri or Max Bense, who are able to characterize the quality of information passing though poetic language and, on the other, the greatest example of re-creation who is Ezra Pound, whose "poetic path," according to Haroldo de Campos, "was always dotted with adventures in translation, through which the poet criticized his own linguistic instrument, subjecting it to the most varied dictions, and stockpiling material for his poems in preparation." Brazilian examples range from Oswald de Andrade to João Cabral de Melo Neto, from *Memórias Sentimentais de João Miramar* and *Serafim Ponte Grande* to Mário de Andrade of *Macunaíma* and João Guimarães Rosa of *Grande Sertão:Veredas*. All are theoreticians and creators for whom, or over whom, the creation of poetry or of creative prose always involves the questioning of the limits of language and of communicability and, therefore, of the difficult as a parameter of poetic reading and criticism.

In the same way that criticism is *partial* because it is crossed by that sense of the poetic that has already been singled out as a quality, so also is translation, which seeks to restore that same sense in another language; this is not a criticism of numerous and rare meanings but of concrete elements of construction. Or, as Haroldo de Campos says:

> The translation of poetry (or prose equivalent to it in problematics) is above all a habitation in the interior of the world and technique of what is translated. It is as if one disassembles and reassembles a machine of creation, that most fragile beauty, apparently untouchable, that offers us a finished product in a strange language. And which, in the meantime, shows us that it is open to a fearless vivisection, that turns over its insides to bring it back to life in a different linguistic body. This is why translation is criticism.

This is what Haroldo de Campos brings about in his reading of passages of Homeric translations by Odorico Mendes: the translation made by the writer from Maranhão serves as a trigger for reflections about the state of poetic criticism in Brazil, even coming to propose a pedagogical plan for an apprenticeship in a "laboratory of texts." The critical reading of poetry, as he repeats on various occasions, would be accomplished "by translation" because it would allow for dismantling and reassembling the machine of creation to which he referred. And his conclusion about reading the translations by Odorico Mendes reveals not only the critical but also the historiographical reach of his vision:

> Naturally, the reading of the translations by Odorico is a bizarre and difficult one (more difficult than the original, so thinks João Ribeiro, with some irony, although he treats him with understanding). But in the creative history of Brazilian poetry, a history that still is waiting to be made, many verses or excerpts from poems, "touchstones" rather than entire poems, have a guaranteed place. And for whoever becomes wrapped up in a theory of translation, exposed to fragmentary comments on the translated *cantos*, that reading will be transformed into an intriguing adventure in which he can follow the successes and failures (more failures than successes perhaps) of the poet in his committed task and in the arena of his linguistic conventions and special inventions. To the contrary of how it appeared to historian Sílvio Romero, the fact of Odorico having started cold ("without emotion") and armed with a preconceived system is, in our view, precisely what is most seductive about his great task.

IV

It is not difficult to see the opening of a wider angle of thought about the historicity of poetry being born here: the suggestion of a "creative history of Brazilian poetry" runs against the grain of a historiography that simply erased the presence of Odorico Mendes, not the important literary historian that he also was, author of critical-historical essays on Portuguese and Brazilian literatures, which would have guaranteed him a place in that historiography, but the disabused reader of the classical tradition in poetry.

In theoretical texts written in 1967, "Por uma Poética Sincrônica," in *A Arte no Horizonte do Provável*, and "Texto e História," the opening essay in *A Operação do Texto,* the poet elaborated his thought more explicitly. I say explicitly in order to differentiate what in terms of critical-historiographical practice is patent in the revindicatory reading made with Augusto de Campos of the romantic poet Sousândrade, in *Revisão de Sousândrade*, whose original edition is from 1964. (An identical practice will later take Augusto de Campos to the revindicatory re-readings of the symbolists Pedro Kilkerry and Ernani Rosas, of the modernist Patrícia Galvão, the celebrated Pagu).

In the first case are two essays ("Poética Sincrônica" and "O Samurai e o Kakemono") and "Apostila: Diacronia e Sincronia," in which, putting Saussurian terms to new use, as re-read by the structural linguistics of Roman Jakobson, he meditates on the question of literary history, above all the Brazilian, insisting on the idea that a re-reading, based on synchronic, aesthetic values in relation to the present of the historian-analyst, should be coupled to the evolutionary diachronics imposed by traditional literary historiography. And, as a preliminary result of what could come to be a structural history of literature, in the terms of Gérard Genette shared by the poet-critic, the first outlines are offered of what is called an "anthology of Brazilian poetry of invention": Gregório de Matos, the *Cartas Chilenas*, Sousa Caldas, the translator Odorico Mendes, the satirical and burlesque poet Bernardo de Guimarães and the Symbolism of Cruz e Sousa and Pedro Kilkerry would all be indispensable names, without forgetting Sousândrade for romanticism, of course, or even Alvarenga Peixoto from the eighteenth century, who in his belatedly discovered sonnets belies the reputation of faint praise with which he appears in the literary histories.

This is not to mention the other readings of Brazilian writers that he published in 1967 in *Metalinguagem*: Drummond, Guimarães Rosa, Murilo Mendes, João Cabral, Oswald de Andrade, poet and prose writer, Manuel Bandeira (to which would be added in *Outras Metas* from 1992 José de Alencar of *Iracema*, Mário de Andrade of *Macunaíma*, Clarice Lispector, Mário Faustino and Paulo Lemínski or even Raul Pompéia of *O Ateneu*), all marked by the singularity of being treated by a criticism that rescued them for the strict vision of creative invention and, thus, as possible members of that "anthology."

We are dealing, therefore, with a criticism of choice, *partial* in the Baudelairean sense, marked without a doubt by that essential quality of poetic sense of language to which I have constantly been referring and to which I will now add a specific historical sense. But it is a sense that comes out of the interstices of the first, that is, from the articulations or intervals between diachrony and synchrony. Or, in the words of Haroldo de Campos:

> The concept of synchronic poetry, as I understand it, comes from a free application of Roman Jakobson's formula, restated recently by Gérard Genette, about what could be considered a "structural history of literature." The latter would be nothing if not a diachronic perspective (historical-evolutionary) of successive synchronic phases. Diachronic poetics, thus reformulated, would then become, as Jakobson desired, "a superstructure to be edified about a series of successive synchronic descriptions." As a corollary, the synchronic cuts, enacted according to criteria of variable functions, would judge not only by the "present moment of creation" (the literary production of each epoch) but also the "cultural present" (the tradition that remained alive, the revision of authors, the choice and reinterpretation of classics).

In the second case, in the introductory essay to the book *A Operação do Texto*, at the same time that he emphasizes the theoretical hypotheses of his previous book, even discussing textual history in a footnote, he adds at least two authors to the projected anthology: Manuel Antônio de Almeida of the *Memórias de um Sargento de Milícias*, which seems to result from the re-reading by Antonio Candido in his essay "Dialética da Malandragem" ("Dialectics of Malandroism"), and the final Machado de Assis of *Brás Cubas*, *Quincas Borba* and *Dom Casmurro*, "that metalinguistic triad" by our "nineteenth-century Borges," as the poet described him.

V

In two texts written in the early and late 1980s, the sense of articulation between poetics and history is intensified: the first, "Da Razão Antropofágica: Diálogo e Diferença na Cultura Brasileira," published in a journal in 1981 and later in many others and in different languages, today part of the book *Metalinguagem e Outras Metas*; the second, the book *O Seqüestro do Barroco na Formação da Literatura Brasileira: O Caso Gregório de Matos* (1989).

In both, the polemical defense of a radical historicity in Brazilian poetry, whether to dislocate the theme of foreign influence to one of difference and that of the precariousness of the antonyms provincial/cosmopolitan, local/universal, in this way recovers the question of nationality in our modernism through the essential contribution of *antropofagia* ("cannibalism"), as it may be viewed in the Brazilian critical tradition since romanticism. One should remember the singular essay by Santiago Nunes Ribeiro, young Chilean-Brazilian critic, ("Da Nacionalidade na Literatura" (1843), seconded by Machado de Assis in "Instinto de Nacionalidade" (1873), broadening the contents of the first essay by problematizing the theoretical arsenal of a basic work in our literary historiography, the *Formação da Literatura Brasileira: Momentos Decisivos*, by Antonio Candido, through the critique of what he calls "logophanic substantialism" that generally characterizes Brazilian literary historiography. Campos analyzes the poetic logic that would lead to the *kidnapping* of the work of Gregório de Matos and the baroque in Candido's book, which seems to have been conceived, as he states, "with the elegance and internal coherence of a mathematical construct."

The essays are actually complementary in the sense that the argument of the first, on the one hand, is supported above all by its denial of an ingenuous origin to Brazilian literature, which develops under the sign of the baroque:

> I will say that the baroque, for us, is its non-origin, because it is a non-infancy. Our literatures – that is, the Latin American – emerging from the baroque, never had an infancy (*infans:* one without speech).

They never were aphasic. They were already born as adults (as certain mythological heroes) and speaking a highly elaborate universal code: the baroque rhetorical code (with late medieval and renaissance survivals, already filtered in the Brazilian case by Camonian mannerism, itself an influence on Góngora). To have articulated itself as difference in relation to this panoply of *universalia* is to describe the "birth" of our literature: a sort of parthenogenesis without any ontological egg...).

The central argument can be found in what the poet calls the kidnapping of the baroque, a consequence of the assumption of an "ontological nationalism," patterned after the biological-organicist model of the evolution of a plant ("a model inspiring, surreptitiously, all literary history concerned with the individuation of a 'classical nationalism,' as the height of a process of gradual flowering, fed by 'objectivist pretensions' and by the 'immanent teleology' of nineteenth-century historicism"), "privilege of the referential and emotive functions" in detriment to the poetic and metalinguistic functions of language. His conclusion to the essay is faithful to this idea:

> The exclusion – the "kidnapping" – of the Baroque in the *Formação da Literatura Brasileira* is not, however, merely the objective result of adopting a "historical orientation" which separates literature, as a "system," from incipient and asystematic "literary manifestations." Neither is its perspective "historical," in a univocal and objective sense, in the disappearance of Gregório de Matos at the foundation of our "literary system." That exclusion – that "kidnapping" – and also his literary non-existence, given as "historical" evidence, are effects on a profound latent level, following a "deconstructive" vision, of the semiological model artfully articulated by the author of *Formação*. This model confers on literature as such, *tout court*, the peculiar characteristics of the literary project of ontological-nationalistic romanticism. It emphasizes the "communicational" and "integrative" aspect of literary activity, as would have occurred within the special Brazilian synthesis of classicism and romanticism ("mixture of neo-classical artisanship with romantic bards") from which a committed literature would emerge, with its "sense of mission" elevated to such a high degree that at times it would become an "exercise of fantasy", but which at other times was able to overcome its "historical sense

and special communicative power" and then become the "general language of a society searching for self-recognition." It has been shown that the baroque does not fit into this model, since baroque esthetics emphasize the poetic function and the metalinguistic function, the auto-reflexivity of the text and the inter-and-intratextual working of its code (meta-sonnets that disarm and denude the sonnet"s structure, for example; citation, paraphrase and translation are plagiotropic views of literary dialogism and rhetorical benefits of codified elements of style). The baroque, an esthetics of "super-abundance and excess," as Severy Sarduy defined it, does not fit here.

Whether or not one agrees with the poet's tight argumentation, he comes to a balanced and just conclusion of the book when he points to the enriching exception that Antonio Candido himself made in relation to what the poet calls the "royal road" of method adopted in the *Formação*, on validating the marginal reading of the "rogue" ("malandro") in the novel by Manuel Antônio de Almeida, as revealed in Candido's essay "Dialética da Malandragem." The fact is that the convergence of the poetic and the historical senses of language, a result of a long experience with poetry and reflection upon it, doubtless adds to this text by Haroldo de Campos the flavor of a seminal rehearsal for all future re-readings that may occur of our historical-literary tradition.

As if the historical-cultural practice that resulted in the re-evaluation of authors and works (such as Sousândrade, Odorico Mendes, José de Alencar, Oswald and Mário de Andrade) were not enough, the poet now adds a theoretical-historiographical reflection capable of shaking the very center of an accepted *impasse* as a tradition that has dominated our historical-literary scenario since the nineteenth century. Through the baroque, a tradition that is also an antitradition either can be instituted or restored, as the poet says:

> It is an antitradition that passes through the rafters of traditional historiography, that filters through its seams, that seeps through its cracks. This is not an antitradition as a direct derivation, which would be only to substitute one linearity for another, but arises from the recognition of certain designs or marginal patterns along the preferential routes of a normative historiography.

VI

Haroldo de Campos's *O Arco-Íris Branco: Ensaios de Literatura e Cultura* (1997) and his collection of poems *Crisantempo: no espaço curvo nasce um* (1998) help to show in an overall way that convergence of the poetic and the historical senses of language, at the same time, *et pour cause,* attests to the universality of his practice and his reflections.

In *O Arco-Íris Branco*, essays spread across linguistic and cultural fields (German, Chinese, Spanish and French), criticism of poetry is also practiced "via translation," to use the poet's preferred expression. We see, on the one hand, those insides of the creating machine, as Haroldo de Campos himself said in a text on translation and criticism published in 1962, and, on the other hand, how he obliges historicity to revise itself according to the postulates of that same text in a way that harmonizes with the poetic operation.

In this way, in the first of those fields, for example, Goethe, Arno Holz, Morgenstern, Stramm, Kafka and Brecht are not chosen only for a supposed representativeness but because of the challenge that they offer, whether through textuality or as the articulators of a solid historicity of poetry. And what is there to say about a text as surprising as "Hegel Poeta," which I deliberately omitted in my list of German authors treated in the book, which in a certain way seems to re-read the philosopher's twisted insides, that illuminating relationship between "poésie et pensée abstraite" that Paul Valéry captured in his famous essay of 1939?

The oldest essay collected in this field is on Christian Morgenstern, whose first publication dates from 1958. Here one already perceived the reading of poetry, a poetry of *nonsense* like that one, that *by way of translation* is not satisfied with the easy paraphrase of meanings. Haroldo the poet-critic seeks rather to confront the complexity of verses that "reveal a series of experiences with deformations of words, portmanteau words, humorous effects generated by the absurd and by paradox, typographical inventions, use of sonorous materials and of the possibilities of the visual field, which would only later be taken up in a systematic way, but not always successfully, by the revolutionaries of futurism and Dadaism." And what he calls *amostragem,* actually a beam shining through that complexity, offers information to the attentive reader that can be used to reconfigure not only the concrete space of a poem but time, or the curve of time that it describes, in which for that very reason the poetic function is intensified by the metalinguistic. An exercise in *amostragem* occurs in the following text, "O Teixugo Estético" ("The Esthetic Badger"), which functions as a *leitmotif* for the whole essay:

O TEIXUGO ESTÉTICO	DAS AESTHESTETISCHE WIESEL
Um teixugo sentou-se num sabugo no meio do refugo	Ein Wiesel sass auf einem Kiesel inmitten Bachgeriesel.
Por que Afinal? O lunático Segredou-me estático:	Wisst ihr, wes halb? Das Mondkalb verriet es mir im Stillen?
o re- finado animal acima agiu por amor à rima.	Das raffineir- te Tier tats um des Reimes willen.

Haroldo de Campos's commentary is in itself a beautiful example of how criticism of poetry, that is, its reading by a critical tradition, can bring about the basic suturing between what is concrete in the poem, its constructive space, and its historical fissures, poetic time. He says:

> In this poem, Morgenstern also lets fly a biting satire against Parnassian estheticism, the chain of cultivated rhyme as a touchstone of the poetic. I translated *Wiesel* (maiden) as *teixugo* in order to maintain the strangeness of the rhyme and to communicate the ironical atmosphere. In the three first verses – introducing the "esthetic badger" – I departed from the original text, setting up a much more grotesque scheme, but one that was in a certain way authorized by the sequence. In the original, there is a pseudobucolic aura: the "esthetic maiden" sits down on a boulder, surrounded by the murmur of the brook. More or less like (in a *tour de force*):
>
> *Um teixu-*
> *go sentou-se num seixo*
> *à sombra de um freixo.*

Whether by reading China's Wang Wei, Spain's Julián Ríos or France's Ponge and Maurice Roche, Haroldo constructs a broad arch of a relationship, so to speak, with universal poetry, omnivorous and, considering its Latin-American condition, "anthropophagic"; from this he chooses what is in fact nutritive, insinuating a basic selection by relativizing the first term, always working in my view to control that complementarity between the poetic and historical senses of language that ends up conferring on his essays a basic unity where it is difficult and even unnecessary to distinguish the poet, the critic, and the translator.

Navigating through this sea of signifiers that seem to be the last and most radical signified of that poem at which all poets dock, bringing their meanings – once I called him a *cosmonaut of signifiers* – courageously crossing the mists of utopia and stamping his foot down on a *nowness* that is also agonistic. In a comparable way, coming out of the broad meditation found in the text that closes the volume, "Poesia e modernidade: da morte do verso à constelação. O poema pós-utópico," Haroldo de Campos performs a last, certainly and happily not the last, convergence: that of space-time that exists as much in a curvature as in that most fragile delicacy that many years ago, in a text from 1960 quoted here, he saw as the principal task of the poet-critic-translator to extract: such is the poetry collected in *Crisantempo: no espaço curvo nasce um*. The reasons of a master in the center of literature.

Translation by K. D. Jackson

PART III

Concrete Prose: *Galáxias* and After

Facing *Galáxias*

Wladimir Krysinski

MANY THINGS MAY be said about what makes the work of Haroldo de Campos so novel. Allow me to draw your attention to his extraordinary "polyglottism." To paraphrase Fernando Pessoa, "A pátria de Haroldo não é só a língua porrigineuse, mas também as línguas do mundo." Jacques Roubaud has demonstrated what constitutes Haroldo's novelty in his numerous "transcreations." I would like to underline the fact that throughout his poetic and critical work, Haroldo has aimed for the universal medium of poetry. Taking into account Mallarmé's syntax and functional discontinuous space, Haroldo attempts to integrate Ezra Pound's *logopeia* ("dance of intellect") and Fenellosa's ideas about the ideogrammic language of poetry. Haroldo's work embodies what Goethe conceived of in 1827 as *Weltliteratur*, or world literature. The creative tension between Brazilian local and world global opens unto the universal, understood as a syncretic and cognitive, an intertextual and interdiscursive synthesis.

Although we may agree with Jacques Roubaud that truly original poems do not exist, we can still understand poetry's evolution as a cognitivized process implying novelty. In this sense, a newly created poem refers to the textual and discursive totality of poetry seen as a set of functional and permutational elements. Roubaud's book, which bears as title the mathematical sign of belonging, formalizes and signifies the evolutionary process of poetry.

Analogically, poetry fulfills itself as *ars combinatoria*; in other words, as an all-encompassing and ever-growing combination of sentences or signs. The sentences and signs contain cognitive messages that may be understood in terms of a given state of affairs. The evolving poetry is not a linear dialectical process but rather a locally tabular and universally ironic digressive process. Paradoxically, one can understand the evolutionary poetic process as a constant extension and amplification of one of the definitions of irony given by Friedrich von Schlegel in his fragments: "Ironie ist eine permanente Parekbase," which may be translated as "Irony is a permanent digression." If we recall Wittgenstein's affirmation that "the limits of my language are the limits of my world," as quoted by Jacques Roubaud, we may also assume that language exists and functions as both game and unfinished potentiality of sentences which constitute poetic images and propositions as spatio-temporal interlocking of form understood in terms of Aristotle's *entelechia* (ideal form) and *morphe* (circumstantial form, understood as contour and irregular line).

My references to classical poetics and language in general lead me back to the title of Haroldo's work and my own title. As the choice of title "Facing *Galáxias*" indicates, I would like to raise a number of questions linked to a possible reading process for this text.

Reading *Galáxias*

This reading process also involves the act of understanding and interpreting *Galáxias* as a literary object or discursive phenomenon. Be it literary object or discursive phenomenon, *Galáxias* belongs to a rare category of texts which intentionally overcomes norms, traditions, influences, intertextualities, or poetics. Among the examples that come to mind are *Finnegan's Wake*, *Cantos*, *The Waste Land*, *Champs magnétiques*, Pessoa's *Maritime Ode*, Rilke's *Duino Elegies*, Ruben Dario's *Azul*, Octavio Paz's *Blanco*, or Khlebnikov's poetry, John Ashbery's *The Self-Portrait in a Convex Mirror,* and Jacques Roubaud's *Trente et un au cube*. *Galáxias* refers to all literature but at the same time it refers only to its own referentiality. However, simultaneously and functionally, *Galáxias* also inscribes in its textual body, norms and traditions, influences and intertextualities. Beneath and beyond any anxiety of influence, Haroldo's "poetro-prose" – prosaically uttered poetry, or poetically narrated fiction – seems to speak about all that which concerns poetry and prose. It expresses everything that poetry means in the way that it existed and pre-existed before *Galáxias*, any atomistically distinguished element of poetic discourse and of narrative discourse.

Here I should like to confess what I immediately felt as a reader of *Galáxias*. For me, this mono-polymorphous text is a remarkable demonstration of a graceful if not gracious state of creation – a gracious, creative gesture. It provides an all-encompassing epiphany of becoming discourse that constantly feeds off the intelligence of the world as the return of *Eros* and *Thanatos*. A progressing epiphany is constantly striving for the triple dimension of the poetic and of the prosaic object grasped as the solidarity of *claritas, consonantia* and *integritas*. The self-reflexivity of this work may be seen in the imperatively existing and functioning conventions and structures, e.g., rhythm, anaphor, repetition, tyranny of rhetoric and freedom of execution. There is a perfect state of happiness in which the artist whose accomplishment reveals both his masterful control of the material and an extraordinary force of inventiveness. The strange albeit splendid Italian word *sprezzatura* best characterizes an exactitude of style and a rightfulness of technique, a knowledgeable complexity of the thematic basis and a gracious formal performance of *Galáxias*.

Seeking *Galáxias*

To face *Galáxias* is not an easy task. The problem may be stated as follows: how to go beyond what is obvious? What is obvious is the whole panoply of poetic and of prosaic signs: *captatio benevolentiae* and *narratio, elocutio* and *dispositio* and rhythms, repetitions, *mots-valises*, quotations, allusions, explanations, references, self-explanations and self-refutations. There is polyglottism and mono-playfulness. There are traveling points of views and *métaphores filées* played out as puns and as repetitions. There is also erasure of the lyrical "I" and imposition of an external perspective. What is obvious is the repetition of literature as literariness. Yet at the same time, this literariness undergoes multiple deformations. The fictional *topoi* of beginning and end do not pertain to the traditional plot or story. Lines are equally structured in terms of rhythmical length, but do not communicate a unified message. What is being said tends to be functional in other ways. However in what way? This is the question. Is the message a meta-message; that is to say, some meta-critical way of expressing the possible future of literature and the rejected way of making literature in present time? The uttering "I" is by no means that of a narrator or poet. The splitting ego of the *persona*, of the *prosopon*, serves a different cause, one which is not that of traditional literary discourse. The uttering "I" acts as a versatile, well-informed voice in the modern if not postmodern fulfillment of the idea of polytropic, semiotic and textual storyteller. This is obvious, too. What is traditional lost its legitimacy after the experimental and cognitive inventions and creations of the poets grouped around *Noigandres*. Let us recall what Augusto de Campos has observed so well in the poem "America Latina: contra boom da poesia":

> de oswald à poesia concreta
> de joao cabral e joao gilberto
> da pc à tropicalia
> criou-se uma outra linha experimental
> antropofago-construtivista
> que nao tem paralelo
> na américa espanhola[1]

Augusto summarizes the Spanish-American poets' traditional way of doing poetry ironically and somewhat cruelly:

> claro, existe um grilo
> entre nós e eles:
> o surrealismo
> (qualquer que seja o nome que lhe dêem)
> impregna a massa dos poemas hispano-americanos
> de uma insuportavél retorica metaforizante
> que não questiona a linguagem [2]

What Haroldo undertakes in *Galáxias* is a prosaico-poetical synthesis of the modern as opposed to the traditional. Here modern signifies questioning language. It also signifies rejecting "understandable metaphorizing rhetorics." *Galáxias* may thus be defined as a verbal icon of the modernity understood as an invention and a practice in an idiom apt to express the function and meaning of poetry problematically. At the same time, it should underline the function of the fiction that must demonstrate its mobility and flexibility, which lies in the capacity of dissipation. Fiction is therefore an episteme of poetry and a dissipative idiom. Mallarmé emphasizes an important element of his poetic and fictional creation of the Book. In this spatial and mobile configuration, a Page is a measure, a unity, at least as important as the Verse (*Vers*).

---

1 Augusto de Campos, *O Anticrítico* (São Paulo: Companha das Letras, 1986), 162.
2 Op. cit., 161.

Haroldo, therefore, constructs a syncretic idiom through which he expresses a variety of things. First of all, the functionality of the Mallarméan aesthetic postulate. Mallarmé says in his preface to "Un Coup de Dès Jamais n'Abolira le Hasard": "Fiction will emerge and will disappear, quickly, as a consequence of the mobility of the writing, around the fragmentary stops of a key sentence which has been introduced and continued since the very title."[3]

Here we must recall that Haroldo stops the Mallarméan sentence after the word *l'écrit*. In other words, the Mallarméan motto of *Galáxias* expresses only one part of this sentence: "La fiction affleurera et se dissipera, vite, d'après la mobilité de l'écrit." Here Haroldo puts a full stop. And what is not said in the motto is the following: "autour dès arrêts fragmentaires d'une phrase capitale dès le titre introduite et continuée." Does *Galáxias* have a key sentence? It is hard to say. What is striking is Haroldo's ingenious interpretation of Mallarmé's manifesto. Fifty pages of *Galáxias* are much more than eleven pages of Mallarmé. Nevertheless, the difference does not consist in the number of pages alone. Mallarmé's poem draws on some continuity around the key sentence. *Galáxias* flows as galaxies, and each page should be taken separately as its own principle of organic, prosaic, poetic and discursive unit. Haroldo proceeds according to the principle of the dissipative fiction. What functions as a constructive principle is discontinuity. Having followed Mallarmé's postulate that the Page is a measure and a unity, Haroldo strongly emphasizes discontinuity, which separates one page from another on the basis of the narrative inconclusiveness of each page. Discontinuity is functional since fiction does not constitute itself in a continuous narrative. In this manner, Haroldo achieves a textual embodiment of Mallarmé's aesthetics, which relies on the spatial mobility of the writing. Consequently, Haroldo's Mallarméan teaching overcomes the traditional vision of Mallarmé, as theorized and developed by Hugo Friedrich in his influential book, *The Structure of Modern Poetry*. Friedrich deals with modern poetry by establishing its origin in Hölderlin, Novalis, Schlegel, Baudelaire, Rimbaud, and Mallarmé and by insisting on the fact that it could be appropriately understood and fittingly described by some negative categories. Those categories are

---

3 Stéphane Mallarmé, "Préface" in "Un Coup de Dès Jamais n'Abolira le Hasard" in *Oeuvres complètes de Stéphane Mallarmé* (Paris: Éditions Gallimard, 1945), 455.

definitional and not pejorative. As Friedrich puts it, "They are, in fact, applied as a result of the historical process by which modern poetry has departed from older literature."[4]

To grasp the definitional and descriptive importance of these categories, one has to take into account the fact that, for Friedrich, it is Baudelaire who founded modern poetry and the central element of this founding is a dissonant imagination. According to Baudelaire the destructive imagination decomposes everything ("Elle décompose toute la création," he says in his critical text *Salon of 1859*). As Jonathan Culler reminds us, in reference to Friedrich and in agreement with his interpretation of Baudelaire's poetry and modern poetry:

> The two main techniques and negative categories are 1) a process of *Entrealisierung*, whereby imagination transforms reality and makes it unreal; and 2) there is *Entpersönlichung*: "Baudelaire sparked off the depersonalization of modern poetry."[5]

From Friedrich's perspective, what counts in modern poetry is its overtly negative disposition towards the world and the act of writing poetry. Thus to complete Baudelaire's vision, one has to assume the definitional function of such categories as "Deformation, depersonalization, obscurity, dehumanization, incongruency, dissonance, and empty ideality...." Jonathan Culler recalls that for Friedrich, "The key terms from German, French, Spanish, and English writings on modern poetry, (...) are largely negative ones: Disorientation, disintegration of the familiar, loss of order, incoherence, fragmentation, reversibility, additive style, depoeticized poetry, bolts of annihilation, strident imaginary, brutal abruptness, dislocation, astigmatism, alienation."[6]

If these categories may be also applied to Mallarmé's poetic writing before *Un coup de dès*, they are not sufficiently functional to account for the meaning, the technique and the dynamics of the Book such as it is described or dreamed by the poet. The merit of Haroldo resides in the fact that Friedrich's vision of modern poetry is put into brackets. It is not

---

4 Hugo Friedrich, *The Structure of Modern Poetry*, translated by Joachim Neugroschel (Evanston: Northwestern University Press, 1974), 7.
5 Jonathon Culler, "On the Negativity of Modern Poetry: Friedrich, Baudelaire, and the Critical Tradition," in *Languages of the Unsayable. The Play of Negativity in Literature and Literary Theory*, ed. by S. Budick and W. Iser (New York: Columbia University Press, 1989), 189–208; 191.
6 Ibid., 8–9.

viable any more after the last, spatially oriented Mallarmé, after Pound and after the experiences of concrete poetry. The reader who faces *Galáxias* should keep in mind that it is about writing and not about the negative categories, as propagated by Friedrich. Haroldo bases his reading of Mallarmé on the problem of the Book. It is topographically understood as a discontinuous flux of words and signs expressing the idea of totality encompassing poetry and world, fiction and reading, cosmos and writing.

Conclusion

Facing *Galáxias* is tantamount to asking some questions concerning such matters as the text's literary status, its intertextuality, thematics, form and playfulness adopted as an infinite game and as a circumstantial performance. In order to grasp its specificity, can we refer to some literary identities pre-existing in Haroldo's construction? It is hardly plausible. I have mentioned some long poems or cycles of modern poetry. Naturally one could recognize that *Galáxias* belongs to this poetic discourse which, since Hölderlin and Baudelaire up to Enzensberger, John Ashbery and Jacques Roubaud, has expressed itself through the category of long poem. To the titles that I mentioned earlier, we could add such poems as Apollinaire's "Zone," Majakowski's "Cloud in the Trousers," Stevens's "Sunday Morning," Seferis' "Mythostirima," Yannis Ritsos's "The Moon Sonata" and C. Milosz's "Moral Treatise" and Rozewicz's "Falling Down."

Haroldo's fifty unnumbered pages break down the principle of thematic and formal continuity and, by the same token, any given identity which one could attach to *Galáxias*. If a rose is a rose is a rose, *Galáxias* is galáxias is galáxias. It has not just the willingness to be tautological but the drive to be unique. The same applies to the intertextualities of this construction. The reader facing *Galáxias* will recognize many other voices. They formally and vocally cohabit with the voice that voices "I". Again, one hears Pound, Mallarmé, Paz, some Chinese poets and some other Brazilian voices. One hears so many quotations; nevertheless, *Galáxias* stands as an independent structure. It is held together and uttered through the implicit author who is either an explicit narrator or an inverted semiotician, a distributor of signs and practitioner of music. Herein lies the truth of the reading process that I mentioned earlier.

Once the parameters have been recognized, traveling through *Galáxias* implies becoming pliable to its multiple intensities. It also implies acknowledging the "undecidability" of its literary status. In the fictional reaffirmation of poetry lies the poetic illustration of prose. The two meet each other in the turbulent and galactic utterances of the discourse, which cannot conceal its stochastic, antitelic, and apodictic nature. The double dynamics of this text is nothing other than *la doppia danza*, the last syntagm of *Galáxias* denoting prose and poetry in the reciprocal dissipations. It is also an open recognition of the performative dimension of *Galáxias*. The sayings of the leading voice pass through the different stages of mimicry (imitation), of *illinx* (vertigo), of *alea* (hazard) and of *agon* (struggle).

Apart from the conventional gesture to say "Now I begin" and "Now I stop," both what was began and what was ended belong to the epiphanic universe of writing; that is to say, to the pure affirmation and pure dissipation. This discourse is not apophantically oriented. It triggers no *alethea*, no *Entdeckung*. It is pure reminiscence of various multiplicities and of numerous memories. Galactically feeling and galactically speaking, this meta-poetry and this meta-prose corroborate the idea of poetic and of prosaic object as constellation. Indeed, this was relevantly expressed by Jacques Roubaud in his text DORS (Sleep) preceded by DIRE LA POESIE (Recite poetry).

> La voix de poésie appelle son objet...comme la constellation... l'étoile elle n'en contemple ni la lumière ni les lois[7]
> (The voice of poetry calls its object...as the constellation...the star it does not contemplate neither the light nor the laws).

The *topos* of the beginning and the *topos* of the end begin nothing and finish nothing. They are stars in the passage of constellations and constellations call the stars.

Galáxias fulfills Borge's definition of poetry marvelously well. His definition: "Dos deberes tendría todo verse comunicar un hecho preciso y tocarnos físicamente como la cercanía del mar."

---

[7] Jacques Roubaud, DORS précédé de DIRE LA POESIE. (Paris: Éditions Gallimard, 1981), 21.

Translation as Creation and Criticism: *Galáxias* as Text and Theory of Translation

Inês Oseki-Dépré

> mais uma vez junto ao mar polifluxbórboro polivozbárbaro polúphloisbos polyfizzykboisterous weitaukfrauschend fluctissonante esse mar esse mar esse mar esse martexto por quem os signos dobram marujando num estuário de papel num mortuário num monstruário de papel múrmur-rúmor-remurmunhante...
>
> Haroldo de Campos, from *Galáxias*

THIS ESSAY SEEKS to illustrate Haroldo de Campos's hypothesis of translation as a critical reading and as a means of creating a new poem. The first point deals with the fact that translation presupposes a grammatical organization, in spite of the meteoric dispersion of the book of prose fragments, *Galáxias*. Since I have already developed this point in an earlier study, I will merely consider this aspect briefly.[1]

The second point that will be made here is a more exciting one. It deals with the question of intertextuality – latent in the fragment "mais uma vez" (the 45th of 50) – as knowledge about literature. Intertextuality in the *Galáxias* is related to the past and to the future, hybridizing the Homeric tradition, via translation and parody, in a poem *en devenir*.

Finally, if Haroldo's text features knowledge about what we term literature, it also contains cognitive elements that have to be decoded when one reads the poem. This element of the analysis takes into consideration both languages and makes the aporia of translation explicit: indeed, in spite of its impossibility ("translation is impossible" as Derrida would say), translation becomes more necessary since it transforms both the author and the reader.

---

1 Inês Oseki-Dépré, "Lecture finie du texte infini: *Galaxies* de Haroldo de Campos," *TTR: traduction, terminologie, rédaction: Études sur le texte et ses transformations*, Québec, 12.1, 1999: 131–54.

The grammatical organization

If we follow Jacques Roubaud's idea that the poem frames the features of language and becomes the memory of language, and if we adopt Roman Jakobson's idea that the poem is primarily a work on the materiality of language as well as a series of recurrences and superposition of codes (parallelisms), we can establish that the fragment 45 of the *Galáxias* mobilizes all the structures of language, both the organized and hidden ones.

Starting from the verse-line considered as a rhythmical regulation and from the sentence-unity (syntactic and semantic unities) as the main element of the analysis (which allows the translation to happen), we can divide the text into four principal and distinct phrases:

1 (a) *"uma vez mais junto ao mar... você converte estes signos... papel"* ("once more by the sea... you turn these signs... paper") (line 1 to line 6);
1 (b) *"estes signos você os ergue... ibericaña"* ("these signs you shore them... ibericaña") (line 6 to line 9).

2 (a) *"na primeira posição do amor... ou foi não sendo"* ("in the first position of love... or was without being") (line 9 to line 13);
2 (b) *"pois os signos dobram... num livro de viagens"* ("for the signs toll... in a travelogue") (line 15 to line 19).

3 (a) *"na segunda posição... regiões escuras"* ("in the second position... dark regions") (line 20 to line 22);
3 (b) *"dizer que essas palavras... os festins floriletos"* ("tell that these words... the floriligea feasts") (line 22 to line 27) ;
3 (c) *"pois a linguagem é lavagem...abcesso obsesso"* ("for language is ashwashing...obsessive abscess") (line 27 to line 30);
3 (d) "e houve também... quello tedesco" ("there was also... quello tedesco") (line 30 to line 36);
3 (e) *"pois não se trata... cartapáceos galácticos"* ("for it's not a question... galactical voluminous thousands tomes") (line 36 to line 43).

4 *"na terceira posição ela... e por quem dobra"* ("in the third position she... and for whom tolls") (line 44 to end).

The syntactical criterion allows us to divide the text into four complex parts in which other divisions are hidden: (Introit), first movement, second movement, parenthesis, and finale. The first movement is, indeed, different from the others, as is the parenthesis (introduced by "for"). The sentences beginning with "she" have the same structure, and we can see a change of verbs: the action verbs disappear and become "to be," pointing to the fact that the subject has vanished. It would be superfluous to show how much these parallelisms are over-determined by the prosodical level (rhyme, sounds). We shall not insist on the details except only on this point: this subdivision clearly shows the parallelisms (correspondences) in both the large unities and the small ones. Therefore, this pattern of units does not necessarily imply linearity or boundedness (closure), but rather it endows this organized text with a dynamics that transforms it as a performative text, while it is being read.

The text as theory and knowledge about literature

The second goal of my analysis is not the text itself as a semiotic object (poetical), but its position in the historical and literary context, that is, in the tradition on the one hand, and in intertextual forms, on the other. This interpretation may, of course, be induced by the previous analysis.

We shall first examine how the original (and translated) text contains its own theory and, second, to what degree it transforms literature and reality.

I. The "metalanguage"
Let us look at the beginning of the poem, which we call introduction (line l) :

mais uma vez   junto   ao mar   polifluxbórboro
*   polivozbárbaro*
*   polùphloisbos*

polyfizzyboisterous
*   weitaufrauschend*

fluctissonante

esse   mar
esse   mar
esse   mar

Inês Oseki-Dépré

        esse martexto
        por quem os signos dobram

marujando

         num estuário de papel
         num mortuário
         num monstruário de papel
         múrmur-rúmor-remurmunhante

once more………..by the sea……….. polyfluxborborous
           polivoxbarbarous
           polùphloisboios
           polyfizzyboisterous
           weitfrauschend
           fluctissonant
     this sea

           this sea
           this sea
           this textsea
           for whom the bells toll

sailoring

           in its papermade estuary
       in a mortuary

           in a monstruary of paper
           murmur-clamor
              roaring-

 Many phonetic and semantic paradigmatic equivalences are juxtaposed on the syntagmatic sequence. Some remarks should be made about the syllabic regularity of the adjectives qualifying the "sea" in the first two lines (6, 6, 5, 7, 5 syllables respectively), about its invariant meaning in opposition to its multilingual and homophonic signifiers.

 The same recurrence may be found in the expression "this sea" and in the adverbs of place. Here we find an amplifying enumeration, whereas the final sequence "murmur-clamor-roaring" goes in an opposite way: starting with a half-word it becomes a complete word and then an action verb. The *sea pattern* is essential.

From the very beginning the poem is addressed to "you." "You" is the very ambiguous subject of this movement, referring to both you-reader or to you-who-are-writing (the two occurrences being deliberately confused and mutually identifiable). Thanks to Émile Benveniste, we know that when the "you" appears, the "I" is presupposed. The pronoun "you" places the question of the speech act (enunciation) in the action of what is called in French a "parole-écriture." The text is placed at the level of utterance (interactive discursivity) and no longer at the diegetic or narrative level, which is often identified with the truth (objectivity). Indeed, the only truth of the fiction is that it allows us to see fiction in the making. This fact is confirmed by the massive presence of shifters (these, your, your...): The subject of the process remains implicit in the interlocutor's ("you") but essentially in the first person shifters. It becomes explicit at the end, under the expression "I want" that indicates not only the presence of the subject but also the simultaneity of saying and acting: telling "I want," I am indeed acting.

In the final sentence, however, the text recovers its namelessness, the absent one ("she") and denies, while bringing the text to a conclusion, the appropriation of the speech by a subject "I." This non-appropriation, apparently at the level of the statement, is metalinguistic and takes the form of an intertextual quote.

II. At the same time, the first movement introduces the non-person, "she," about whom something is said in the text. This fictional embryo whose overtones are erotic, merges into and disappears in the act of writing ("the same brown-smooth hand") in the typewriter.

The continuation of the text insists on the return of the implicit subject, but especially on a metalinguistic and almost theoretical lucidity about the productive activity of the signifying practice which is mobilized here: "for the bells toll to this text which subsumes the contexts and produces them as script figures...."

The second movement introduces "she" again, who will appear in the Finale, in the same context:

" in the ... position" (first, second, third)
"She" – a mysterious victim of a "mise-en-scène/ mise-en-signe," who is passive and aggressed, is transformed into signs. "She" is no longer the actress, but may be *one* actress in the memory's script. She represents the fiction's tenuous clue that is created, re-created, and

consumed in the speech. In this text, the reference to a literary discourse is explicited all the time:

"a typewritten text... memory..."(I)
"say that these words..."(II)
"she is sign" (III)

The third paradigm (present in the three movements) demonstrates the particularity of showing, clarifying the text by placing it on a more theoretical level. We can, indeed, translate the three sentences:

I – for the bells toll
II – for the language is ashwashing
III – for here it's not question of a pink-book
into : the signs, transformed by "you-I" toll; she, a sign, transformed by "you-I" tolls, but the signs-bells toll for the signs-sounds transformed by "you-I."

In other words, language is memory, and because of that it is the locus of coexistence between mud, dirt, *cloaca*. But at the same time, it is only in language that the work on the signifying material is able to "clean" language, to deny "civilization" (the traditional culture). Only the language can erase the useless words while creating others and keep Homer's sea traces (trails?), his vowels and consonants.

The last phrase defines the book – for the *Galáxias* are the book: a "blackbook," a "pestseller," a "horreaderdigest," the book which refuses happy beginnings and ends and destroys the logocentric conception of literature as a fable, the Author as a subject, and the usual ingredients of the canonical literary repertoire. If, as Jacques Roubaud suggests, poetry in free verses anticipates the work of the Prague linguistic circle, the post-utopian poetry of Haroldo de Campos develops in the direction of what Derrida has analyzed under the category of "dissemination."

It only remains for us to comment on the parenthetic narrative unity, which has the formal appearance of fiction. We have already mentioned the relation between:

      in the... position   / for
              I   II

in which I and II include a theoretical conception of literature. At this level, the subject that is in the third person ("the German's story") can be opposed to the others, as being negatively denoted from a semantic point of view. The object here is a silly person who personifies the consumer of the language as a catalogue of words or a dust dictionary: word by word, the man tries to get hold of another language. His attitude is the opposite of the theory of the text, which makes other languages speak from inside. This is what explains why there is a break between the story and its continuation: "quero que se danem" ("I want them to go to hell").

> excessos de linguagem abcesso obsesso e houve também a estória daquele alemão que queria aprender o francês por um método rápido assimil de sua invenção e que aprendia uma palavra por dia un mot par jour zept mots jaque zemaine e ao cabo de um mês e ao fim de seis meses e ao fim e ao cabo deum ano tinha já tudo sabido trezentas e sessenta e cinco palavras sabidas tout reglé en ordre bien classé là voui là dans mon cul la kulturra aveva raggione quello Tedesco e a civilização quero que se danem...

In a word, the text, relived by the recurrences, the preservation and the cyclic transformations of its units, offers a theory of literary practice (of writing and translating) backed by a set of pronominal persons that works like a thread. Hence, if the subject of the uttering hides himself, it reveals and contributes to its own "occultation" thanks to the dialectical play of the various persons which are put into play:

THEORY	PRACTICE	FICTION
you	this	she
you	these	bells-signs
your	this	wail(ing)-hand
your	that	saliva-text-your
I		homere-faun-
here	the language	
now	linen-all-nightmare	

	WANT	

the story of
(associated to the negative conception of the idiom as words depot)
(ZERO)
the subject's vanishing in the text)

Tradition and intertextuality

(a) The itinerary mapped out by the subject that includes (as Lautréamont does) the reader in his practice throughout the pelagos-language, the sea in which the old fashioned culture of linguistic capitalism (by the German) drowns itself in the production of signifier, let us see a female presence as fictive and vague. It remains in its enunciation of the text – in which a wish-desire is affirmed, in a flash of lightning.

> No mais
> Profundo fundo do pélago-linguagem onde o livro faz-se pois não se trata
> Aqui de um livro-rosa para almicândidas e demidonzelas ohfélias nem de
> Um best-seller fimfeliz para amadores d'amordorflor mas sim de um
> Nigrolivro um pesteseller um horrídeodigesto de leitura apfelstúrdia
> Para vagamundos e gatopingados e sesquipedantes e sestralunáticos
> Abstractors enfim quintessentes do elixir caximônico em cartapáceos
> Galáticos na terceira posição ela é signo e por quem dobra

The text belongs in this way to traces that, while being contemporary, do not disown their history. Traces of a scripture that produces its own theory, a new theory of language-thinking. The literature (the poetry) continues in the direction of the odd structure's transformations, while canceling by this motion the subject as a supreme conscience (logocentric), master (boss) of his *dramatis personae* and his fables.

This dis-appropriation of statement appears also through a network of quotations, so "for whom the bells toll," a verse from John Donne, reemployed by Hemingway in his novel and later by Hollywood. In the same way "these signs you have shored them against your ruins or these ruins against these signs-sounds" is the quotation from Eliot "These fragments I have shored against my ruins" (*The Waste Land*), to which Pound answers in counterpoint (*Canto VIII*): "These fragments you have shelved (shored)."

(b) At the same time another setting (mise-en-scène) of the intertextuality is outlined via translation. "Polyspeech" designates "polúphloisbos," Homer, but the whole literature in its historical process and development of "translation vowels floating against the mobile springing of consonants." Besides that, this Homeric word works like the touchstone of the text – Ezra Pound (who uses it in his poetics and criticism) – by the phonetic paradigm and also through Joyce's translations ("polyfizzyboisterous") and those of Voss ("weitaufrauschend") and the Brazilian poet Odorico Mendes ("fluctissonante"): all poetic transcreations. It means that the text includes also a theory of translation as a poetic medium.

Moreover, "polyspeech" means the succession of Homeric sea-epithets and the succession of "vowels floating," "travel re-travel all along a travel-book" mixes with other texts of the *Galáxias*, in the same inspiration.

>…essas palavras convivem no mesmo mar de sargaços da
>Memória é dizer que a linguagem é uma água de barrela uma borra de
>Baixela e que a tela se entretela à tela e tudo se entremela na mesma
>Charade charamela de charonhas carantonhas ou carantelas que trelam…
>…pois a linguagem é lavagem é resíduo
>De drenagem é ressaca e é cloaca e nessa noite nócua é que está sua
>Mensagem nesse publiexposto putriexposto palincesto de todos os passíveis
>Excessos de linguagem abcesso obsesso…

The same recurrences are found in the second movement, with a chiasmatic configuration, rendered by my attempted transcreation in French:

> "*uma água de barrela uma borra de baixela*"
> "*a tela se entretela à tela*" with rimes and echoes or
> "*charonhas carantonhas ou carantelas que trelam e taramelam*"

Or in

> "*pois a linguagem é lavagem é resíduo de drenagem*" (line 27/28) :
> "for the language is washing is residue of drainage"
> "*é ressaca e cloaca.*"

(c) Text as questioning of reality

It is difficult to separate this fragment from the entire *Galáxias,* and it is even more difficult to isolate the *Galáxias* from Haroldo de Campos's whole project. Started in 1963, in a period of political hope in Brazil (the *Noigandres* group, 1955; Brasília and the Pilot-Plan, 1962; political and cultural effervescence), the work was being written until 1976, our fragment being from 1970, the moment of the hardening of the military dictatorship in Brazil, with a neo-fascist tendency.

A certain despair can be found in it, the only remaining consolation being the *poien,* the "doing" – "because it's more difficult than doing nothing" – as João Cabral de Melo Neto would say. We cannot be satisfied just by this semiotic reading; a reading which would confirm its belonging to the poetic domain, even if it is an homage to literature, coupled with a convocation/denunciation of the political and ideological reality of the times. Indeed, the *Galáxias* project is wider since it ties the ancient and the new, but mainly since it proposes a new reading of literature and of reality.

In reference to Haroldo de Campos's *Galáxias*, critics often associate them with a baroque writing, not difficult to accept if we define baroque by its superabundance of strained words, by the antithesis between high and low, and mainly by the "breath." Certainly Haroldo de Campos alludes to the baroque, but rather as a regret (as a motif) than as a script form, and if we had wished to interpret the expression "your baroucous deadepic ibericana," it would be in considering alike as much "baroucous" as "deadepic."

For the Brazilian poet, indeed, contrary to set ideas about national culture (which would be a Portuguese sub-culture trying to affirm its national specificity since the nineteenth century), Brazil was born baroque: "I will say that the baroque is for us the non-origin: our literatures, which were born with the baroque, do not have an infancy (*infans*: the one who does not speak). They were born adults (like certain mythological heroes), speaking a universal language, extremely elaborated: the rhetorical baroque language...." But this baroque epic is definitely dead.

To make up for it, there are many references to the epic genre, first in a literal way – "A horn-word blown by Homer and which can be transflown" ("*uma palavra búzio que homero soprou e que se deixa transsoprar*") – then, in an intertextual way. We have evoked the homages rendered to the English idiom poets like John Donne, T. S. Eliot and Ezra Pound. In the same way, we could see in this fragment a tacit homage to Mallarmé and a less tacit homage to Fernando Pessoa, to whom Haroldo comes closer with regard to the fictional dimension. Pessoa is the author of a poem called "Ulysses" about the myth "that is nothing that is everything" and where the one who "without existing filled us and created us." And which we could consider as the origin of literature.

As for Ezra Pound, the problem is to do like Homer, to write the epic of modern man starting from Homer and following his itinerary through time (Homer, Propercius, Di Cavalcanti, Dante, the troubadours), to be the "arts minister without a ministry" (Horace Gregory), to be a kind of a spokesman for Western man.

That said, if Ezra Pound is named, translator (and re-animator) of the past, our translation (as a critical medium, close reading) allows us to gain another parameter of Haroldo's text. I am clearly thinking here of James Joyce. It is interesting that Haroldo de Campos himself comments on the "ideogrammatic" method recommended by Pound and which consists in measuring the influence between two scripts via the translation. Here we are faced with a reference to a common *koiné*, the voyage of Ulysses which became an interior voyage/journey in Joyce's work, but a poetical project as well in all the meanings of the word: the origins of the narrative, the origins of poetry, but also of the Joycean proceedings which tell this origin: barbarous words, neologisms, puns, citations, the outside, the inside, the irony of the infinite phrase. At the same time, it is a question of putting together Pound and Joyce, these two giants of poetry who were so close and so far away from one another.

According to Forrest Read, "Pound and Joyce are the only ones who decided from the beginning to follow the classical vocation and to prepare themselves to write an epic (...) whilst being modern and classic. Both have developed just one idea in regard to a synthetic form wider and wider, integral" and Pound can say: "Ulysses is my answer."[1]

So, the reference to the baroque belongs to this propaedeutic intention: the post-Utopian poem is the rewriting of Homer (via Odorico Mendes's translation, via Joyce's hyper-translation, via Pound's inter-translation), an homage rendered to the future and to the tradition.

Conclusion

To conclude, I recall a passage from Haroldo de Campos's preface to his translation of *Finnegans Wake*:

> The rhythm of this prosepoetry – *riverrun-rivercurrent* – is something like a global and continuous flux. *Durchdringung*... A texture where the notion of the linear development of the narrative is

---

1 Forrest Read, *Pount/Joyce; the Letters of Ezra Pound to James Joyce, with Pound's Essay on Joyce* (New York: New Directions, 1967).

no longer true. Everything happens in a total time and in a total space. Spacetime. The real character is language.

We could parody Voltaire as mentioned by Jacques Delille, one of the *Aeneid*'s French translators – another hypertext of the Homeric epic: "if it is Homer who made Virgil, it is his most beautiful work." Indeed, if it is Homer who made Pound, Joyce, Pessoa, Haroldo de Campos, they are his most beautiful works, except for this small detail: that to the Brazilian poet, Ulysses is not a character, but the poet himself.

Music of the Spheres in *Galáxias*

K. David Jackson

> ...one's entire ambition being not to live all life
> or to feel all life but to organize all life, to consummate it
> in intelligent Harmony and Co-ordination.
> The longing to understand... belongs to the sphere of sensibility.
> *Book of Disquietude.* Fernando Pessoa

> Everything is music, my friend.
> *Dom Casmurro.* Machado de Assis

> He said that the people of their island had their ears adapted
> to hear the music of the spheres, which always played at
> certain periods...
> *A Voyage to Laputa*

HAROLDO DE CAMPOS's fragmentary poetic prose novel, *Galáxias* (1984), composed between 1963 and 1976, is approached as a musical composition, in which movement and form are translated into isomorphic ideogrammes or visual "constellations" and different kinds of harmonic relationships give shape to the poetic materials. The musicality of *Galáxias* is a contemporary contribution to the theme of "music of the spheres," in which musical intervals were thought to correspond to celestial mechanics, as in Paul Hindemith's opera about the astronomer Johannes Kepler, *Die Harmonie der Welt* (1956–7). In the prose, inconclusiveness, play, and awareness of language as a body are the characteristics used to follow how Haroldo de Campos established correspondences between the harmony of the world and the harmony of the word.

Literature and music: concepts of movement

In an interview in the São Paulo press with Rodrigo Figueira Naves, Haroldo de Campos describes his relation to artistic tradition as musical, speaking of his way of relating concepts through movement and form, as in the isomorphic ideogramme or visual constellation (Campos, 1987). Through music, he affirms, history itself can be understood as movement. Choosing to relate the cultural past to the present through music rather than memory, Haroldo de Campos describes his method of composition as a selective translation or harmonization, extracted from works of world literature that reply poetically to a contemporary creative question. To read literature as a trans-temporal musical score, Campos continues, often produces the effect of a mosaic. His own interest, however, does not lie in the linearity or accumulation of contents intrinsic to the mosaic, but rather in the simultaneity, temporal-spatial synthesis, and harmonic relationships of the musical-poetic materials of his compositions. Music provides an aesthetic foundation for his poetics, which in the fusion of a selective reading of tradition with the creative present suggests a universal or world harmony of materials.

Galáxias (1984), the book of poetry in prose, or prose fragments, composed over more than a decade (1963–76), embodies the trans-temporal reading of tradition and the musical foundations of composition found in the work of Haroldo de Campos. Related to the oral epic and saga, the fifty fragments of *Galáxias* frame the mythical beginning and end of speech, or song, which represents all story and flows uninterruptedly from its origin to apotheosis: "e aqui começo a fala/aqui me fino…não canto não conto." Within the song itself, the singer of tales further relates episodes of an archetypal voyage through 46 geographical locations encompassing his epic travels, which are cast as an underworld where a Ulysses, Faust, or Riobaldo passes, each with its peculiar musical tonality of enticement or enchantment. Here lies the passage from the voyage to the underworlds of negative language: "nada e néris e reles e nemnada de nada e nures de neeris de reles de ralo de raro… nenhumzinho de nemnada nunca…" (from the first text, "e começo"). The rhythm of the world, "o ritmo das coisas do mundo…," may symbolize both the chaos of totality, through sounds of anarchical cacophony, and the ritual of rebirth: "num círculo fálico como um xiva de luz neon… nesta anarcopédia de formas volúveis." Recapitulating

Sousândrade's *O Guesa*, the poet condemns history's moribund circles of inferno: "neste eldorido feldorado latinoamargo tua barrouca mortopopéia ibericaña" ("mais uma vez").

The disharmony of experience in the underworlds, the negative dimension of the narrator's life quest, stands in counterpoint to the harmonization of the overarching narrative, the story of story and sound of language itself, of which it is a part. In the narrative tale of *Galáxias*, voice equals story and universe. In its primal sea of song, sound propitiates the existence of the world, while harmony and rhythm reproduce the inner tensions of its dualistic structure. The word flow, as Walter Moser observed, produces sensual delight in that it uses all the registers and full vocal range of musical song. Campos's translation of a primal creation and voyage myth into a contemporary literary constellation involves, in Moser's definition, a "semiotic proliferation triggered by the body of words and sustained by chains of signifiers" (149). In the words of the teller, it is a "chuva de palavras" ("rain of words"). The score of *Galáxias* is then the topographical projection of a universal music, both archetypal and experiential. Our purpose here is to analyze the correspondence between Haroldo de Campos's "harmonizations" and the linguistic mechanics of his galaxies.

Music and the natural order

The correspondence between music and the laws of mathematics and the physical universe pertains to what Jamie James (*The Music of the Spheres: Music, Science and The Natural Order of The Universe*) describes as the great theme running throughout Western civilization, the belief in the sublime harmony of the cosmos. Likewise, in a recent text meditating on his secret life as an amateur cellist, the rhetorician Wayne C. Booth reflects on the universal scope once attributed to music, a value now seemingly antithetical to our own age:

> From the ancient philosophers until two or three centuries ago, innumerable writers have claimed that music was not just what musicians play but the very foundation of all things: the universe was itself playing music at every moment, the "music of the spheres," and the resulting "heavenly Harmony," though in a sense silent, was itself responsible not just for actual beautiful sounds but for everything

good, true, or beautiful in the world. It was in our bodies as we do gymnastics or have sex; it was/is the spheres as they create and enfold us.

That harmony was not ever something invented anew in any fresh musical moment: it was discovered and joined, or at least aspired to, not only by musicians but by all creatures whenever they lived in harmony with the creation... (205)

James's study develops the history of Pythagorean "music of the spheres" – or "harmony of the world" – which is the concept that basic mathematical truths observed in the intervalic relationships of the musical scale also explain the nature of the physical universe. Numbers also represent mystery, which is their emergence from unity and infinity to permanence in a dualistic world. Measuring the relationships of harmonic intervals – primarily the fourth, fifth, and octave – the Pythagoreans theorized an exact correspondence between the numbers of the musical scale and the cosmos, between musical intervals and heavenly motion. As Aristotle wrote, "...they supposed the whole heaven to be a musical scale and a number" (*Metaphysics*).

In the early fifth century, Boethius codified the three classes of music as *musica mundana* (harmony governing the universe), *musica humana* (harmony governing the human body and soul), and *musica instrumentalis* (harmony of audible sounds produced by instruments or the voice) in his work of music theory, *De institutione musica*. With the astronomer Kepler's *De harmonice mundi*, in the early seventeenth century the theory of music of the spheres becomes polyphonic and is joined to the scientific search for a mathematical pattern of harmonization in the planetary system, to which Leibnitz and Schopenhauer also contribute. What is of most importance here is the scope of Kepler's project, his attempt to calculate an infinite and perfect polyphony of movement and thereby synthesize the cosmos both in number and symbol. In his musical and astronomical theory, each of the planets produces a scale; to unite the sounds of the spheres would be to construct polyphonic harmony as a celestial synthesis.

Twentieth-century composition, to follow James's essay, again takes up the relationship between musical proportion and physics in Arnold Schoenberg's attempt to express musical ideas in the least possible space and without tonality. His innovation in composition is the tone row, a mathematical ordering of the twelve half steps of the chromatic scale. Once the row is established in any order, it is subject to variation by inversion, reversal, or reverse inversion. Both cosmic scope and esoteric symbolism remain a part of Schoenberg's synthetic atonal structures, however, and become principal themes in the massive compositions, *Gurrelieder*, an oratorio based on medieval legend, the opera *Moses und Aron*, or the mystical oratorio *Die Jakobsleiter*.

Of twentieth-century compositions, Paul Hindemith's opera *Die Harmonie der Welt* (1956–7), based on the life of Kepler, is considered to be the major contemporary transposition of the concept of music of the spheres. Florence Malhomme studies Hindemith's fascination with Kepler and music of the spheres, making it clear that Hindemith likewise founds his aesthetics on numeric, intervalic proportions that express in music the rational, natural, and universal laws of harmony. He considers tonality to be a fundamental force comparable to gravity and as mysterious as the creation of the world:

> ...we shall observe in the tiniest building unit of music the play of the same forces that rule the movements of the most distant nebulae... Without such organizing harmony how would the cohesion of the entire universe be possible?

In the opera, composed in rhyming archaic German poetry, there are eight major characters who represent planets of the Keplerian system, each possessing a distinctive tonality. The intervals and relationships of these tonalities function symbolically and are related to celestial motion. In the finale, the character-planets in the form of a constellation of the zodiac, surrounded by the chorus whose robes with pinpoints of light represent the Milky Way, sing an octet in praise of the harmony of the world.

Literary experimentation and musicality

Because of its conceptual scope and poetic language, its telescoping of primal myth into expressive vocalic forms, the *Galáxias* may be interpreted as a contemporary literary contribution to the theme of music of the world. Specifically, it may be understood as correspondence between the body of poetic materials of language and its world of reference in archetypal story and pure vocal sound. The poet's "galactic" interests had previously been foregrounded in his earlier poetry: the poem "o â mago do ô mega" directly addresses themes of totality and eschatology, while the series of "semantic variations," based on a given word or phrase, alters form and meaning through mathematical re-combinatory or dialectical possibilities derived from the given linguistic materials: the adjective "admirável," for example, is transmuted to "admerdável." In "anamorfose," the common expression "sem sombra de dúvida" ("without the shadow of a doubt"), implied but never actually written, is constantly suggested by a set of variations cum re-combinations, such as "sombra sem dúvida na sombra / shadow without doubt in the shadow." Preparatory to *Galáxias*, this kind of experimentation works at the limits of the signifying function of language, and its spatial representation on the page engages its materials in constantly changing forms.

Haroldo de Campos's experimental writings have been characterized technically by Moser as "literary experimentation of the second kind." In experimentation of the first kind, writers may use language to explore scientific or social purposes, a concept such as that of music of the spheres, or even to experiment with language itself, with the goal of revealing truths about its employment, reference, or function. The school of self-referentiality specializes in manipulating stereotypes of language in ways that reveal their control over us. There are limits to this approach, however, which in terms of Moser's types mark the borders of a second kind of experimentation. Limits are reached when the search for a truth or referential function begins to be overridden by language per se. The very concision of "concrete poetry," for example, along with its work with spatial objects, has the tendency in Moser's view to concentrate meaning within the world of language itself, beyond any controllable semantic context. More interior and self-contained, literary experimentation of the "second kind" has three main attributes: it stresses the inconclusive and processive nature of language; the author-creator relinquishes agency in favor of forms of radical play; and the body of language becomes an experience of sense perception that engages the body, our body as readers. These are the parameters of Haroldo de Campos's musical prose in *Galáxias*.

Contagious signifiers, phonic surfaces

A reading of *Galáxias* is proposed here to determine how Haroldo de Campos's contributions to a more radical literary experimentation "of the second kind" account for its musicality; and, further, if the harmonic relationships of the work as radical experiment with indeterminacy, play, and the body constitute a new galactic "music of the spheres." Consonant with the twentieth-century musical background of Schoenberg and Hindemith, Campos's massive novel of fragments speaks not only to the exuberant, full dimensions of the artwork as performance, but also to the precise, synthetic, and technical arrangement of sound and timbre. In the fragment "tudo isto" an orientalist legend is invoked to expound the author's musical art of composition, based on "contagious signifiers" and "phonic surfaces:"

> tudo isto tem que ver com um suplício chinês que reveza seus quadros em disposições geométricas pode não parecer mas cada palavra pratica uma acupunctura com agulhas de prata especialmente afiladas e que penetram um preciso ponto nesse tecido conjuntivo quando se lê não se tem a impressão dessa ordem regendo a subcutânea presença das agulhas mas ela existe e estabelece um sistema simpático de linfas ninfas que se querem perpetuar por um simples contágio de significantes essa torção de significados no instante esse deslizamento de superfícies fônicas...

> (all this has to do with a Chinese torture that alternates its applications in a geometrical order it may not seem like it but each word practices acupuncture with silver needles especially sharpened and that penetrate a precise point in that conjunctive cloth when one reads there is no impression of that order directing the subcutaneous presence of the needles but it exists and establishes a sympathetic system of lymph nymphs who wish to perpetuate themselves by a simple contagion of signifiers that sudden twisting of signifieds that slipping of phonic surfaces...)

With this legend-theory as a guide, Campos applies some of the principal techniques in twentieth-century music to the composition of *Galáxias*. As in the earlier poetics of "semantic variations," the basis of the writing is numerical permutation. A letter, a word, or a phrase is formed to state a theme or motif and to establish a basic sequence in prose, comparable to a musical tone row. The twelve tone technique of row, inversion, and retrograde, applied in prose to the motif-row, is a mainstay of *Galáxias*. In the fragment "esta é," the text itself confirms this mode of operation: "alealenda ler e reler retroler... girar regirar retrogirar;" or from "nectarstrasse," "delida, deslida, treslida." When based on a dominant vowel sound, the permutation acts to reinforce the tonality of a prose fragment. The novel begins with a series of permutations based on "começo" and the vowel tones of "e" and "s": "e começo aqui e meço aqui este começo e recomeço e remoço e arremessa e aqui me meço." In "e brancusi" the closed vowel "o" both sounds and symbolizes birth and innovation: "o ovo do vôo o vazio do vôo o vôo do vôo." When the motif is a word, as "mar" in "multitudinous seas," it is likewise subjected to sequential permutation, in this case rhyming verbal suffixes that invert the meaning of the original "mar": "mareando marujando marlunando marleando marsoando...." In a phrase or word sequence, as in "no jornalário," the permutations may vary different elements to create juxtapositions and portmanteau words, by which "o depois e o antes" becomes "antesdepois depoisantes transantontem transantemanhã." Although systematic, permutations in series have the effect of freeing language from its instrumentation, as the listener becomes aware of order, sound, and variation before meaning.

Experimentation recovers the unused or forgotten potential of language in musical forms that challenge common reading for meaning. In "cadavrescrito" the narrator invokes a "babelório" of unexpected temporal-spatial forms, as in the series "núltimo noutubro nãovembro," or surreal harmonies of meanings, as in the image "tocando num piano sem cordas." The poetic function of language demands different voices of reading, following Portuguese poet Ana Hatherly's essay on the necessity to "reinvent reading" in order to hear all the voices of meaning (71). In "cheiro de urina," the beauty of the poetic over the referential function, of sound over sense, is incorporated in the multilingual phrase, "colorless green ideas sleep furiously" "incolores idéias verdes dormem furiosamente." Clusters of tone-colors likewise indicate the tonal and harmonic dimensions of language, as in the arabesque in "reza calla": "o branco do branco do branco y calla no branco no branco no branco a cal um enxame de branco o branco um enxame de cal."

The dimension of language as physical sensation, a utopia or Eros of desire, runs through *Galáxias*; it is both the language that reconstructs the thousand and one nights and the universal body of story, "umbigodomundolivro...umbigodolivromundo." The book, its materials, and its language are made physical, "nudez o papel...branco osso." In his solitary play with paper, the writer broods that he alone must cover it "como se cobre um corpo" ("eu sei"). Another orientalist legend develops the image of the book as muse, "a mulher livro em papel-japão." The muse is a "quimono-borboleta," and to read each page is to see her body written in red and gold filigree, posing in each poem like a butterfly seeking honey. In the underworlds, the muse of writing is the world's lover: "a bacante hippie de tranças sujas," a "pantera na pele... peitos pop... gorducha rubicona em calcinhas... com mamilos de borracha... bebendo coca-cola." The pan-erotic language of the world's great nude brings the narrator into contact with the occult center of meaning, "a mandala o om o centro o umbigo de tudo...." Hyperforms equate language with experience, as in the onomatopoetic "balibadalandobimbalindo" of a Basque flock of sheep ("um avô de estória"). The om-navel-book orders, unifies, and centers all sound into one, which is the harmony of being.

"Words or stars"

The musical aesthetics of *Galáxias* unites the cosmos with the fragment, the symphony with the solo. The incessant flow of words is a presence as well as a meaning, made intelligible by the variable grammatical, semantic, and phonic borders of language itself. Counterbalancing geometry of form and mathematics of permutation is a whirling movement of word, sound, and story that exploits a full repertoire of linguistic expression. Experimental language addresses the three kinds of Pythagorean music – *musica mundana*, *musica humana*, and *musica instrumentalis* – while radicalizing their function: freeing language from meaning, exploring its forgotten expressive potential, and foregrounding its physical presence, performance, and instrumentality. The primacy of archetype and pattern is a principle inherited from the historical avant-gardes, expressed aphoristically by poet-artist Almada Negreiros: "We do not invent words; we only invent the words that have already been invented." Music always retells the primal story in a contemporary form, in which the song is the world: "...cantando cantava o sol contando contava o mar contava um conto cantado de terra sol mar e ar meu canto não conta um conto só canta como cantar" ("cadavrescrito").

As in the finale of Hindemith's opera, Haroldo de Campos's *Galáxias* features a final chorus composed of "myriads of faint stars" which are made equivalent to words: "palavras ou estrelas... lampiros no empíreo galáxias...." Their song, heavenly and worldly, reconfirms the presence of the music of the spheres and reaffirms the lost identity between harmony of the world and harmony of the word.

Bibliography

Backès, Jean-Louis, *Musique et Littérature: Essai de Poétique Comparée* (Paris: Presses Universitaires de France, 1994).
Booth, Wayne, *For the Love of It* (Chicago: University of Chicago Press, 1999).
Campos, Haroldo de, "Minha Relação com a Tradição é Musical," in K. David Jackson, *Transformations of Literary Language in Latin American Literature: From Machado de Assis to the Vanguards* (Austin: Abaporu, 1987), 145–51.
——, *Galáxias* (São Paulo: Ex-Libris, 1984).
Celis, Raphaël, ed., *Littérature et Musique* (Brussels: Publications des Facultés Universitaires Saint-Louis, 1982).
D'Angelo, James P., "Tonality and its Symbolic Associations in Paul Hindemith's Opera *Die Harmonie der Welt*," Ph.D. dissertation, New York University, 1983.
Escal, Françoise, *Contrepoints. Musique et littérature* (Paris: Klincksieck, 1990).
Hatherly, Ana, "Voices of Reading," in *Experimental, Visual, Concrete: Avant-Garde Poetry Since the 1960s*, ed. by K. David Jackson, Eric Vos and Johanna Drucker (Amsterdam: Rodopi, 1996), 71.
Hindemith, Paul, *A Composer's World* (Cambridge, MA: Harvard University Press, 1952), 7.
Hindemith, Paul, *Die Harmonie der Welt*. Opéra en cinq actes (1956–57).
James, Jamie, *The Music of the Spheres: Music, Science and The Natural Order of The Universe* (New York: Springer-Verlag, 1993).
Malhomme, Florence, "Hindemith et le Concept Pythagoricien de 'L'harmonie du monde': Fondement d'une Esthétique," *Ostinato rigore. Revue Internationale d'Etudes Musicales* (Paris) 6/7 (1995–96): 135–45.
Moser, Walter, "Haroldo de Campos' Literary Experimentation of the Second Kind," in *Experimental, Visual, Concrete: Avant-Garde Poetry Since the 1960s*, ed. by K. David Jackson, Eric Vos and Johanna Drucker (Amsterdam: Rodopi, 1996), 139–54.
Padmore, E., "Hindemith, Weill," *A History of Western Music* (London: Sternfeld, 1973), 111.
Pessoa, Fernando, *The Book of Disquietude*, trans. Richard Zenith (Manchester: Carcanet, 1991), 75–6.
Piette, Isabelle, *Littérature et Musique. Contribution à une Orientation Théorique (1970–1985)* (Namur: Presses Universitaires de France, 1987).
Ruwet, Nicolas, *Langage, Musique, Poésie* (Paris: Seuil, 1972).
Spitzer, Leo, "Classical and Christian Ideas of World Harmony (Prolegomena to an Interpretation of the World 'Stimmung')," *Tradition* 2 (1944): 409–64; 3 (1945): 307–64.
Tranchefort, François-René, "Paul Hindemith," *Guide de la Musique Symphonique* (Paris: Fayard, 1986), 358.
Wilder, Thornton, *The Long Christmas Dinner* (London: Longmans, Green, 1931).
Wilder, Thornton, *Pullman Car Hiawatha* (London: S. French, 1931).

Arabesques in *Galáxias*

Luiz Costa Lima

LET US BEGIN with a simple comparison. In 1797, in what would be the famous "Kritische Fragmente", the then young Friedrich Schlegel wrote: "Also in poetry the greatest good could be half and all half, in fact everything" (*Auch in der Poesie mag wohl alles Ganze halb, und alles Halbe doch eigentlich ganz sein*).[1] For his part, Haroldo de Campos said in a newspaper interview: "Monologically, in each fragment are found all and each one of the *Galáxias*."[2]

The coincidence between these affirmations would be casual and its verification only a curiosity were it not possible to develop it from a third term, the arabesque, which although valued by Schlegel never assumed theoretical importance in the reflections of Haroldo de Campos. Our intention is to point out, on one side, what the term arabesque meant for Schlegel and, on the other, for its presence in the textuality of *Galáxias*. This is a doubly complicated task, since it must be done concisely and because Schlegel never actually conceptualized it. To the contrary, he begins as if certain that to affirm its presence is to highlight a positive value. Taken as a synonym of chaos or its hieroglyph, its field addresses both poetry in general – "In the style of a true poet nothing is ornament, everything is an essential hieroglyph," one reads in fragment 173 of "Athenäum Fragmente"[3] – as well as the theory of the novel.[4] If opposing

---

1 Friedrich Schlegel, "Zur Poesie und Literatur," (1797) in *Kritische Ausgabe seiner Werke*, vol. XVI, ed. by Hans Eichner (Munich: Verlag F. Schöningh and Zurich: Thomas-Verlag, 1967), fragment 14, II, 148.
2 Haroldo de Campos, "Entrevista a J. J. de Moraes," *Jornal da Tarde* (São Paulo), 6 October, 1984.
3 Friedrich Schlegel, "Athenäum Fragmente" (1798), in *Kritische Ausgabe seiner Werke*, vol. II, ed. by Hans Eichner (Munich: Verlag F. Schöningh and Zurich: Thomas-Verlag, 1967), 193.
4 Cf. "Letter on the Novel", in "Conversation on Poetry," Friedrich Schlegel, "Brief über den Roman", 3rd part of "Gesprach über die Poesie" (1800), *Kritische Ausgabe seiner Werke*, vol. II (Munich: Verlag F. Schöningh and Zurich: Thomas-Verlag, 1967), 329–39.

it to the ornament offers some support, that is amplified on our verifying that in the "Letter" his consideration of the arabesque is derived from *Tristram Shandy,* about which he says that the delight that it offers the reader is comparable to the "scenes of jokes and caprice (*witzigen Spielgemälde*) that we call arabesques."[5] One final characterization will be enough. In fragment 274 of the series of hundreds still unpublished, one reads: "What is essential in the novel is its chaotic form – arabesque, fairy tale."[6]

Bringing the quoted passages together, we can infer that the arabesque is placed at the highest level of poetic and fictional values, because in place of the most common and acceptable extremes of the decorative and linear, the arabesque deals with the sinuous and complex. The complexity of the arabesque is what separates the poetic and fictional from the imitative, or what will later be called realism. Its proximity, on the contrary, is to chaos, from which it still differentiates itself because it supposes the delimiting of a form – "die chaotische Form" – capricious as in a fairy tale, witty as in Sterne.

Passing to the *Galáxias,* we must ask ourselves how the theoretical operator of the arabesque can augment the intelligence of the text. But let us not convert our conversation with Haroldo's text into what may seem to be a juridical opinion. This is, in fact, the first lesson to be learned from the arabesque. The arabesque has rather more to do with excess than with containment. The ideal for our reading will be to locate it, without its being necessary to point it out at every turn.

In Western literature, there is no older or clearer theme than that of the voyage. In Homer, the voyage had been defined as the noblest *topos* of tradition. A voyage out, which supposes a circumnavigation, is simultaneously an internal voyage, since it occurs both in luminous memory and dark forgetfulness. As Harald Weinrich appropriately says: "Homer is truly the first, although not the only, Greek poet who grants a place of honor in literature to memory and along with it to forgetfulness."[7] Begun in a port familiar to the traveler, the latter would have to fight against monsters, giants, and seductive forces opposed to the return of No-name

---

5 Ibid., 331–2.
6 Friedrich Schlegel (1799), "Zur Poesie und Literatur," in *Kritische Ausgabe seiner Werke*, vol. XVI, ed. by Hans Eichner (Munich, Verlag F. Schöningh; Zurich, Thomas-Verlag, 1967), 276.
7 Harald Weinrich, *Lethe. Kunst und Kritik des Vergessens* (Munich: C. H. Beck, 1997), 29.

to Ithaca, where his absence threatened to break down the old order. Odysseus' return signifies the victory of Mnemosyne over *lethe*, forgetting, and it makes explicit, as Auerbach demonstrates in the first chapter of *Mimesis*, one of the veins in which Western expression would become rooted, opposed to the mysteriousness of Biblical stories. These two veins, still, are one common form: over them the powers of divine Mnemosyne and of earthly forgetfulness equally dominate. The force of both will make itself felt in the galactic voyage, where Mnemosyne assures their companionship with other trajectories, whereas *lethe* makes the new voyage forget the established genres and the search to create multiples of them.

With his frequent allusions to the Greek ocean and to the Homeric text itself, Homer is certainly the first reference incorporated into *Galáxias*. The second is no less apparent: the Joycean parody that shortens and brings Odysseus' navigation back to earth, internalizing it in the streets of Dublin and exposing the new Ulysses to the most terrible of gods: the quotidian. To this second mark it would not be arbitrary to add Pound's *Cantos*. Homer is changed once more. *Lethe* now operates by transforming what was a continuous narration, where, as Auerbach had shown, nothing is left unexplained, into a collage of scenes and memories. In *Galáxias*, Mnemosyne, memory, establishes another relationship with *lethe*, forgetting. Instead of being opposing powers, they are superimposed. The collage, instead of narration, is the consequence.

Homer, Joyce and Pound thus form the axles of the voyage as memory. These poles are at the same time permeated by an equivalent feature, seen through the work with language: Homeric clarity is in the ascendant as much in the crude realism maintained by Joyce as in the Poundian conception of form in which, as Marjorie Perloff says, "form *is* that reality."[8]

To point out such different foci here serves the function of dislocating attention from the content of the voyage to the language of the voyage. This is exactly what should be emphasized: in *Galáxias*, it is not the narration that matters. It is not what one remembers, with the help of language, but what is planted in it. In the narration-that-narrates, language is subject to memory. Is language a faithful servant of its

---

8   Marjorie Perloff, "Pound / Stevens: Whose era?," in *The Dance of the Intellect. Studies in the Poetry of the Pound Tradition* (Evanston, IL: Northwestern University Press, 1985), 14.

capricious traitor? That question obsessively runs through the narration-that-narrates, regardless of whether it is a log of journeys throughout the world or of travels for the very life of what they narrate. To what extent did the scenes described by Marco Polo or Fernão Mendes Pinto report what they had seen and lived? It doesn't seem by chance that the narratives of travelers in the New World aroused suspicions about their veracity and, thus, indirectly contributed to the distinction between the documentary and the novelesque. As for autobiographical narratives, remember Schlegel's observation, which said to prefer, among the novels of Rousseau, his *Confessions*: "To my eyes, the *Confessions* of Rousseau are an excellent novel; *Héloïse*, only mediocre."[9] In both, this is the case because, in a more or less disguised way, the fictional appears on the horizon of the narration-that-narrates. In order for the risk of fraud not to burn all who narrate, confidence in memory will have to be aided by the use of archives, documents, live testimonies, in sum, by kinds of proof. This is the way that the historian tries to de-cogitate the ghost of the fictitious that covers his objective and threatens its loss.

A very different attitude toward language comes out in the narrative whose theme is its own composition. Glossing Perloff, where is reality to be found if not in form itself? But, if there is form, i.e., delimitation, can reality *be* in the form? Yes, to the contrary of the deconstructionist position, one may think so, as long as one understands that to have form means that one does not conceive of a reality independent of it. My reservations about deconstructionism do not necessarily imply the adoption of a realist point of view. And what I said just now about Joyce and Pound will lead to misunderstandings if one does not keep in mind what I said about the relationship between form and reality. Let us return to the argument at the beginning of the paragraph, which stated that the position of language changes when the narration thematicizes its own composition. Now, for the very reason that one no longer counts on the mnemo-technique of oral culture, Mnemosyne loses her status as a goddess and memory no longer assumes the proud position of teacher or guide. She is comparable, rather, to a patient weaver, who combines what she lives with the experience of the word. The voyage thus becomes the relation, a voyage of narrative and no longer a narrative of the voyage. It is a voyage of writing that begins rather than recapitulates.

---

9   Schlegel, "Brief über den Roman" (1800), 338.

O que importa não é a viagem mas o começo da[10] *(What matters is not the voyage but the beginning of)*

As a result, the relation with the horizon assumes a different guise than that of the narrative-that-narrates. In the latter, the horizon was filled with the fictitious, a source of disturbance for the narrator and of doubt for the reader. For that reason, the horizon is something that puts the narrator on his guard – the typical case of historical fiction – or something whose threat is "forgotten" or whose immanence is feigned not to exist – the case of illusionist works. In the opposite modality, where *Galáxias* is inscribed, the fictional horizon transmutes into what it aspirates into speech and which is fulfilled in the choice of each word. This aspiration, in the double meaning of what one tastes and what one searches for, is the fictional, which is the product of transforming the fictitious. Here, the keyboard of rhetoric is typed not to persuade or dissuade, or to deceive, but rather to make the materiality of its sign concrete, to explore, as the poet said, the prismatic divisions of the idea; or, to be coherent in terms of the distinction made above concerning the prismatic divisions of reality. What was a threatening horizon is converted into a desired presence. The threat is transmuted into theme, whether an insupportable or a radiant presence to the eye that touches and thinks. Rather than be persecuted by the risk of the fictitious, whose workings would bore the reader aware of it, the words seek to become fictional. The hand no longer deflects the arrow that wounds; rather it activates the arrow-word, the one that inscribes. The word no longer refers to a genre that is necessarily a plot. The plot, no longer being narration, is converted into a *mise-en-scène* and becomes part of a strategy of "as if." The plot can be as much potentially illusionary, which happens when the word pretends merely to recuperate reality, or totally denuding of the reality that was its *materia prima*. In the first case, it intends, consciously or unconsciously, to persuade the reader – transporting us to the place where such and such events happened. In the second, it is as if to say: let us suppose that in place X, already invented in itself, such as Yoknapatawpha, or to be invented, like Dublin of *Ulysses*, there was

---

10 Haroldo de Campos, *Galáxias* (São Paulo: Editora Ex Libris, 1984), 1. Since the pages of the complete editions of *Galáxias* are not numbered, from here on we will use the letter F for each citation from the book, accompanied by the number of the corresponding fragment. Thus, the above entry, "1," following the author's name, refers to the first fragment.

someone who.... To accept the rules of the game implies coming to read actions that could have been real or, if they were, in fact only became so when they were reconverted into words. Thus there is the simultaneous proximity and distance between total denuding and illusionism.

The "mined prose" of *Galáxias* makes the second strategy explicit and then throws itself into a wrestling match with the fictional where there are no previous truths; in its place, there is syntactic complexity being produced, united only by the image, in the precise sense defined by Pound: "that which presents *an intellectual and emotional complex* in an instant of time."[11] Let us briefly exemplify this with an arabesque, found in the short phrase, "Tudo isto não passa do eco fechado na palavra beco" (F 36) ("All this is no more than the closed echo of the word 'beco'").

"Beco" is no longer what is designated by a referent. Without shifting its own weight, its semantics changes direction and starts to point toward the interiority of the word itself. More explicitly: through a lexical understanding, "beco" supposes a certain kind of narrow closure. To use it to designate means to spatialize it (for example: "be careful, this is a dead end!"). In *Galáxias*, "beco" has its semantic charge internalized, i.e., one sees the word, i.e., its reference is twisted when the word is converted into a thing, *mot-chose*. Upon doing this, the reader is enabled to find the "eco" that until then was lost inside the "beco." Such is the wit of the arabesque. Internalization of semantics means nothing more than emphasis on the materiality of the sign. The "eco" was already in the "beco"; however it could not be heard. This writing supplements meaning by concretizing what could not be extracted from the sign through designation. But does the "beco" listed in the dictionaries have an "eco"? No, its definition shows that it does not. The *mot-chose*, however, is not truly enunciated. (Our reason could be expanded if we remembered that in Sartre, in whose work the expression is found, it has as its opposite the *mot-monnaie*. *Pace* Heidegger, truth is thus a coin, a mode of exchange... This reflection would need space.) The *mot-chose* of poetry exalts neither truth nor non-truth. It is simply that in its non-designative use, its relation to truth passes to a second plane.

To say that *Galáxias* lies in the common berth that stretches between the opposite shores of the Homeric epos confronting Joycean parody and Poundian collage is only to proclaim its origins, so as to offer a partial

---

11 Pound, Ezra, "A few don'ts," (1913) in "A Retrospect," *Literary Essays of Ezra Pound* (London, Faber, 1960), 4, my emphasis.

approximation. To go beyond, we must consider another element: the presence of the baroque – although not the Baroque in its historico-social context but rather only as a stylistic configurator. To speak of the baroque will seem strange for those who are used to identifying the concrete poetry project with a spatialized arrangement, having words either disconnected from their syntactical connections or having them reduced to an indispensable minimum. From this perspective *Galáxias* was either praised as liberation from a straightjacket or treated with irony as the return to a Rabelaisian cornucopia. It is fitting for the proposal to accentuate along with the Spanish critic Andrés Sánchez Robayna that "a good part of the galactic fragments was written at the same time as the most radical expressions of the 'concretist displacement'."[12] As the critic says, the primary position of the baroque in the concretist project constitutes "a surprising mistake": "[…] Such a paradox becomes dissolved inside the Baroque itself, as the omphalic center of an alliance of 'cornucopia' and 'economy', whose greatest example is, perhaps, Góngora, a kind of mathematical state of Baroque excess […]"[13]

It is certain that Góngora was introduced in that way to a *paideuma* that previously had not included him. Even so, Sánchez Robayna rightly points out that combinations such as "verbal and stylistic concretion of phonic contiguities," typical of Góngora, should not be considered to be heterodoxies in the concretist project.

It would be less relevant to question whether that expressive modality was foreseen in the "heroic" phase of the concrete movement. What would it mean if it were not present except that one of its members was then able to bring about an elective affinity previously uncalculated? If we judged by the other concrete founding fathers, Augusto de Campos and Décio Pignatari, we would see that each one took on his own derivations, which made it impossible to view the initial project as something that had stagnated. There remains above all the case of Haroldo: is it not contradictory that those who accuse concretism of being too rationalist now may criticize it for expanding the "five senses"? But there is nothing to be gained by attributing greater importance to inevitable literary polemics. What is important is the baroque rigor of *Galáxias*.

12 Sánchez Robayna, Andrés, "Lectura de *Galáxias*, de Haroldo de Campos," *Diario*, 16–25 August, 1984, IV.
13 Ibid.

Their baroque characteristic carries us to the introduction of a more problematic reflection. We refer to the divergence that he establishes with poetic practice of Mallarmean lineage. So improbable is it that this divergence is intentional, given the constant importance of Mallarmé for Haroldo and the concretists, that I hesitate to carry it forward. *È pur si muove*? We shall see.

In Mallarmé, as in Valéry, verse becomes inverse in the course of life. If such is a legacy of accidents, of small deceptions and tiny joys, verse distances itself from its smallest dimension and favors the pure naming of the shipwreck, of the "désastre obscur"; instead of being small and contingent, general and insignificant, it verticalizes the word. Its taste is for abyss. The mediocrity of the quotidian is reserved for the antipode of the verse; at best, for verses of circumstance. The white of the page will barely contrast with "le sacre" of the language. The movement that repulses the quotidian mediocre is, at the same time, one of attraction, because of the impoverishment of the environment in which the word is inscribed. The poet Antonio Machado saw it well. After citing the phrase by Mallarmé – "parler n'a trait à la réalité des choses que commercialement" – he added: "In his lyrics and further in his precepts, he announces the superstitious belief in the magical virtue of the enigma."[14]

Such, therefore, is the counter position between the disdain for commercial speech about things – the currency of daily life – and the cult of the enigma, as a form and manifestation of the worthy, if not of the sacred. The writing of *Galáxias* is too notoriously vitalist to participate in such an ascesis. We spoke just now about a Rabelaisian cornucopia. We could have been more precise by referring to the Pantagruelian nature of its lines. The voyage that begins in each fragment calls forth a thousand and one accidents into a festival of language. The sinuosity of the arabesque becomes one with the curves of beings, of dialects, of languages, of encounters and of things. "Le sacre du langage" is separated from any "sacré", "trop sucré" to explain the diverse iridescence of life, from "the hands (that) melt like wax in the sun" to, in the continuation of the phrase, the "half of a smooth and beautiful face like the skin of a fruit", which is extended into the "other half crumpled like wrapping paper torn, ripped gnawed spit into an empty skull" (F 17), into the infinite of the interminable arabesque.

14 Antonio Machado, "Sobre las Imágenes en la Lírica," (1916) *Los Complementarios y Otras Prosas Póstumas* (Buenos Aires: Losada, 1957), 33, my emphasis.

The divergence now emphasized, more a practice than intellectually conceived, irradiates far beyond the mere aesthetic. In order for us to approach its cosmovision, compare Mallarmé's affirmation – "Le vers [...] philosophiquement remunère le défaut des langues, complément supérieur"[15] – with Gottfried Benn's meditation. The modern poem, says Benn, shortly before his death, is invested with an evident monological direction (*monologischer Zug*). And he continues: "Monological art, which rises from the, so to speak, ontological vacuum, underlying all conversations, insinuates the question whether language, in general, in the metaphysical sense of the term, still has a dialogic character. Does it still produce, in sum, an alliance, bring abnegation, transformation, or is it just an instrument for business and the emblem of a tragic ruin?"[16] The answer that the poet offered to his own question reaffirmed the tragic disaster ("tragischer Verfall") and empire of monology in modern art: "All humanity feeds on some encounters with itself. But who can encounter the self? Only some few who are then alone."[17] The way words are treated, being the little left to us, is imperious. Only the word eroticizes the world: "Das Wort ist der Phallus des Geistes."[18]

This is not the place to reflect on the state of affairs that led to sacred monology that found its greatest poet in Mallarmé. One should only not forget to point out that he is the product of the loss of belief that only a few centuries ago was deposited in disenchanted reason, which replacing faith by confidence in human reason and enriching the capacity of science, thought to assure the progress of the human species. Rabelaisian laughter and voracity create in *Galáxias* an extremely meaningful detour. Verbally, they are formulated by a continuous arabesque, which does not fear to distance itself from its favorite poet so that other wills, other paths, other plots can come into being. The phallic word, as we remember Benn's image, needs the rugged surface of the earth. In the smallness of the quotidian there are treasures hidden to which our depressive monology makes us deaf and blind. As fragment 1 declared, "Há milumaestórias na mínima unha da estória" ("There are athousandandonestories in the smallest fingernail of the story"). The

---

15 Stéphane Mallarmé, "Le Livre, instrument spirituel," in *Variations sur un Sujet, Oeuvres Complètes*, ed. by H. Mondor and G. J.-Aubry (Paris : Pléiade, 1956), 364.
16 Benn, Gottfried, "Probleme der Lyrik," in *Gesammelte Werke*, ed. by D. Welershoff (Wiesbaden: LIMES, 1968), 4, 1092–3.
17 Ibid., 1093.
18 Ibid., 1074.

baroque legacy then comes to the aid of the poet of *Galáxias*. The Iberian presence interacts with the reception of Mallarmé and transforms his ascetic profile, as this is the only profile that the arabesque does not assimilate. The arabesque diverts the Mallarmean ascetic and transforms it into a text open to the world, inscribed in the event-word. For to the contrary of its Islamic variant, the galactic arabesque is not abstracted from the mundane.

Translated by K. D. Jackson.

Concrete Prose in the Nineties: Haroldo de Campos's *Galáxias* and After

Marjorie Perloff

– [Gertrude Stein's] prose is a kind of concrete
poetry with justified margins.
David Antin, "Some Questions of Modernism"

– The language act is also an act of survival.
Word order = world order.
Steve McCaffery and bpNichol, *Rational Geomancy*

ON THE FACE of it, concrete poetry and prose poetry (or poetic prose) would seem to represent two extremes, with the lyric (lineated text framed by white space) as middle term. The concrete poem is, by common definition, a visual constellation in which, as the "Pilot Plan for Concrete Poetry" published by the *Noigandres* poets of Brazil put it, "graphic space acts as structural agent."[1] Indeed, in the words of Dick Higgins, the concrete poem characteristically "defines its own form and is visually, and if possible, structurally original or even unique. And further, unlike the Renaissance pattern poem or the Apollinairean *calligramme* – forms which are in many ways its precursor – the concrete poem's "visual shape is, wherever possible, abstract, the words or letters within it behaving as ideograms" (233). But unlike, say, Ezra Pound's ideograms in the *Cantos*, the text from which the *Noigandres* poets of Brazil took their name,[2] the concrete poem is usually short: its most obvious

---

1   For Solt's discussion of the "Pilot Plan," see her introductory survey, "A World Look at Concrete Poetry," (7–8). In a similar vein, Draper writes "The sine qua non of concrete or visual poetry is that the visualization of the text cannot be dispensed with….the use of space is untranslatable into any other dimension" (330). See also Drucker 39–40.
2   Solt explains: "In 1952 […] three poets in São Paulo, Brazil – Haroldo de Campos, Augusto de Campos and Décio Pignatari – formed a group for which they took the name *Noigandres* from Ezra Pound's Cantos. In Canto XX, coming upon the word in the works of Arnaut Daniel, the Provençal troubadour, old Lévy exclaimed: "Noigandres, eh,

feature," as Rosmarie Waldrop puts it, "is reduction [...] both conventions and sentence are replaced by spatial arrangement" (143–4). "We do not usually *see* words," Waldrop remarks, "we *read* them, which is to say we look through them at their significance, their contents. Concrete poetry is first of all a revolt against this transparency of the word" (141).[3]

Take, for example, Haroldo de Campos's well-known concrete poem (Solt, 101–2) "fala/prata/ cala/ouro" ("speech/silver/ silence/gold"), which plays with the hackneyed proverb "Silence is golden" as well as the classical epithet "silver-tongued":

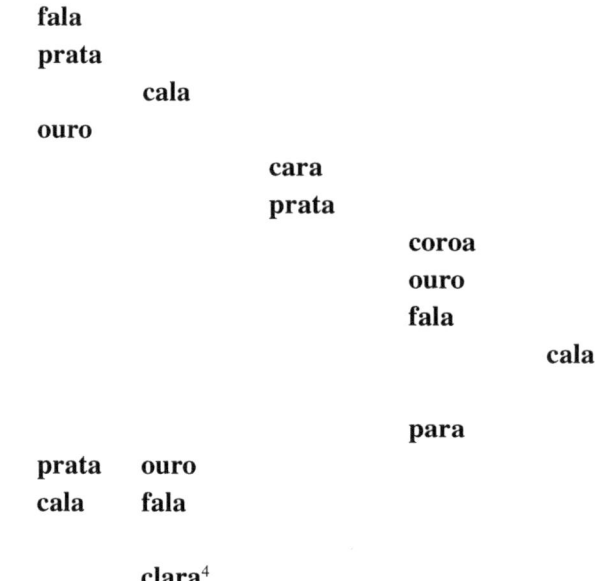

Of the constellation's sixteen words, four, "fala," "prata," "cala," and "ouro" ("speech," "silver," "silence," "gold"), appear three times each: "fala" (speech) is first "prata" ("silver"), and its rhyming partner "cala"

---

noigandres / Now what the DEFFIL can that mean!' This puzzling word suited the purposes of the three Brazilian poets very well; for they were working to define a new formal concept" (12).

3   The "Pilot Plan" of *Noigandres* similarly talks of "space-time structure instead of mere linear-temporistical development" (Solt, 71).

4   In a short note Solt gave to Haroldo, and which he made available to me, Solt gives the following verbal equivalents. "Fala" means both "speech" and "speak" (imperative verb); "cala" is also an imperative verb which means "be quiet," and, by analogy to "fala," can be read as "silence." "Cara" = "heads" (literally "face"), "coroa" = "tails" (literally "crown"), "para" = "to stop" and "clara" = "clear." The poem dates from 1962.

("silence") is "ouro" ("gold"). But the application of epithets seems to be no more than a matter of chance – "heads" ("cara") or "tails" ("coroa"): and so the fifth pair – "fala" / "cala" – joins the two contraries ("speech"/ "silence"), and is followed by a stop ("para") that disrupts the poem's staircase structure. Accordingly (below stairs, so to speak), a double reversal sets in: "silver" ("prata"), in a reversal of noun and adjective, is now "silent" ("cala") and it is gold ("ouro") that speaks ("fala"). Indeed, what is "clara" (the poem's final word, used for the first time here, combines "cala" and "cara" both visually and phonically), is that "ouro" is the dominant, the one word that doesn't match any of the others, containing as it does the only "u" in the poem and being the only word that doesn't end in "a" and has no rhyming partner. Silence, Haroldo implies, may be golden but, at least in our culture, it is gold that speaks![5]

The poem is a good example of the reduction Waldrop speaks of: it has only eight different words (the count is 4 x 3 + 4 = 16), and its syntax is minimal, there being no connectives relating paired nouns and adjectives. Visual placement is central to meaning: the possible pairs – almost nudes descending a staircase – are blocked in line 11 by the isolated word "para," followed by the reversed matching pairs of the penultimate lines, which yield to the final "clara." The modulation from the initial "fala" / "prata" to the final "clara" is certainly temporal, but the text is also self-reflexive, each item pointing back to its previous partner as well as forward, the constellation as a whole resembling, as Haroldo himself notes, serial structure in music – for example Anton Webern's "Klangfarbenmelodie" (see Solt, 12).

Whereas a concrete poem like this one is to be understood as what the *Noigandres* poets, following Joyce, called *verbivocovisual*, (see "Pilot Program", 72), the prose poem, read as it must be from beginning to end, is primarily temporal. No matter how disjunctive or semantically open it may be, no matter how fully it is constituted by what Ron Silliman has called "the new sentence,"[6] the prose poem is usually a

---

5 Solt, according to the manuscript cited in note 4, reads the poem somewhat differently: "When the play stops, silence may turn to silver, speech may turn to gold (but only if speech is clear)." The reference to the clarity of language makes this, according to Solt, a reference to the concrete poem itself.

6 In a very good summary of Silliman's argument, Bob Perelman writes, "a new sentence is more or less ordinary itself, but gains its effect by being placed next to another sentence to which it has tangential relevance.... Parataxis is crucial: the autonomous meaning of a sentence is heightened, questioned, and changed by the degree of separation or connection that the reader perceives with regard to the surrounding sentences. This is on the

block of print whose words, syllables, and letters have no optical significance. In the case of Western prose, as R. P. Draper notes, "it is an automatic assumption that letters forming words are separated by space from other letters forming words, that these letters march across the page from left to right, and that the lines so formed are strictly parallel and progress downwards at equal intervals" (337).

In their *Rational Geomancy,* Steve McCaffery and bpNichol remind us that the conventional book "organizes content along three modules: the lateral flow of the line, the vertical or columnar build-up of the lines on the page and thirdly a linear movement organized through depth (the sequential arrangement of pages upon pages)." Practically speaking, this means that "the book assumes its particular physical format through its design to accommodate printed linguistic information in a linear form" (60). And further, "Prose as print encourages an inattention to the right-hand margin as a terminal point. The tendency is encouraged to read continually as though the book were one extended line" (60). The page, far from being a visual unit, thus becomes "an obstacle to be overcome" (61). Even when the prose poem avoids narrative, it generally exhibits the very continuity concretism rejects in favor of spatial form.

Here, for example, is James Tate's prose poem "Casting a Long Shadow," which appears in the journal *The Prose Poem*:

> This is where the child saw the vision of the Virgin Mother. She was standing right here and the Blessed Mother was up there on that rock (smoking a cheroot – but we don't believe that part). The child wept for joy and ran to get her mother. The mother was watching her favorite soap opera and accused the child of playing pranks. When the soap opera ended the mother agreed to go outside. Several ravens were talking to one another. Storm clouds were moving in. The mother suddenly slapped the child across her cheek.[7]

The subgenre of prose poetry represented by Tate's piece is that of the sardonic fable, the seemingly casual little tale that leads up to an ironic epiphany – in this case the reality of motherhood that deflates the child's dream. Max Jacob was an early master of this form. In this

---

immediate formal level. From a larger perspective, the new sentence arises out of an attempt to redefine genres; the tension between parataxis and narrative is basic" (61).

7 In *The Prose Poem* (Providence, RI) no. 8 (1999), 78.

parabolic variant of the prose poem, the semantic dominates, the visual playing no appreciabk ¿art: the reader's eye moves from start to finish without paying attention to the right margin. Indeed, the narrative ("This is what happened...") demands continuity and hence there is little internal sound play or eye rhyme. The page, as McCaffery and Nichol put it, is little more than an obstacle to be overcome.

But, as the authors of *Rational Geomancy* argue, there can be prose that doesn't satisfy these conventions. To begin with, the prose poem is itself a calling into question of lineation. *Verse*, even free verse (the word *verse* [Old English *fers*] comes from the Latin *vertere*, "to turn," which is to say, to move from *a* to *b* and, in turn, from *b* to *c*) is by definition a kind of container, and hence poets from Baudelaire to the present have tried, at particular junctures, to circumvent it. "Linear progression," McCaffery notes, "we have come to understand not merely as a spatial arrangement but as a way of thinking" (Jackson, 372). A way of thinking, one might add, called into question as long ago as the 1860s, when Baudelaire, in the dedication to Arsène Houssaye (1862) that prefaces *Le Spleen de Paris*, (*Les petits poèmes en prose*) declares, "Which of us in his moments of ambition, has not dreamed of the miracle of a poetic prose, musical, without rhythm and without rhyme, supple enough and rugged enough to adapt itself to the lyrical impulses of the soul, the undulations of reveries, the jibes of conscience?" (ix–x).

Baudelaire's own prose poems are set as normal printed pages: visual design plays no appreciable role. Paragraphs are often quite short, and the longer ones are often interrupted by snatches of dialogue. Indeed, since the narrative element is so marked here, *Le Spleen de Paris* poems might more properly be designated short fictions. Neither Baudelaire's nor Rimbaud's (nor even Mallarmé's) prose poems, for that matter, set the stage for concretist experimentation with prose. Rather, the *Noigandres* poets looked to two prose writers: Gertrude Stein and especially James Joyce. The de Campos brothers had been translating *Finnegans Wake* since the late fifties, and in 1962 they brought out a book called *Panorama do Finnegans Wake*, which contains, among other things, what Haroldo calls "the creative transposition ('transcréation') of eleven fragments (bilingual presentation), accompanied by interpretative comments" ("Sanscreed", 56). Indeed, Haroldo reminds us, "the 'verbivocovisual' elements of Joyce's prose, the 'montage word,' regarded as a composite mosaic unit or a basic textural node ('silvamoonlake,' for instance) –

were emphasized from the very beginning of the concrete poetry movement" ("Sanscreed", 55). And he cites an earlier formulation by Augusto de Campos: "The Joycean 'micro-macrocosm,' which reached its pinnacle in *Finnegans Wake*, is another excellent example [of proto-concrete poetry].... Here counterpoint is *moto perpetuo*. The ideogram is obtained by superimposing words, true lexical montages. Its general infrastructure is a circular design of which every part is a beginning, middle, and end" (*Theory of Concrete Poetry*, 48).[8]

It may seem strange that concrete poetry, with its emphasis on graphic space as structural agent and its conviction that, in the verbivocovisual constellation, form and content are isochronous, would take as its exemplar a 628-page work of continuous prose – a "novel" that, except for Book II, Chapter 2 ("UNDE ET UBI"), with its marginal glosses, pictograms, musical scores, and geometric forms, does not seem to exploit the visual dimension of the text at all. But perhaps it is the word *visual* that needs reconfiguration here. A hint is supplied by Haroldo in his essay "The Open Work of Art" (which, incidentally, preceded Umberto Eco's well-known *Opera aperta* by a number of years).[9] In discussing the "circular organization of poetic material" in *Un coup de dés*, Haroldo adds:

> The Joycean universe also evolved from a linear development of time toward space-time or the infusion of the whole in the part ("allspace in a notshall" – nutshell), adopting as the organogram of *Finnegans Wake* the Vico-vicious circle. [...] each "verbi-voco-visual" unit is at the same time the continent-content of the whole work and instantly myriadminded.... a whole metaphoric cosmos is contained in a single word. This is why it can be said of Finnegans [sic] that it retains the properties of a circle, of the equidistance of all points on it from the center. The work is porous to the reader, accessible from any of the places one chooses to approach it. ("Open Work of Art", 6)

---

8 In the "Yale Symphosymposium," Augusto cites "the vocabulistic kaleidoscope of *Finnegans Wake* and its textual polyreadings" and the "experimental, minimalist, and molecular prose of Gertrude Stein" as important sources for *Noigandres* (*Experimental–Visual–Concrete*, 376).

9 Campos notes that in his preface to the Brazilian edition of his *Opera Aperta*, Umberto Eco wrote, "It is certainly curious that some years before I wrote *Opera Aperta*, Haroldo de Campos, in a short article, anticipated my themes to an astounding degree, as if he reviewed the book which I had not yet written and would yet write without having read his article" ("Open Work of Art", 5).

The implication of such "allspace in a notshall" is that, for Haroldo, concrete poetics is not a matter of word placement or innovative typography (as it is for some of his colleagues), but rather the phonemic, ideogrammic, paragrammatic character of the morphemes and words themselves. Accordingly, the distinction between "visual poem" and "prose" break down. Consider the following passage from the *Anna Livia Plurabelle* section of *Finnegans Wake*. Haroldo's translation, which becomes Fragment 8, covers the better part of page 202 (seven lines from the top of the page and three from the bottom). Here is the original:

> Tell me, tell me, how cam she camlin through all her fellows, the neckar she was, the diveline? Casting her perils before our swains from Fonte-in-Monte to Tidingtown and from Tidingtown tilhavet. Linking one and knocking the next, tapting a flank and tipting a jutty and palling in and pietaring out and clyding by on her eastway. Waiwhou was the first thurever burst? Someone he was, whuebra they were, in a tactic attack or in single combat. Tinker, tilar, souldrer, salor, Pieman Peace or Polistaman. That's the thing I'm elwys on edge to esk. Push up and push vardar and come to uphill headquarters! Was it waterlows year, after Grattan or Flood, or when maids were in Arc or when three stood hosting? Fidaris will find where the Doubt arises like Nieman from Nirgends found the Nihil. Worry you sighin foh, Albern, O Anser? Until the gemman's fistiknots, Qvic and Nuancee! She can't put her hand on him for the moment. Tez thelon langlo, walking weary! Such a loon waybashwards to row! She sid herself she hardly knows whuon the annals her graveller was, a dynast of Leinster, a wolf of the sea, or what he did or how blyth she played or how, when, why, where, and who offon he jumpnad her and how it was gave her away. She was just a young thin pale soft shy slim slip of a thing then, sauntering, by silvamoonlake and he was a heavy trudging lurching lieabroad of a Curraghman, making his hay for whose sun to shine on, as tough as the oaktrees (peats be with them!) for forstfellfoss with a plash across her. She thought she's sanhk neathe the ground with nymphant shame when he gave her the tigris eye!

Reading this "chattering dialogue across the river by two washerwomen," as Joyce himself described it (*Letters*, 213), one cannot proceed from left to right and from top to bottom as one does in the case of standard "see-through" prose. Since the page is not broken up by dialogue, paragraphing, or indented quotation, the reader intuitively searches for configurations that might "organize" the verbal flow that is equivalent to the river Anna Liffey, which is its nominal subject. Punctuation marks – exclamation points, question marks, capital letters – become important as do proper names, both real and those created by punning, especially when they alliterate. Consider the following sentence which comes roughly in the middle of the sequence:

> Fidaris will find where the Doubt arises like Nieman from Niergends found the Nihil.

The eye moves up the page past "Flood" to "Fonte-in Monte" (Fountain in the Mountain) in line 2; the coinage *Fidaris* contains the morpheme Fid that gives us *Fides* (faith) and *Fideles* (faithful). Faith is thus pitted against "the Doubt that arises," but the capitalization of Doubt suggests that this is also one of the myriad river names in the sequence, as in "the Doubt river rises." The first half of the sentence is, in any case, put into question by the second in which *Nieman* (*Niemand* = no one) from *Niergends* (nowhere) finds Nihil. But – and here the "vocovisual" comes in, there can be no "Doubt" about the intricate relationship between words:

> *Fid*aris (with "Flood" in the sentence right above it) → *find* → *f*rom → *found* (alliteration of *f, d, n*)
> Fidar*i* – aris*es* (rhyme)
> *N*ieman – *N*iergends – *N*ihil (anaphora)

There is, further, assonance of *I* – the letter appearing ten times in the space of fourteen words. The "Fidaris" cluster thus stands out as do "Albern, O Answer" and "Qvic and Nuancee" in the next lines. "Nuancee" is a particularly complex compound, containing "nuance" and hence "Quick (with a German accent) and with nuance" as well as "Nancy," "antsy," and "see."

The opposite of such cluster effect is to have a clause comprising the most ordinary of monosyllables, as in:

> She was just a young thin pale soft shy slim slip of a thing then...

Cliché piled on cliché with all the connectives in place! But the sentence now shifts from these clipped words to further compounding, neologism, and play on proverbial wisdom, in the phrase "sauntering, by silvamoonlake and he was a heavy trudging lurching lieabroad of a Curraghman, making his hay for whose sun to shine on, as tough as the oaktrees (peats be with them!) used to rustle that time down by the dykes of killing Kildare for forstfellfoss with a plash across her." The punning here must be *seen*, especially "peats [peace] be with them!" – a perfectly reasonable reference to the care of oaktrees, "killing Kildare," where the first morpheme in the proper name of the county is taken literally, and "for forstfellfoss," perhaps just a tongue twister when heard, but visually a pun on such phrases as "first fell frost" or "forced [and she] fell [in the] foss." The *ru* of "*tru*dging" reappears chiastically in "l*ur*ching" and "Cu*rr*aghman," and "us" in "*us*ed" reappears in "r*us*tle."

In his study *Ideograma: Lógica / Poesia / Linguagem* (a section of which has been translated into English), Haroldo discusses Ernest Fenollosa's study of the Chinese written character. Unlike Pound, who took Fenollosa at face value, Haroldo recognizes that the Sinologist's notion that in Chinese, words are much closer to things than in English, that there is a natural connection between the ideogram and what it represents, is incorrect. Rather, using Roman Jakobson and Charles Peirce's theories of semantic and syntactic motivation, Haroldo argues that Fenollosa's argument must be understood somewhat differently:

> Since ... at a second level, poetry "naturalizes" (reifies) the sign by virtue of its "self-reflecting" function and the emphasis on the materiality of the message .... Fenollosa's genetic *parti pris*, highlighted by his "magic realism," loses in importance to the formal (intrinsic) pertinence of the description. At this point the Peircean notion of diagram makes it possible to transfer ("translate") the Fenollosian (and Poundian) conception of the ideogram and the ideogrammic method of composing (relational, parallelistic, paratactic syntax) to the sphere where the palpable side of the sign comes to the fore), wherein Saussure (the Saussure of anagrams as "asyndetic successions" of paradigms) and Jakobson (above all the Jakobson of the poetry of grammar) are privileged mediators. ("Poetic Function", 14)

For Haroldo, in other words, the interest of the ideogram is not in its status as a visual sign that stands for a particular meaning; rather, the ideogram brings to our attention the "palpable side of the sign" in its "relational, parallelistic, paratactic syntax." *Relationality* becomes the key term, and the units to be related are phonemes and morphemes as well as words and phrases.

From this perspective, concrete poetry is less a matter of spatial form and typographic device than of "ideogrammatizing" the verbal units themselves. The *ru* /*ur* constellation in "and he was a heavy t*ru*dging l*ur*ching lie*abr*oad of a Cu*rr*aghman," with its punning on "lie" and "broad" – these are items that must be seen. But – and this has been the role the *Wake* obviously played for Haroldo and the other concretists – the ideogrammic method, reconceived as it is in Haroldo's study, can be used in "prose" quite as easily as in verse or in the spatial constellation characteristic of the concrete poem.

Now we are in a better position to understand the following statement in Haroldo's 1977 essay "Sanscreed Latinized:"

> In 1963 I began to write my BOOK OF ESSAYS / GALAXIES…. The book was conceived as an experiment in *doing away with limits between poetry and prose* [my emphasis], and projecting the larger and more suitable concept of *text* (as a *corpus* of words with their textual potentials…. The *text* is defined as "a 'flux of signs,' without punctuation marks or capital letters, flowing uninterruptedly across the page, as a *galactic* expansion. Each page, by itself, makes a "concretion," or autonomously coalescing body, interchangeable with any other page for reading purposes. There are "semantic vertebrae" which unify the whole…. [The book] constitutes a search for "language in its materiality," without "beginningmiddleend." "Exterior monologue" was the phrase I used to express this "materiality" "without psychology," that is, *language that auto-enunciates itself.* (58, my emphasis)

The notion of the "galaxy" as *limit text* is reiterated in Haroldo's afternote to the *Galáxias*, where he refers to his text as operating "at the extreme limits of poetry and prose."[10] And in an interview with Roland Greene, Augusto similarly endorses a writing "where the criteria of poetry and prose co-exist in a boundary-situation, where the words of

---

10 In the Afterword, unpaginated, reprinted as the headnote to Oseki-Dépré's French translation, Haroldo writes that the *Galáxias* were first published in the journal *Invenção*, São Paulo, 1964 and were subsequently published irregularly in various places until 1976.

prose are as though ionized by their poetic function." "Such," adds Augusto, "is the case in *Finnegans Wake*, in many texts of Gertrude Stein, and in the *Diaries* of John Cage, which are analogous to those lyric works that incorporate the language of prose, such as certain passages in the *Galáxias* of Haroldo de Campos" (Greene, 120).

The case of Gertrude Stein is especially interesting because, unlike the concretists or Joyce before them, Stein does not use innovative typography and rarely includes foreign words, proper names, or allusions – in other words, the exotic items whose coordination makes for visual interest in *Finnegans Wake*. Yet consider the following paragraph from "Regular Regularly in Narrative," from Stein's 1931 text *How To Write* (248):

> They be little be left be killed be left be little be killed be killed be little be little be left be killed be his father be his mother be his father be little be left be killed be his mother be his father be left be killed be little be his father be his mother. Be little be his mother be left be his father be little be his father be left be killed be his father be left be killed be his father be his mother be killed be his mother be left be his mother be little be killed be left be his mother be his father be his father be his mother be his father be left be his mother be killed be left be his father.
>
> This is what did not happen to happen to be this brother to his brother to his father to his father to be left to his mother to his father.

"Successions of words," remarks Stein at the opening of "Arthur a Grammar," "are so agreeable" (35). And so they are in the faux-narrative above, which alludes mysteriously to a "they" who are "little" and have been "left" to "be killed," possibly by their father and/or mother but then again mother and father are themselves evidently there to be killed. We "see" these verbal configurations before we take in their meaning – no doubt because, for Stein, narrative is not nearly as interesting as description, and here the wholly reductive vocabulary – there are only eight different words in this 131-word paragraph – forces the reader's eye to dwell on the visual design produced by the ceaseless conjunction of *little* and *killed*, *little* and *left*, with *father*, *mother*, and especially the word *be* placed at key junctures of the word square.[11] The only punctuation Stein uses here is a period, and in the paragraph before us, there are only two sentences and hence two periods. Accordingly, when the second paragraph introduces a succession of new words – *"This is what did not happen to happen"* – followed by reference to another new word, *brother*, the "plot" thickens, almost as if Stein were about to recount the tale of Cain and Abel, only to "sacrifice" these characters to her abstract and minimalist grid.

Haroldo de Campos has clearly learned from both Joyce and Stein. Here is the opening text of the *Galáxias*, "e começo aqui," as translated into French by Inés Oseki-Dépré and into English by Suzanne Jill Levine.[12]

> e começo aqui e meço aqui este começo e recomeço e remeço e arremesso
> e aqui me meço quando se vive sob a espécie da viagem o que importa
> não é a viagem mas o começo da por isso meço por isso começo escrever
> mil páginas escrever milumapáginas para acabar com a escritura para
> começar com a escritura para acabarcomeçar com a escritura por isso
> recomeço por isso arremeço por isso teço escrever sobre escrever é
> o futuro do escrever sobrescrevo sobrescravo em miluminoites miluma
> páginas ou uma página em uma noite que é o mesmo noites e páginas
> mesmam ensimesmam onde o fim é o começo
>
> et ici je commence et ici je me lance et ici j'avance ce commencement
> et je relance et j'y pense quand on vit sous l'espèce du voyage ce n'est
> pas le voyage qui compte mais le commencement du et pour ca je mesure et
> l'epure sépure et je m'élance écrire millepages mille-et-une pages pour en
> finir avec en commencer avec l'écriture en finir commencer avec l'écriture
> et donc je recommence j'y reprends ma chance et j'avance écrire sur écriture
> est le futur de l'écriture je surécris suresclave dans les mille-et-une
> nuits les mille-et-une pages ou une page dans une nuit ce qui se ressemble
> s'assemble pages et nuits se miment s'ensoimêment où le bout c'est le début

---

11 For an excellent discussion of Stein's abstract visual word designs in various texts, see Dydo, 15–27.
12 There is, to date, no complete translation of the *Galáxias* into English.

and here I begin I spin here the beguine I respin and begin to release
and realize life begins not arrives at the end of a trip which is why I
begin to respin to write-in thousand pages write thousandone pages
to end write begin write beginend with writing and so I begin to
respin to retrace to rewrite write on writing the future of writing's the
tracing the slaving a thousandone nights in a thousandone pages or a
page in one night the same night the same pages same semblance
resemblance reassemblance where the end is begin

Galáxias is, loosely speaking, written in prose, although its jagged right margin reinforces the notion of the page as "constellation," its look perhaps more Steinian than Joycean, created as it is primarily by rhyme (both auditory and visual) and what we might call hyper-repetition. Haroldo's text permutates the words *começo* (*commence, begin*) and its variants like *meço, recomeço, remeço, acabarcomeçar, arremeço*, as well as two other galaxies, the first referring to writing – *escrever escritura, sobrescrevo, sobrescravo* (this last item punning on the notion of writing as slaving) – and the second to the page in its isolated or multiple incarnations: *uma pagina em una noite, or milumanoites, milumapáginas,* the page and the night becoming interchangeable. The image of the circle, *onde o fim é o comêco, (ou le but c'est le début, where the end is begin)* is enacted phonemically and visually by the elaborate turn and return of words and morphemes. In the words of Eliot's *East Coker*, "In my beginning is my end": *acabarcomeçar, finircommencer, beginend.*

The long word *acabarçomeçar*, with its internal rhyme stands out visually on the page, leading the eye in various directions that follow the paths of *começo* and related words containing *e*'s and *o*'s. As the eye moves down the page, the notion of writing as circularity – the tracing and retracing of words on a hitherto blank page – is conveyed not only by the meanings of the words but by their visual configurations. In the Levine translation, the emphasis is on the second syllable of *begin*, which leads to *in* and *spin*, and, further down the page to *finish, fine, line*, and so on. The latter are eye rhymes only, suggesting what care is taken to ensure *seeing* rather than *seeing through* on the reader's part.

Galáxias can thus be regarded as a visual poem – visual, not in the sense of calligrammatic, as in the case of Apollinaire's "Il pleut" or Eugene Gomringer's "Wind," but in its attention to letters and morphemes

Marjorie Perloff

as well as paronomasia and paragram. A series of "exterior monologues" in prose, *Galáxias* thus points the way from the "prose" of Modernists like Joyce and Stein to the new prose poetry of the late twentieth century. I am thinking less of the current predilection for fusing prose with pictogram, the alternation of prose and verse, or the use of typography (different font size, boldface, italics, lines reversed or upside-down) for "special effects" in the great tradition of Futurist page design. Such design, as I suggest in *Radical Artifice* (115-20), all too easily shades into the now familiar formats of advertising, billboard, magazine, and webpage layout. Rather, I want to look at some "limit-texts," at "prose poems" that, like the *Galáxias*, challenge the distinction between poetry and prose and emphasize the materiality of the text.

Consider, for example, the seemingly normal "prose" of Rosmarie Waldrop's sequence *Lawn of Excluded Middle,* published in 1993. Waldrop, herself one of the early theorists of concrete poetry, has experimented with various verse and prose forms; in *Lawn*, the norm is the short verse paragraph, one per page. Here is section 3 (13):

> **I** put a ruler in my handbag, having heard men talk about their sex. Now we have correct measurements and a stickiness between collar and neck. It is one thing to insert yourself into a mirror, but quite another to get your image out again and have your errors pass for objectivity. Vitreous. As in humor. A change in perspective is caused by the ciliary muscle, but need not be conciliatory. Still, the eye is a camera, room for everything that is to enter, like the cylinder called the satisfaction of hollow space. Only language grows such grass-green grass.

When we look at this block of print, with its justified left and right margins, at first nothing especially stands out, except perhaps the first letter, a boldface capital "I," and even this is a well known print convention. And, as in the case of normal prose format, we read the text from left to right and from sentence to sentence to its conclusion. Waldrop's is not primarily a paragrammatic text where morphemes or phonemes within a given word split off and form new constellations, although of course the book's title is a play on the law of the excluded middle, the law of formal logic that everything must be either true or false, which Waldrop herself rejects as a falsification of experience.

Language is just as important to Waldrop as it is to Haroldo de Campos, only for her, as for the Wittgenstein she cites in her Endpaper, "Poetry [is] an alternate, less linear logic." "Wittgenstein," she writes, "makes language with its ambiguities the ground of philosophy. His games are played on the Lawn of the Excluded Middle," which "plays with the idea of woman as the excluded middle.... more particularly, the womb, the empty center of the woman's body, the locus of fertility." Accordingly, the "logic" that governs Waldrop's prose poem is absurd in its hyper-literalism. The poet puts a ruler in her handbag, "having heard men talk about their sex." "Now," the poet notes proudly, "we have correct measurements" but the "stickiness" that results seems to be in the wrong place: "between collar and neck." The next sentence derives, I would guess, from Wittgenstein's proposition that "A picture held us captive. And we could not get outside it, for it lay in our language" (115). "It is one thing," we read, "to insert yourself into a mirror, but quite another to get your image out again...." One can generate one's own image merely by placing oneself in front of a mirror, but of course one can't "get" that image "out again" and still have it, for a mirror image obviously has no life of its own. Then, too, from the woman's perspective, "to insert yourself" is a male prerogative, one that calls into question the woman's efforts to "get your image out again" and to "have your errors pass for objectivity." The situation, as the next word tells us, is "Vitreous," as glassy and slippery as the "grass-green grass" – a phrase defying the rule of logic that an attribute of a thing can't be identical to that thing.

"Vitreous. As in humor." What does that "As" mean? Is humor glassy? Transparent? Brittle? In Waldrop's poem, a given phrase or sentence only seems to "follow" its predecessor, either logically or temporally. Indeed, the familiarity of the print block on the white page turns out to be as open to question as is the law of the excluded middle. For one thing, the very fixity of Waldrop's grid is contradicted by her phrasing, the words, not cut into syllables at the margin, fitting into the confined area only by allowing for uneven spacing that leaves prominent white gaps. In her new book of "prose poems," *Reluctant Gravities,* Waldrop refers to this practice as "gap gardening which, moved inward from the right margin, suspends time. The suspension sets, is set, in type, in columns that precipitate false memories of garden, vineyard, trellis" (4).

Thus, in this particular passage, the characters per line vary between 45 (line 1) and 53 (line 4). The wider spacing of certain words like *conciliatory* emphasizes their phonemic and visual relationship to other words, in this case *ciliary* (of an eyelash) in the fifth line and *cylinder* in the seventh. The spacing of line 8 (it has only 47 characters), moreover, creates the very "hollow space" that is its reference point, and the reader's eye is inevitably drawn to the words "Only language grows" that follow and that have no words beneath them on the page. There is only the "grass-green grass" on the left. And that *grass* points back to *grows* so as to create a "galaxy" on this lawn of excluded middle.

A second example of a prose block that is attentive to the right-hand margin is Steve McCaffery's "Aenigma":

> when i am read i am sentenced and detached from equivalence when the shadow lifts its box i'm light when my fingers turn to foreheads i'm an eagle's heart instructing scorpions to dance when there are cities i'm the colour grey when there's a national blaze i am a bed of shared water wherever i am tempted by precision i become a wrinkle elsewhere if they modify my centre i repeat a word before the next word has a meaning should my voice be grafted to a question then the third persona will replace a cardboard cover if i tell myself these possibilities i tell myself a canvas has subsided so that when i am eaten in the answer i am still proposed. (38)

The key phrase in this 12-line composition here is "I am" (used twice in the first line and twice in the last), the "Aenigma" (archaically spelled) of the title being "what am I?" The answer depends upon adverbs of time and place: direct at dead center, we see the phrase "wherever I am," and the reference to "elsewhere" right beneath it follows hard upon five instances of "when." "My centre," "my voice," "if I tell myself," "I tell myself": self-reference is foregrounded throughout the piece. And yet, this is the least personal of poems, an "exterior monologue," as Haroldo would call it, in which "language autoenunciates itself." Indeed, the ubiquitous "I" is not a particular individual but a function of the larger language game.

The opening, "When I am read I am sentenced and detached from equivalence," sets the stage for the poem's paragrammatic activity. To be

Concrete Prose in the Nineties

"read" is inevitably to be sentenced: readers of prose process consecutive sentences – but that demand (which this poet cannot fulfill) also becomes a kind of death sentence. Furthermore, the text is "detached from equivalence" – from equivalent line lengths, equivalent statements. And since there is no punctuation, the "when, then" constructions become equivocal, clauses often pointing both forward and back, as in "when there are cities I'm the colour grey when there's a national blaze." Indeed, throughout the text, *post hoc* is never quite *propter hoc*. Punning, moreover, regularly undermines the possibility of communication. "When the shadow lifts its box I'm light," for example, plays on the gerund "shadowboxing," and perhaps, more specifically, on the well-known Duke Ellington song "I'm Beginning to See the Light," which contains the stanza, "Used to wander in the park / Shadowboxing in the dark, / Then you came and caused a spark, / That's a four-alarm fire now." That fire becomes, in line 5, a national blaze, and *when* that occurs, *then* "I'm a bed of shared water." Nice for putting out the flames, but how does one share water? McCaffery's mode, as line 8 puts it, is one of suspension: "I repeat a word before the next word has a meaning." Thus, "sentenced and detached from equivalence," the text must fend for itself. If the "aenigma" of the title is never resolved, textuality nevertheless forces itself on the reader: "when i am eaten in the answer I am still proposed."

Note that this last line is the only one that fails to meet the justified right margin, calling the reader's attention to the proposal. McCaffery's "Aenigma" thus enacts its meanings visually, concretely, even though it looks like an ordinary prose paragraph. Typography, we see, has come a long way in deconstructing the categories "prose"/ "verse."

A somewhat different "Galaxial" prose is that of Joan Retallack in a piece from her book *How to Do Things with Words* called "Narrative as memento mori" (105–6):

> At breakfast in the Ramada Inn Paul
> needed to test the procedure for de
> veloping a photogram. (He does not
> wish to call it a Rayograph for pol
> itical reasons.) Doug ordered 2 egg
> s sunnyside up with ham. I ordered
> Special K and a banana. Paul ordere

d French toast and began the photog
ram placing a blue rectangular piec
e of sensitive paper on his noteboo
k, sticking push pins in each of th
e four corners to hold it in place.
He placed a spoon, an ashtray, and
4 packets of sugar on the sensitive
paper and then took it outside to d
evelop, returning a few minutes lat
er without the photogram, but with
a rectangular aluminum pan filled w
ith water. He placed the pan on the
table next to his French toast. Dou
g said he was embarrassed by all th
e food on his plate. I was disappoi
nted because the waitress didnt br
ing me a whole banana. I told the s
tory of the flying banana sighted I
n the same village in Russia (Voron
ezh?) where aliens were recently re
ported strolling in the park with t
heir robot. Paul went out to check
the photogram. He said when the sen
sitive paper turns pale the images
are developed. He was worried there
might not be enough light. It was a
foggy morning. Doug said he had tal
ked with Marcia on the train coming
up about her daughters post-punk r
ock band. He said they were into vi
olent lyrics. Somehow the subject o
f misogyny arose. Paul came back an
d said the photogram wasnt ready a
nd he was *really* worried there wasn
t enough sun. I thought the slices
of banana on my special K were less
than 1/3 of a whole banana. Paul we
nt back out to check the progress o

> f the photogram. Doug had finished a
> ll the food on his plate. I realiz
> ed I didnt want the orange juice I
> had ordered, but I drank it anyway.

Retallack's "narrative" – an account of breakfast in the Ramada Inn with Paul and Doug – is a story that goes nowhere, except on the page, but on the page, there is plenty of verbal "action." If Waldrop and McCaffery adjust spacing so as to meet the demands of the justified right margin, Retallack begins with a specific constraint, 35 characters per line, including spaces that function as rests. When a sentence reaches the margin formed by this firm rule, the word in question must be spliced, giving us such items as "ordere/d, "noteboo/k," "w/ith," "Dou/g," "br / ing," "t/heir", "a/ll", "wasn/'t". The left margin thus becomes a letter column, vertically producing words like "eke" and "pee." How strange, the poet suggests, word formation really is. Throughout, Paul's making of the photogram ("he said when the sen/sitive paper turns pale the images / are developed") is analogous to the poetic process itself, where words are endowed with a new life by their decomposition and placement on the "light sensitive" page. Decisions: what to order for breakfast, what to do to the paper – these come together in quirky ways as the woman who speaks expresses her disappointment that "the waitress didn't br/ing me a whole banana," an item that somehow becomes conflated with the potential misogyny of her two male companions. Like the photogram (which can't be called "a Rayograph for pol/itical reasons," evidently to avoid reference to the inventor of this art form, Man Ray, Retallack's "memento mori" memorializes, not death, but everyday trivia: "I realiz/ed I didn't want the orange juice I had ordered, but I drank it anyway."

My fourth and last example is taken from Kenneth Goldsmith, *No. 111 2.7.93–10.20.96*, chapter II:

> A door, à la, a pear, a peer, a rear, a ware, A woah!, Abba, abhorred, abra, abroad, accord, acère, acha, Ada, ada, add a, adda, adore, Aetna, afford, afire, afore, afyre, ah air, ah car, ah ere, Ah Ha, ah ha, ain't tha, air blur, air bra, airfare, alder, all ears, all yours, alla, Allah, aller, allya, alpha, alswa, ama, amber, ambler, AmFar, amir, amor, Ana, ana, and ka, and uh, and war, anear, Anka, Anna, anvers, apes ma, appeere, aqua,

ara, arbour, archer, ardor, ardour, are our, are there, Are there?, Are uh?, arm bears, armoire, armor, armour, arrear, as far, ashore, asper, ass tear, asthore, atcher, atma, au pair, au poivre, auntre, aura, austere, Auxerre, aw arrgh, aw awe, aw war, award, aware, awed jaw, Ayler, bazaar, baba, babka, bacca, baga, bagba, bagger, baiter, bamba, bancha, baner, bang your, bania, banker, banter, bar burr, bar straw, barbed wire, barber, barbour, bare rear, bare tears, Barère, batter, baxa, be here, be square, Beans Dear?, beau-père, beaver, BeavHer, bedder, bedsore, beeba, beemba, been there, beer blare, beer blur, beer here, begba, beggar, beggere, Bel Air, Bela, bela, belcher, ben wa, Ben-Hur, bencher, bender, Bernard, Bertha, bestir, beta, betcha, betta, better, bettre, bever, beware, bezoar, bibber, bicker, bidder, biddler, bider, bien sûr, bifore, Big Star, Big Sur, bigga, bigger, bim-ba, bird's rear, bismer, BiStar, biter, bitter, bittre, blabber, black tears, blah corps, Blair's, blare, blanca, blare blur, blaster, blather, blazer, bleahhh, blear corps, bleeder, bleeper, blender, blinder, blisker, blisper, blister, blixa, blobber, blonder, bloomer, blooper, blubber ... (103)

Goldsmith's prose is the most rule-generated of the four, although, like John Cage, in many ways his mentor, Goldsmith has obviously "collected" his words and phrases "according to taste." The amazing 606-page "useless encyclopedic reference book" that results was composed by collecting all the phrases the poet came across in the given time period of the title (whether in books, on radio or TV or on the internet or in actual conversation), words and phrases that end in the common sound of American English linguists call *schwa* (*er*). The phrases are organized alphabetically by syllable and letter count, beginning with one syllable entries for Chapter 1 ("A, a, aar, aas, aer, agh, ah, air...") and ending with the 7,228 syllable "The Rocking Horse Winner" by D. H. Lawrence, which is never identified. The page in question is the opening of Chapter 2, where the units are two-syllable. Recitation of the passage is a great feat but note that when the page is seen, the words and phrases create all manner of rhymes and repetitions, as in "be here, be / square," "Beans Dear, beau-père," "beaver, BeavHer, bedder, bedder, bed-/sore, beeba, beemba, been there." The reader's eye can proceed vertically ("betcha," "bicker," "bigga," "bittre," "blare") as well as horizontally and even diagonally as we move from "A door" to "Blue Cheer." Capitalized words stand out ("Anka, Anna, anvers, apes ma" or "Big Star, Big Sur, / bigga") creating fascinating disjunctive inventories of the language we actually use today in the U.S.

The absurdist cataloguing that is the basis of *No. 111* – for example, "Are there?, Are uh?, arm bears, armoire, armor, armour, arrear, as far, ashore, asper ass tear, asthore atcher, atma, au pair, au poivre, auntre, aura, austere, Auxerre" – and, as the syllables get longer, such units as "How do you spell 'onomatopoeia'? How long do you plan to be 'almost there?'" (from Chapter X, 137) – constitutes a socio-poetic document, a *memento mori*, as it were, for the discourses that characterize the 1990s, from those of the *National Enquirer* and the TV talk shows to the *argot* of daily conversation and the beautiful prose of D. H. Lawrence. Along the way, Goldsmith gives us passages in which the faulty transmission of verbal information (usually the transcription from oral to written which is such a common phenomenon today) produces language like the following:

> CXCV
>
> My son is under the doctor's care and should not take P.E. today. Please execute him. Please excuse Mary for being absent. She was sick and I had her shot. Please excuse Fred for being. It was his father's fault. Please ackuse Fred being absent on Jan. 28 29 30 31 32 and 33. Mary could not come to school today because she was bothered by very close veins. Mary was absent from school yesterday as she was having a gangover. Please excuse Mary from Jim yesterday. She was administrating. Please excuse Fred for being absent. He had a cold and could not breed well. Please excuse Mary. She has been sick and under the doctor. Please excuse Mary from being absent yesterday. She was in bed with grandpa; (No. 111 490).

This parodic catalogue of standard medical excuses produced by the parent for the teacher – I especially like "She was sick and I had her shot," "she was having a gangover," and "she was bothered by very close veins" – is nothing if not a verbovisivocal construct. What Haroldo de Campos perceived in the early sixties, when he produced such concrete poems as "fala / prata," is that the technological revolution of our time would produce a situation where "reading" increasingly means "seeing," where the dichotomy is less between "poetry" (verse) and "prose" than between *seeing* and *seeing through*. "Please excuse Fred for being absent. He had a cold and could not breed well."

Works cited

Antin, David, "Some Questions about Modernism," *Occident* 8, new series (1974), 7–38.
Baptista, Josely Vianna, ed., *Desencontrários / Unencontraries: 6 poetas brasileiros / 6 Brazilian Poets* (São Pãolo: Bamerindus, 1995).
Baudelaire, Charles, *Le Spleen de Paris* (1869), ed. by Y. G. Le Dantec; révisée par Claude Pichois (Paris: Gallimard: Bibliothèque de la Pléiade, 1961), 227–319.
——, *Paris Spleen*, trans. by Louise Varèse (New York: New Directions, 1970).
Campos, Augusto de, "Dos Fragmentos do *Finnegans Wake*," *A Margem da Margem* (São Paulo: Editora Schwarcz, 1989), 35–48.
——, "gertrude é uma gertrude," *O Anticrítico* (Sao Paulo: Compagna Das Lettras, 1986), 173–89.
——. "Theory of Concrete Poetry: Introduction," trans. by Jon M. Tolman. *Studies in the 20th Century*, no. 7 (1971), 31–49.
——, Décio Pignatari and Haroldo de Campos, *Plano-Piloto Para Poesia Concreta* ["Pilot Plan for Concrete Poetry"], *Noigandres* 4 (1958). Reprinted in Solt 70–72.
—— and Haroldo de Campos, *Panaroma do Finnegans Wake* (São Paulo: Perspectiva, 1971).
Campos, Haroldo de, *Galaxias* (São Pãulo: Ex Libris, 1984).
——, *Galaxies*, trans. by Inés Oseki-Dépré and Haroldo de Campos (Paris: La Main Courante, 1998).
——, "De Galáxias," trans. by Suzanne Jill Levine (from a basic version by Jon Tolman), *Desencontrários / Unencontraries*: 70–3.
——, *Ideograma: Lógica / Poesia / Linguagem*, 3d ed. (São Pãulo: Editora da Univ. de São Paulo, 1994).
——, "Poetic Function and Ideogram: the Sinological Argument," *Dispositio: Revista Hispánica de Semiótica Literaria*, 6, no. 17–18 (1981): 9–39.
——, "Sanscreed Latinized: The *Wake* in Brazil and Hispanic America," *Tri Quarterly*, 38 (1977), 54–62.
——, "The Open Work of Art," trans. by Maria Lucia Santaella Braga, *Dispositio: Revista Hispánica de Semiótica Literaria*, 6, no. 17–18 (1981), 5–39.
Draper, R.P. ,"Concrete Poetry," *New Literary History* 2, no. 2 (1971), 329–40.
Drucker, Johanna, "Experimental, Visual, and Concrete Poetry: a Note on Historical Context and Basic Concepts," In *Experimental–Visual–Concrete*, 39–61.
Drucker, Johanna, K. David Jackson and Eric Vos, eds, "Yale Symphosymposium on Contemporary Poetics and Concretism," *Experimental–Visual–Concrete*, 367–416.
Dydo, Ulla, "Stop Look and Listen: a Digression on the Picture of a Page of Gertrude Stein," *Big Allis*, 6 (1993), 15–27.
Goldsmith, Kenneth, *No. 111 2.7.93–10.20.96* (Great Barrington, MA: The Figures, 1997 and http://www.ubuweb.com).
Greene, Roland, "From Dante to the Post-concrete: an Interview with Augusto de Campos," Special Issue: "Material Poetry of the Renaissance / The Renaissance of Material Poetry," ed. by Roland Greene, *Harvard Library Bulletin*. 3, no. 2 (1992), 19–35.
Higgins, Dick, "Concrete Poetry," *Encyclopedia of Poetry and Poetics*, ed. by Alex Preminger and T.V. F. Brogan (Princeton: Princeton University Press, 1993).
Jackson, K. David, Eric Vos and Johanna Drucker, eds., *Experimental–Visual–Concrete. Avant-Garde Poetry since the 1960s* (Amsterdam–Atlanta, GA: Rodopi, 1996).
Joyce, James, *Finnegans Wake* (1939) (New York: Penguin, 1976).

——, *Letters*, Vol. 1, ed. by Stuart Gilbert (New York: Viking Press, 1957).
McCaffery, Steve, "Hegel's Eyes," *Theory of Sediment* (Toronto: Talon Books, 1991).
McCaffery, Steve and bpNichol, *Rational Geomancy: The Kids of the Book-Machine. The Collected Research Reports of the Toronto Research Group 1973–1982* (Vancouver: Talon Books, 1992).
Perelman, Bob, "Parataxis and Narrative: the New Sentence in Theory and Practice," *The Marginalization of Poetry: Language Writing and Literary History* (Princeton: Princeton University Press, 1996), 59–78.
Perloff, Marjorie, *Radical Artifice: Writing Poetry in the Age of Media* (Chicago and London: University of Chicago Press, 1991).
Retallack, Joan, *How To Do Things With Words* (Los Angeles: Sun & Moon, 1998).
Silliman, Ron, "The New Sentence," *The New Sentence* (New York: Roof Books, 1992), 63–93.
Solt, Mary Ellen, ed., *Concrete Poetry: A World View* (Bloomington and London: Indiana University Press, 1971).
Stein, Gertrude, *How to Write* (1931) (Los Angeles: Sun & Moon Press, 1995).
Tate, James, "Casting a Long Shadow," *The Prose Poem: An International Journal*, 8 (1998), 78.
Waldrop, Rosmarie, "A Basis of Concrete Poetry," *Bucknell Review* (1976), 141–51.
——, *Lawn of Excluded Middle* (Providence, RI: Tender Buttons Press, 1993).
——, *Reluctant Gravities* (New York: New Directions, 1999).
Wittgenstein, Ludwig, *Philosophical Investigations*, 3d. ed. and trans. by G. E. M. Anscombe (New York: Macmillan, 1958).

PART IV

Concrete Poetry: from Noigandres to Finismundo

Brazilian Concrete Poetry: How it Looks Today

*Haroldo and Augusto de Campos
Interviewed by Marjorie Perloff**

THE BRAZILIAN POET-BROTHERS Haroldo (1929–2003) and Augusto (b. 1931) de Campos first attracted world attention when, in 1952, they formed, together with the poet Décio Pignatari (b. 1927), a group called *Noigandres*, the name deriving from Ezra Pound's Canto XX, where the old Provençal scholar Levy says: "Noigandresi NOIgandres! / You know for seex mon's of my life / Effery night when I go to bett, I say to myself: / Noigandres, eh, noigandres, / Now what the DEFFIL can that mean!" The indefinable but suggestive word *noigandres* suited the poets' purposes perfectly, their aim being to foreground the materiality of the signifier, the actual physical material from which a poem or text is made. So the Brazilian concrete poetry movement based in São Paulo was launched.

The *Noigandres* poets took their inspiration not only from Pound's *Cantos* and Joyce's *Finnegans Wake*, but also from Anton Webern's "Klangfarbenmelodie," from Mondrian's space-structures, from John Cage's sound experiments and, above all, from Mallarmé's *Un coup de dés*, which they regarded as the first great "verbivocovisual" poem. But the Campos pantheon also includes Brazilian modernist poetry: the work of Oswald de Andrade and João Cabral de Melo Neto, as well as that amazing Whitmanian epic, *The Inferno of Wall Street* (1877), by the poet Sousândrade (Joaquim de Sousa Andrade), a poem the Campos brothers rescued from oblivion and reprinted in 1965.

From the 1950s to the present, Augusto and Haroldo de Campos have each produced dozens of volumes of poems, manifestoes, theoretical and critical writings, artists' books, broadsides and translations. And they have single-handedly (or, should I say, double-handedly) introduced the

---

* Interview first published in *Arshile. A Magazine of the Arts* (Los Angeles), no. 3 (1994).

work of Pound, Stein, Cage, Cummings, Schwitters, Duchamp and other avant-gardists into Brazilian literature. In recent years, Haroldo has devoted his attention to the larger issue of semiotic theory, while Augusto, fascinated by the possibilities of computer art, has experimented with what he calls "digital poetry" – computer-animated graphics, video poems and so on. And he is collaborating with his son, Roland Azeredo de Campos, a professor of physics at the University of Brasília, on what the latter calls the "synchronous trans-semiosis between art and science."

Trained as lawyers, both Augusto and Haroldo have held various positions so as to "support their habit." Their oeuvre, now forty years in the making, has been the subject of a number of exhibitions, most recently in Milan in 1990. And the international literature devoted to their work continues to grow.

This interview took place in the late afternoon on 20 August 1993 at Haroldo de Campos's town house in downtown São Paulo. The house, wedged between large commercial buildings and apartment complexes, has the feel of a small museum: every available inch of wall and table space is covered with books, paintings, graphics and posters, and an elaborate sound system has been installed in the living room. Augusto de Campos lives nearby in a very different environment: a modern condominium, elegantly furnished and, again, containing many works of art. On the dining table, for example, stands one of the rare copies of John Cage's Plexiglas "sculpture," *Not Wanting to Say Anything About Marcel.*

I had had the good fortune to be invited to São Paulo to celebrate the publication by EDUSP (University of São Paulo Editions) of the Portuguese edition of my book, *The Futurist Movement.* What interested me the most in my conversations with the Campos brothers, with Décio Pignatari and a number of younger poets, like Arnaldo Antunes and Nelson Ascher, is how alive the traditions of Futurism (both Italian and Russian) and Dada, as well as of the U.S. avant-gardes, are in Brazil. Modernism in this culture has never ended. And poetry, especially in its inter-media aspects, continues to be a subject of intense and passionate debate.

Marjorie Perloff: Let's begin with a broad question. Now that the concrete movement is almost half a century old, how do you think it has evolved and changed, and where do you think it is now going?

Augusto de Campos: Well, outside Brazil, our concrete poetry is best known for what we used to call its orthodox moments, its first moments in the fifties. But in the sixties, concrete poetry in Brazil evolved in different ways. I would say that in my case I kept a great interest in visual poetry, or rather, as we used to call it, using Joycean terminology, "verbivocovisual" poetry. But my own poetry evolved in the sense of appropriating new technologies that were implicit in our theories all along, but that we didn't have at our disposal at the time. When I wrote my first book of poems of the fifties, *Poetamenos* (*Poetminus*), I remember indulging in some wishful thinking: "Oh, if I could only have filled letters, luminous billboard letters, letters that light up!" And now, since the early eighties, we have access to video making and computers. My first experiments with "clip poetry" – clip art poetry – were made in 1984 when Macintosh was beginning to make personal computers, and from then on I worked on experiments using such different means as holography, laser projections and computer graphic systems. So, I think at least one strain of what was called concrete poetry followed in this direction, and this direction has received a new impulse from the technological improvements of the last decades, because now we have letters in movement, we have colors. And the language that was defended by concrete poets – parasyntactical, asyntactical – was most appropriate for this new technological appropriation, whereas long passages didn't work very well.

MP: I want to hear what Haroldo says about this, but I have one follow-up question. Décio Pignatari was telling me you are now doing a lot more performance. What form does this performance take?

AC: In the performance the visual takes part in video and multimedia presentation. But it's much more a matter of the technological use of voice, as in Laurie Andersen's work, but with the difference that we are not working with pop lyrics, but with highly developed non-syntactical or parasyntactical texts, as in the case of *cidade / city / cité,* where a single one-hundred-and-fifty letter word is made of the juxtaposition of several words ending with "cidade."

Haroldo de Campos: My answer to the same question is a little bit different. Since the middle sixties, more fully since the beginning of the seventies, I have no longer been making concrete poems. Rather, I developed the possibilities of concrete poetry in the sense of the larger exploration of syntactic and semantic devices. So to say: I changed from the limited problem of concrete poetry to the larger problem of concretion in language. The poet, in my opinion, has to deal with the concrete face of the language, the materiality of the signifier. So, the famous formula of Roman Jakobson about the poetic function has to do with the materiality of the language. Each poet is by nature a concrete poet. Now, the concrete poetry movement is a limited case, but since its beginning, poetry has been dealing with concretion. For instance, I am now translating fragments of the Bible and there's concrete poetry in the Bible! Not in the sense of visual poetry (although there's also calligraphy in the Hebrew Bible), but the point is that the materiality of the language, the paranomasias, all the elements of the poetic function, we find these in the Bible. Camões is a concrete poet, Dante is a concrete poet, Goethe is a concrete poet, in the sense that each poet who deserves the name of poet has to deal with the *concrete* face of the language. There is always this element and the task of the translator is to capture this concrete face of language. For this reason, the literal translation of poetry, the translation of the content, is of no importance when not followed by the transposition – trans-creation – of the formal elements – either phonic and prosodic, or morpho-syntactic – that inhere in the original and contribute decisively to the semantic effects of the given poem.

MP: I want to ask you about your theory of translation later.

HC: Since 1963, for instance, I began to write a larger text, *Galaxies*. I wrote this text for thirteen years, from 1963 to 1976, and this text has, at the micro level, elements of concrete poetry, but in the larger sense, I intended to do a kind of epic, but I made an epiphanic poem, because it contains vision over narration. It's a kind of experiment between poetry and prose. It's a kind of concretion of language. More important, I believe we are now in a post-utopian moment. We have, of course, been "post-modern" since Mallarmé. Baudelaire was modern, as Walter Benjamin states very well. But we are developing the open field of modernity since Mallarmé, since the *coup de dés,* and concrete poetry is one of the limit cases of this modernity (or post-modernity, if considered in rapport to Baudelaire's paradigm).

But what is in crisis today is not modernity, but ideology and, therefore, also the futurology of the avant-garde, the utopian sense of the avant-garde, with the exception of the very real and concrete work with the new technologies. The idea that the avant-garde would change the world, would function to improve the world, is in crisis. And I am today making poetry, as Octavio Paz says very well, not of the future but of the present, and that poetry has the possibility of all the instruments of modernity and has to select in a precise moment what thing to do. There is no program for poetry. We had in the past the pilot plan for concrete poetry. We were programming the future. Now, it's not possible to program the future, so I am writing poetry that is dealing with the possibilities of modernity, not in a programmatic, but in a critical way. I'm trying to preserve that which remains from utopian thinking, but now from the point of view of critique.

MP: That leads me to an interesting question either one of you might want to answer. If, as you say, poetry has always had a concrete dimension – and I agree with you – why was it so necessary in the 1950s to have a movement called concrete poetry? Why was it so necessary to reassert it just then? Had the nineteenth century, for that matter, not had concrete poetry in the sense you use the term? What's the difference?

AC: There are two questions. One is the question of concreteness, the concreteness of language. Ezra Pound had a point of view, the point of view that was needed at the moment would be concrete language in poetry, and so in *ABC of Reading,* he stated things like "Poetry is language charged with meaning to the utmost possible degree." And with this kind of perspective, he viewed the literature of all times, and he gave more importance, let's say, to Donne than to Milton, and to Catullus than to Virgil, and so this is the thing we tried to restate, reinterpret, many years later.

HC: Just a moment, Augusto. Concreteness, for myself, is not necessarily a synonym of visuality. Visual arrangements in poetry belong to the syntactic aspect of the language. Parataxis is a modality of syntax, a way of organizing words on the page, more or less like montage in cinema, isn't it true? Whereas concreteness in the broader sense is the synthetic aspect of poetry. All the formal aspects of poetry make the concreteness of poetry. The formal aspects have two sides: the phonic and prosodical on one side, and the syntactic, the poetry of *logopoeia* (as in Pound) on the other.

MP: Let me be the devil's advocate for a moment. According to your definition, wouldn't Robert Frost be a concrete poet? He used formal stanza forms, he used meter, he used rhyme. Why wouldn't that be concrete poetry? Isn't his a "language charged with meaning"?

AC: I was saying that, of course. Pound had his particular point of view. He knew very well what he considered to be "concreteness." For Pound, vagueness was condemned, language inversions as in Milton were condemned. And he naturally postulated a language that would catch the fragmentariness of the new vision. And all these things you don't have to the same degree in Robert Frost, but you do have them in Gertrude Stein and William Carlos Williams.

But you were asking about visuality. The emphasis on the visual and phonic was much stronger in concrete poetry than in other movements. You don't have it in Surrealism, for example. You can take one or another example from Bréton, but Surrealists concentrated on psychic automatism, on the unconscious, and interestingly, they used straightforward phrases, normal grammatical phrases, a very conventional structure. Well, concrete poetry emphasizes the problem of syntactical structure, the question of de-automatizing language structures. And at the same time with the emphasis on the visual presentation, new structures of rearranging and recombining the logical and syntactical structures more radically than it had been done. And at this point it approaches the experiments of John Cage, but from a very different point of view. Because Cage said (in the foreword to *M)* that he was interested in nonsyntactical language – what he called "demilitarization of the language" – and he even said that he came a little tardy to it. So, interestingly, he arrived more or less at the same conclusions as the concrete poets. And Cage pinpointed what is still the main question today: how to de-automatize language, why not just go back to orderly structures.

HC: And there is another point: when we talk about tradition we talk about tradition that emphasizes invention. For instance, in the case of Latin American poetry, I am interested in Vallejo, I am interested in Huidobro, but my interest in Neruda is not the same because, although the first Neruda is interesting, the late Neruda is a rhetorical poet. So, there is a big difference when one compares, say, Octavio Paz, who has this element of invention, and the late Neruda, who does not. And in the past, poets that nowadays are considered classics, were avant-garde poets: poets of the *Dolce stil nuovo*, Baroque poets like Góngora, a Roman poet like Catullus – these are all great inventors of language. So, what is for me essential in the appropriation of tradition in the post-utopian moment is not to be merely eclectic. What is important is a critical selection from the past. And a selection guided by invention.

AC: Let me interrupt a moment. You asked why these things happened in the fifties. I think there was a very important demand for change, for the recovery of the avant-garde movements. We had had two great wars that marginalized, put aside for many, many years, the things that interested us. You see, the music of Webern, Schoenberg and Alban Berg, for example, was not played because it was condemned both in Germany and in Russia, the two dictatorships. You could say that all experimental poetry, all experimental art, was in a certain sense marginalized. Only in the fifties began the rediscovery of Mallarmé, the rediscovery of Pound. Pound suffered at that time from the charge of fascism. His work was very much condemned. We participated in an international movement [gathered around *The Pound Newsletter*] that tried to rescue Pound, who was excluded from American anthologies.

HC: By the way, the book by Hugh Kenner, the first one to deal with Pound in any serious way, dates from 1951.

AC: The same happened with *Finnegans Wake,* with Gertrude Stein.

HC: And with Mallarmé. Robert Greer Cohn's book [*The Poetry of Mallarmé*] appeared in 1952.

MP: So, you would say the war put it all on hold?

AC: Yes, it was a traumatic situation. You can extend it to all the arts. Duchamp was rediscovered in the sixties by the Pop movement and by Cage, and then he balanced the influence of Picasso, which was a great phenomenon. With the musicians, it was the same thing. There was a great movement in music, in Europe as in the U.S. – the revival of Charles Ives, Henry Cowell and Cage. So, I think it was a necessity to recover the great avant-garde movements. This is why I am so critical of post-modernism. There is inside the discussion of post-modernism a tactic of wanting to put aside swiftly the recovery of experimental art and to say all this is finished!

MP: I don't really agree. I've just been to a conference on the "Poets of the Thirties," and the whole emphasis was on the derivation of Zukofsky, Oppen, Niedecker, etc., from Pound, Stein and other avant-gardists. But it's true that in certain U. S. circles the avant-garde is currently quite suspect. When I was coming to Brazil, most of my friends immediately asked if I was going to visit the places where Elizabeth Bishop had lived. That's Brazil to them, because she lived here. Yet I doubt you're equally enthusiastic. What's your view of Bishop?

AC: I'm not very interested.

HC: Well, Octavio Paz likes Elizabeth Bishop very much. I met her once in Cambridge (Massachusetts) and we had a nice conversation, but her poetry does not touch me as a kind of invention. She is a presence, though, in Ashbery, who, in my opinion, is also not so important. The main influence on Ashbery, I think, is Elizabeth Bishop – and French poetry. She lived in Ouro Preto and was very retiring. She did some good translations but didn't participate in Brazilian poetic life.

MP: She wasn't very ambitious?

HC: That's right. And I want to add something else. Another book very influential in the fifties was the anthology by Carola Giedion-Welcker, the *Anthology of the Marginal Poets*. It's a beautiful anthology, where she publishes poets of different nationalities, all poets who have been put aside – Hugo Ball, August Stramm, Huidobro – in a bilingual edition. I myself, inspired by this collection, published in 1956 a large article on Kurt Schwitters. I tried to restore all the trends opened up by Carola Giedion-Welcker. Because the curious thing is that in both the futurist and the dada movements, poets and painters were exchanging positions – Klee, for instance, and Kandinsky and Arp were also poets and avant-garde poets. So, this was another very good contribution to the universality of our point of view.

MP: Yes, just recently Jerome Rothenberg and Pierre Joris have put out an excellent large edition of Schwitters in translation. How about the Minimalist movement of the sixties? Did your own work relate to that?

AC: In a certain sense concrete *painting* preceded the concrete poetry movement. There was a group here in the 1950s that called themselves the concrete painting group. The term *concrete* in Brazil was derived from Max Bill's concept. He wanted to distinguish between *abstract* and *concrete* painting. By "abstract" he meant "abstracted" from reality. For example, a red circle as an abstraction from, say, the sun. This would be abstract painting. The other view, the concrete view, would be to see the circle as a visual element, not an abstraction from reality. This was the sense in which "concrete" entered the semantics of poetry. When we saw these new paintings, we decided to use the term "concrete." We wanted to free poetry from subjectivism and the expressionist vehicle.

MP: What about Paul Celan? Is that a poet who's important to you?

AC: For me it was not important, but I know he is a good poet.

HC: I disagree. I like Celan very much, and I even helped to translate his poetry into Portuguese. When, for instance, you compare Celan to Rilke, it's manifest. He had an element of invention! He has the contemporaneity of concrete poetry. He was a poet who was at the same time influenced by the syntax of Hölderlin, by some devices of Trakl, but on the other side, there are visual elements in his poetry, there is a reduction and fragmentation of language typical of concrete poetry. All these elements are present in Celan. Considering the German poetry situation, he is a very important poet. He corresponds in age and generation to João Cabral de Melo Neto, who is, so to speak, our forerunner.

AC: I would say also that Celan is clearly neo-Expressionist. The difference between him and João Cabral is that Cabral is clearly a constructed poet, even dealing with stanzas. His work is constructed with a sense of an engineer. So, this makes him a clearer link to experiment.

HC: It's hard to make a real comparison between Cabral and Celan. Cabral's poetic mode is similar to Williams's objectivism and to Ponge's *chosisme*. But what is the role the poet performs. Because even in concrete poetry, the German tradition was much less interested in the field of semantics than, for instance, Brazilian poetry. The Gomringer poetry is very interesting, but very limited. And between Gomringer and Heisenbüttel there is also a difference. Heisenbüttel is a political poet who manipulates syntactic techniques derived from Gertrude Stein, and so on. And Celan – from the point of view of a new generation and reception – he is the German poet with the most radiance of invention considered most important by the role he performs.

Haroldo de Campos

MP: Both of you speak of invention versus expression. What's wrong with expression?

AC: Nothing's wrong. It's a matter of distinction. I feel that Celan is a very good poet – I don't know his poetry as well as Haroldo does – but I would say he has no place in the experimental ideology. It's like comparing Georg Trakl to Kurt Schwitters. Both are very good poets, but one has nothing to do with experiment.

Maybe I'm too much of a radical, but the first experiments of John Cage, after all, came from the late forties. In the fifties he was making *4'33"*. So, this presence gives a reference to what was possible in the period.

MP: But why is experimentation *ipso facto* a good thing? Suppose I say that Celan is the ultimate poet of the tragedy of the twentieth century, the Holocaust? And that he does this brilliantly? Why then is constructivist experiment better than the "expression" of Celan? What's wrong with emotion?

AC: I think that you yourself have answered this question very well in your book *Radical Artifice* when you posed the question, "Why don't they write like Kafka?" This is not to say that Kafka is not a great writer – one of the greatest of the century. But why do some people not "write like Kafka"? I think that poetry is like nature. There is the rose that is in your hand and there is the beautiful fish inside a phosphorescent coral, but there are always some artists who play different roles, who want not only to express these things, but to change themselves. This was the beautiful answer that Cage gave to someone at the Venice Biennale. Someone asked him, "Why do you do these things?" And Cage said, "Because I don't want to express myself. I want to change myself." And I think that experimental artists are more interested in changing themselves and in changing things than in expressing, however beautifully, that which has already been discovered.

HC: I feel a little differently. I studied German in the fifties, when I was studying law, in order to read Rilke and Trakl. I had, by the way, the first edition in three volumes of George Trakl. I never did translate Trakl. Augusto is now translating Rilke, by the way. But I think there are gradations from the point of view of invention, and Celan is clearly for me an inventive poet. Because his is not the expression of the emotive function, but the emotive function dealt with by the manipulation of the poetic function. He uses resources from the avant-garde. There is a big difference between Celan and Trakl, whose poetry is much more conservative than Celan's. And then you have to see it in the context of the German tradition. One cannot be completely satisfied with Gomringer. Or Heisenbüittel. Or Hans Magnus Enzensberger. Or Brecht. So, Celan is very special.

MP: That's an interesting distinction. What about Aimé Cesaire? Do you like his work?

AC: Doesn't interest me much.

MP: Too surrealist?

AC: Too surrealist. I'm not very fond of surrealism. From the point of view of the avant-garde movements, surrealism was the least interesting. And the one that caused the most trouble.

HC: But in South America the influence of surrealism has been immense.

AC: Yes, a traumatic influence as a kind of avant-garde of consummation!

HC: A kind of conservative avant-garde.

MP: A throwback to romanticism, would you say?

AC: Yes, of course. All the emphasis on the unconscious and on figurality. I think French poetry did not free itself from surrealism until now. They did not understand *Un coup de dés*.

MP: But they now have *Oulipo* and other movements that must appeal to you much more.

HC: Yes, and, for instance, Ponge. But the point is that no poet after Mallarmé was as radical as Mallarmé. Not even Apollinaire. Apollinaire is decorative where Mallarmé is structural. I like Apollinaire, I like for instance "Lettre-Ocean." It's a very important poem. But Octavio Paz, who was connected to surrealism, especially with Bréton, gives the movement great importance and for a good reason. Because South American Spanish poetry was very much influenced by surrealism, whereas in Brazil we have no surrealism at all. We care much more for Italian futurism and dada – they are more radical.

AC: Décio Pignatari has a good phrase for it. He says that Brazil never had surrealism because the whole country is surrealist.

MP: Touché. I want now to come back to the naughty, nasty question of ideology. You have often passed off the question of Pound's fascism. But it's now a burning issue and there are many interesting books on the subject. Doesn't Pound's ideology affect the value of his poetry?

AC: Well, I think it's now clear that Pound had some link with fascism. You can say from our perspective today that this was not a good choice, but at the time when Pound was in Rapallo in the thirties, maybe it was not so easy to see things clearly.

HC: Many poets were affected by fascism. Ungaretti's first book, *Il porto sepolto* (1917), was taken up by Mussolini. Valéry had some inclinations toward fascism, T. S. Eliot was conservative, Fernando Pessoa....

MP: Well, but there are people who argue that therefore Pound can never be considered one of the great poets, that the fascism is *there* in the poetry.

HC: A poet as reactionary as Pound, and who attacked others with the same violence we find in Pound, was Dante. There is a beautiful essay by Edoardo Sanguinetti about this. Dante wanted the Italians to receive with open arms the German monarch, whom he thought reigned by divine right. Dante was one of the first poets to be exiled for political convictions – and very reactionary ones, at that. Pound, a kind of modern Dante, had a corporate conception of society, a medieval one, centered around the "good ruler."

MP: But wouldn't you grant that Dante's ideas, whatever they were, were not *silly*, whereas many of Pound's – like the stamp scrip project and the Major Douglas cult – were?

HC: Yes. When George Steiner wrote about Dante he said the *Inferno* always reminded him of the concentration camps. That Dante anticipated the Holocaust.

AC: There is another issue. The left-wing writers committed great errors, too. Mayakovsky, for instance. Neruda wrote litanies for Stalin. So, if we would make a grand jury to judge writers who were interested in politics, we would have to condemn many great writers.

MP: But why do you think that in the twentieth century writers have made such terrible political mistakes? Surely the British romantics, for instance, were not as out of touch with their culture?

HC: Because they are afraid of being bourgeois!

AC: I would say that everyone was wrong in one sense or another. Everybody was deceived by political utopia, whether from the Left or from the Right. I rather tend to see this question from an ethical point of view. I think that Pound was an ethical man. He was not an opportunist. Neruda, for example, was much more of an opportunist. He had great benefits from his fidelity to the Soviet Union – ambassadorships, and so on. And Jorge Amado in Brazil, who got the Stalin Prize, the Lenin Prize, and all of his work disseminated throughout the world in translation. Pound got no benefit from his political ideas. He was a poor man. His intentions were good.

HC: And there is another point. Pound's fascism came from an anti-bourgeois, anti-capitalistic position. I myself, from the time I was very young, was always for socialism, but for a democratic socialism. I was always against Stalinism. We as a group believed in socialism and so we were attacked by the Socialist realist poets of Brazil, who called us formalists. Even though our public position was clearly defined as a left-wing position.

AC: Even in the sixties, we believed in the Cuban revolution. That was in 1962. When Fidel Castro came with eighteen young men and demolished the dictatorship, it was a fantastic thing.

HC: Cuba in that moment was very much open to the avant-garde. They had fine literary magazines. Even Borges contributed.

AC: There was a moment when everyone was deceived from one or another point of view. I think the most reasonable thing to do is to approach the question from the ethical point of view. To try to understand the motives of the different poets.

MP: That's an interesting distinction. Let's talk a little bit about translation. Both of you are extraordinary translators. Do you want to say something about your theory of translation? In relation, say, to Walter Benjamin's "The Task of the Translator"?

AC: Here in Brazil, the great theorist of translation is Haroldo. I would say for myself that, in matters of translation, I consider myself a disciple of Ezra Pound. In the sense that Pound had the idea that when you translate, you recreate to the point of making a mask. And he did it magnificently.

HC: For me, translation is characterized by hyper-literalism. It has to capture all the elements, the phonic as well as the semantic. So, to be brief, what we rescue from the original text – what Walter Benjamin "sublimates" under the label of "pure language" – is the itinerary of the "poetic function" within a given poem, a sort of design or choreography. If the poet (as Décio Pignatari puts it) is a "designer of language," the translator (trans-creator) is a redesigner of it in his own idiom.

MP: Do you think you've been well served by the translations of your poetry?

AC: The problem is very difficult. At least so far as concrete poetry is concerned. It's very difficult to find equivalents in another language. On the one hand, there was this kind of international flavor in concrete poetry. Especially when you use non-verbal elements. But the problem is that you don't find verbal equivalents. For example, a poem like Pignatari's *hombre, fembre, hembra* could only be written in Spanish.

HC: From the point of view of that orthodox phase of concrete poetry, this was true. On the other hand, I myself and Augusto, too, we work together with our translators to achieve a good result. My *Galaxies* have been translated into French by Inês Oseki-Dépré, who is a professor of Comparative Literature at the University of Aix-en-Provence. She has developed her task with my personal assistance.

MP: I was looking at Augusto's Gertrude Stein translations (a reference to the beautifully produced 1989 bilingual edition of *Porta-Retratos* (*Portraits*)). Is Stein very difficult to translate?

AC: Almost impossible, because Portuguese has very few monosyllables, so it was hard to find equivalents. Think, for instance, of Stein's opening line of the second Picasso portrait, "If I told him would he like it. Would he like it if I told him." In my translation, this becomes "Se eu lhe contasse ele gostaria. Ele gostaria se eu lhe contasse." There are no monosyllables in Portuguese to match the English.

HC: Since we are running out of time [we were due at the book-signing party for *The Futurist Movement* at the Livraria da Vila], let's listen to a recording I think you'll find interesting.

The interview concluded with the playing of recordings of Augusto's and Haroldo's earlier concrete poems.

Concrete Poetry at the Crossroads

Willard Bohn

ALTHOUGH CONCRETE POETRY combines two separate traditions – the European and the Brazilian – few traces of its double origin remain. To be sure, some observers perceive significant differences between the two schools, but these are more apparent than real. In contrast to their European colleagues, the Brazilians have adopted a bold typeface that makes their compositions more forceful. However, this innovation is largely cosmetic. Some critics claim the two traditions appeal to different senses, the one conceiving poetry as a visual experience, the other as a "verbivocovisual" exercise, but this distinction does not seem to hold up in practice. Like the Brazilian poets, the chief theoretician of the first group, Max Bense, affirms that "the word has simultaneously a verbal, a vocal, and a visual positional value."[1]

In truth, the first generation wrote as much for the ear as for the eye. While they experimented endlessly with different visual combinations, they never forgot they were dealing with language. As Rosmarie Waldrop remarks, "Concrete poetry makes the sound and shape of words its explicit field of investigation. Concrete poetry is about words."[2]

This statement bears repeating. For if in theory "la linguistique s'arrête à la phrase" ("linguistics stops at the sentence"), as Roland Barthes puts it, concrete poetry stops at the word.[3] Like the sentence, it is the largest unit that falls within the scope of its respective field of inquiry. This situation is acknowledged at the end of a Brazilian manifesto

---

1 Cited in Mary Ellen Solt, ed., *Concrete Poetry: A World View* (Bloomington: Indiana University Press, 1970), 74. Subsequent references to this volume, abbreviated as MES, will appear in the body of the text.
2 Rosmarie Waldrop, "A Basis of Concrete Poetry," in *The Avant-Garde Tradition in Literature*, ed. by Richard Kostelanetz (Buffalo: Prometheus, 1982), 315.
3 Roland Barthes, "Introduction à l'Analyse Structurale des Récits," *Communications*, no. 8 (1966), 3.

entitled *Plano-pilôto para Poesia Concreta*, where concrete poetry is defined as "uma arte geral da palavra" ("a general art of the word").[4] Despite (or perhaps because of) its abbreviated form, this formula has much to recommend it. For one thing, so many definitions have been proposed over the years that its simplicity is refreshing.[5] For another thing, it stresses the primacy of the word, which is conceived both as a fundamental building block and as an independent entity. In addition, it calls attention to one of the genre's distinctive features: its emphasis on condensation. The traditional sentence is reduced to a few basic words, perhaps to only one word, which tantalize the reader with their brevity. Not surprisingly, since they must bear the whole weight of the composition, these tend to denote objects and/or operations. Like the Italian futurists before them, who also abolished traditional syntax, the concrete poets show a predilection for verbs and nouns. Condensation requires the reader to pay more attention not only to what the poem says but to its individual elements. It foregrounds each word, Waldrop observes, much as indenting both margins emphasizes the poetic line.[6]

The preceding remarks apply primarily to the poem's verbal aspect. However, concrete poetry derives its name not from its abbreviated format but from its appearance on the page. As Bense points out, the meaning of "concrete" is to be understood as the opposite of "abstract" (MES, p. 73). Whereas traditional poetry operates on the conceptual level, concrete poetry is based on perception. Whereas traditional poetry occupies a virtual dimension, concrete poetry possesses an undeniable presence. Where it differs from conventional verse is in its ability to translate abstract ideas into visual images. This ability is precisely what makes it concrete. In addition to condensation, it should be noted, concrete poetry is distinguished by spatialization: the words are arranged to form various patterns. In the absence of conventional grammar, the

---

4 Augusto de Campos, Décio Pignatari, and Haroldo de Campos, "Plano-pilôto para Poesia Concreta," *Noigandres*, No. 4 (1958). Reprinted in Solt, *Concrete Poetry: A World View*, 71. The translation is my own. Cited in the text hereafter as PP.

5 See especially Dick Higgins, "Concrete Poetry," in *The New Princeton Encyclopedia of Poetry and Poetics*, ed. by Alex Preminger et al. (Princeton: Princeton University Press, 1993), 233–4; Peter Mayer, "Some Remarks Concerning the Classification of the Visual in Literature," *Dada/Surrealism*, no. 12 (1983), 5–13; Eric Vos, "On Concrete Poetry and 'A Classification of the Visual in Literature'" in *Verbal/Visual Crossings, 1880–1980*, ed. by Theo D'haen (Amsterdam: Rodopi and Antwerp: Restant, 1990), 241–80; and Jon M. Tolman, "Towards a Definition of Concrete Poetry," *Poetics Today*, Vol, III (1982), 149–66.

6 Waldrop, "A Basis of Concrete Poetry," 316.

poem employs a spatial syntax. The words are liberated from the tyranny of the sentence on both the syntagmatic and the paradigmatic axes. They are free to combine with each other visually as well as verbally, vertically as well as horizontally. Concrete poetry requires "the dynamic utilization of typographical resources," Augusto de Campos explains, because their normal arrangement is "incapable of serving the whole range of inflections of which poetic thought is capable."[7]

In concrete poetry, Rudolf Arnheim notes, each word may combine with several others while retaining its individual autonomy.[8] For better or for worse, visual syntax presents the reader with multiple choices at every turn. One can proceed from left to right, from top to bottom, or diagonally in any direction. According to Michael Webster, this situation represents one of the central paradoxes associated with the genre: "By a reduction of means, it achieves an expansion of possible readings."[9] However, this property is not as paradoxical as it seems. Although the sentence is condensed to only a few words, the syntactic possibilities are greatly expanded. The increase in the second area easily compensates for the decrease in the first. Since words are free to establish multiple relations, concrete poetry is by definition indeterminate. Readers are free to follow alternate paths and to arrive at different interpretations. This does not mean the works are unstructured but that the structure has been redefined, together with its conventional role. With the abolition of linear constraints, the traditional poem has become obsolete. From a circumscribed entity focused inward upon itself, it has been transformed into a work that opens outward to embrace multiple possibilities. It no longer belongs to the author but to its readers.

Whereas poetry has traditionally been the vehicle for ideas, symbolic references, allusions, passionate avowals, and didactic lessons, Mary Ellen Solt points out that concrete poetry disdains this role (MES, p. 8). In keeping with the principles of reduction and condensation, it conceives of its mission in much simpler terms. What the concrete poem communicates above all, the Pilot Plan affirms, is its structure (PP, p. 70). It is extraordinarily successful in realizing this project, I believe, for two

---

7 Augusto de Campos, "Points-Periphery-Concrete Poetry," translated by Jon M. Tolman, in Kostelanetz, *The Avant-Garde Tradition in Literature*, 260.
8 Rudolf Arnheim, "Visual Aspects of Concrete Poetry," *Yearbook of Comparative Criticism*, Vol. VII (1976), 98.
9 Michael Webster, *Reading Visual Poetry After Futurism: Marinetti, Apollinaire, Schwitters, cummings* (New York: Lang, 1995), 147.

reasons. One of these involves its unique verbal properties; the other is related to its hybrid identity. In the first place, deep structure and surface structure are usually congruent in concrete poetry. Indeed, to many observers they appear to be identical. In the second place, this (verbal) structure is projected onto the visual plane for everyone to see. Unlike conventional works, which attempt to obscure their underlying mechanisms, concrete poetry has nothing to hide. Not because it has nothing to say, as some critics have alleged, but because it is incapable of concealment. Each poem is conceived as an autonomous object, as the sum of its various signifiers. From this point of view, as someone has declared, concrete poetry is all surface. What you see is essentially what you get.

Although it is tempting to conclude that its aesthetic and semantic functions occupy opposite sides of the same coin, this metaphor proves to be unsatisfactory. Object and sign are not opposed to one another any more than structure and meaning. While they represent different aspects of the semiotic process, they are intimately related. The poets themselves speak of "isomorphism" in discussing the complex interplay that exists between them. The relation between word and image is isomorphic, they explain, if the visual elements assume a form that is analogous to the verbal meaning. As we will see, this relation varies in degree and kind from tautological constructions to carefully crafted analogies to approximate parallels. Virtually all the poets downplay mimesis in favor of visual analogies and schematic compositions. A careful reading of the Pilot Plan suggests that concrete poetry can be classified as either static or dynamic, representational or non-representational. This means that the genre can be divided into four categories. A poem may be conceived as a passive exercise or as an active demonstration. By the same token, it may portray another object or simply itself.

>paralelamente ao isomorfismo fundo-forma, se desenvolve o isomorfismo espaço-tempo, que gera o movimento. o isomorfismo, num primeiro momento da pragmática poética concreta, tende à fisiognomia, a um movimento imitativo do real (*motion*); predomina a forma orgânica e a fenomenologia da composição. num estágio mais avançado, o isomorfismo tende a resolver-se em puro movimento estrutural (*movement*); nesta fase, predomina a forma geométrica e a matemática da composição (racionalismo sensível) (PP, p. 71).

(parallel to form-subject isomorphism, there is
space-time isomorphism, which generates movement. at
the first stage of concrete poetry praxis, isomorphism
tends to physiognomy, to movement imitating physical
appearance (motion); organic form and phenomenology of
composition predominate. at a more advanced stage,
isomorphism tends to resolve itself into pure
structural movement (movement proper); during this
phase, geometric form and mathematics of composition
(rational sensibility) predominate).

While the vast majority of the poems exploit analogical procedures, a few are unabashedly mimetic. Despite the prohibition placed on figurative compositions, the form has been cultivated by a number of concrete poets. Over time, as the movement acquired additional members from other countries, the original restrictions have become more relaxed. Not unexpectedly, the degree of realism varies from one figurative poem to the next. One of the more successful examples, created by Mary Ellen Solt, depicts a forsythia shrub thrusting its flowering branches toward the spring sun (MES, p. 243). Each of the stems consists of a single letter taken from the word "FORSYTHIA" which generates a string of equivalent letters in Morse Code. In addition, the poem is superimposed on a bright yellow background that evokes the shrub's distinctive color.

Another striking example is provided by Henri Chopin (see page 186), who left concrete poetry to become one of the leading exponents of *poésie sonore* ("sound poetry").

Portraying the Arc de Triomphe, the poem consists almost entirely of two words: "saoul" ("drunk") and "feu" ("fire"). These are repeated over and over to form the linguistic equivalent of bricks. Interestingly, the first word and its replicas are restricted to the arch, while the remaining words form its horizontal base. Although the implications of this arrangement take a moment to register, the portrait is clearly meant to be subversive. The Arc de Triomphe is not just a tourist attraction, after all, but a monument to France's military glory. In this, capacity, it commemorates a whole series of victorious battles and symbolizes French imperialism. In addition to the military establishment, therefore, Chopin is attacking the institutions that are responsible for its existence. If his main target is doubtless the French government, present and past, this is only the tip of the iceberg. The Arc de Triomphe symbolizes a multitude of sins ranging from colonialism to patriotism and perhaps even capitalism.

```
            saoul                                           saoul
            saoul  saoul  saoul  saoul  saoul  saoul  saoul  saoul
            saoul  saoul  saoul  saoul  saoul  saoul  saoul  saoul
            saoul  saoul  saoul  saoul  saoul  saoul  saoul  saoul
            saoul  saoul  saoul  saoul  saoul  saoul  saoul  saoul
            saoul  saoul  saoul  saoul  saoul  saoul  saoul  saoul

            saoul saoul sao          l           oul saoul saoul
            saoul saoul s            e              saoul saoul
            saoul saoul                            saoul saoul
            saoul sao                s                oul saoul
            saoul s                  o                  l saoul
            saoul                    l                    saoul
            saoul                    d                    saoul
            saoul                    a                    saoul
            saoul                    t                    saoul
            saoul                                         saoul
            saoul                    i                    saoul
            saoul                    n                    saoul
            saoul                    c                    saoul
            saoul                    o                    saoul
            saoul                    n                    saoul
            saoul          n              u               saoul
            saoul     b    r    û    l    e    !          saoul
            saoul                                         saoul
            saoul                                         saoul
            saoul s                                     s saoul
            saoul s                                     s saoul
            saoul s                                     s saoul
      feu feu feu feu feu feu feu feu feu feu feu feu feu fe
      feu feu feu feu feu feu feu feu feu feu feu feu feu feu
                                                 (MES, p. 165).
```

More than anything, perhaps, Chopin attacks various myths associated with war that seek to mask its brutality and inhumanity. There is nothing glorious about military conquest, the poem proclaims, no matter how nobly it is depicted on monuments. War simply gives thousands of drunken soldiers an excuse to rape, kill, and loot. The Unknown Soldier, whose tomb lies beneath the arch, is no better than the rest. The central inscription, which appears to be a macabre joke, describes and depicts his body being consumed by the Eternal Flame: "le soldat incon / nu / brûle." Like the base of the monument, the phrase is printed in fiery red letters. Both literally and figuratively it constitutes an inflammatory statement. Appalled by what the Arc de Triomphe represents, the poet has set fire to the structure, determined to raze it to the ground. Before our very eyes the whole monument goes up in flames, together with the Unknown Soldier.

In general, the realistic works undergo remarkably little change or development. They are concerned with how an object appears rather than with how it can be transformed. Like Salette Tavares's realistic spider (MES, p. 190), which consists of variations on the Portuguese word *aranha*, they are caught in an invisible web of their own devising. Like Edwin Morgan's poem in the shape of Scotland, consisting of local names for the chaffinch, they can only map physical features.[10] Whereas Solt's forsythia bush and Tavares's spider utilize outlined forms, Chopin's monument and Morgan's map employ solid forms. The problem with the second style is that it utilizes rectilinear building blocks, which makes it hard to reproduce most shapes. As a result, a number of concrete poets have experimented with solid cut-outs, whose contours are created with a pair of scissors. The Czech poet Jirí Kolár fashioned a replica of a famous sculpture in this manner (MES, p. 142). Beginning with the name "brancusi" printed seventy-three times in tabular form, he trimmed the original text until it resembled the sculptor's *Bird in Space* on its pedestal. As in Morgan's ornithological map of Scotland, the relation between the verbal and the visual elements is metonymic. By contrast this relation is tautological in Reinhard Döhl's apple poem, whose circular shape is filled with numerous "Apfels" (plus one "Wurm" hidden near the center) (EW, n. p.). The same thing is true of Ian Hamilton Finlay's pear composition whose punning text, printed in orange letters, consists of the phrase "au pair girl" repeated over and over.[11]

---

10   Edwin Morgan, "The Chaffinch Map of Scotland," *An Anthology of Concrete Poetry*, ed. by Emmett Williams (New York: Something Else, 1967), n. p. Cited in the text hereafter as EW.
11   Ian Hamilton Finlay, untitled poem in *Concrete Poetry: An International Anthology*, ed. by Stephen Bann (London: London Magazine, 1967), 151. Cited in the text hereafter as SB.

A number of other works manage to exploit mimesis while observing the taboo on realistic portrayal. Several poets have developed strategies for representing an object's appearance, or at least some of its visual characteristics, indirectly. By resorting to schematic depiction, they are able to translate its realistic features into abstract (or semi-abstract) terms. As the following example by Gerhard Rühm demonstrates, reducing the figurative demands on a poem encourages it to develop in other directions.

        die blume

        die blume blüht
        die blume blüht
        die blume blüht
        die blume blüht

        die blume welkt
        die blume welkt
        die blume welkt
        die blume welkt

        die blume
        die blume
        die blume
        die blume
        die blume
        die blume
        die blume
        die blume
        (MES, p. 132).

As the title proclaims, the poem seems to be concerned with some kind of flower ("blume"). Unfortunately, the visual design is so ambiguous – deliberately as it turns out – that the flower is impossible to identify. Although the first two stanzas appear to represent the plant's blossom, and the third stanza its stem, it could belong to any one of a hundred species. Returning to the title in desperation, one perceives that the poet employs "die" ("the") instead of "eine" ("a"). Thus the poem is concerned not with a particular flower but with flowers in general. By a curious process the definite article acquires an indefinite meaning. Like a picture labeled "The Zebra" in an encyclopedia, this is a generic portrait. Reflecting the work's broad focus, the text is no more informative than the design. Like the authors of the previous compositions Rühm, as Stephen Bann points out, "makes full use of the momentum that can be gained from sheer repetition" (SB, p. 12). Unlike them, however, he introduces a note of change. While each stanza repeats a particular statement, the statement changes from one stanza to the next. The poem's shape, one discovers, is motivated as much by verbal as by visual concerns. As the text progresses, it evokes three important stages in the life cycle of a typical flower. First the plant blooms ("blüht"), then it withers ("welkt"), and finally it disappears altogether. All that remains is the bare earth – and the blank page – from which it originally sprung.

Other poems, such as Dom Sylvester Houédard's "Near the Guernsey Coast" (SB, p.161), feature multiple objects but portray them in another manner.

    gulls   bulls

        boats   goats

Whereas the various objects are represented verbally, their relations to each other are depicted visually. From the words' arrangement on the page one can deduce the position of the invisible objects. It is up to us, however, to imagine everything else: the objects' appearance, the physical setting, and what, if anything, is taking place. Although the details naturally vary from one observer to the next, it is surprisingly easy to reconstruct the original scene. The first thing one notices is the picture's balanced composition, which suggests it is unusually harmonious. On the one hand, the visual elements are evenly divided between land and sea. Juxtaposed with several animals grazing on the hillside, a few boats bob gently in the water as gulls circle lazily overhead. On the other hand, the verbal elements are amazingly symmetrical, both in their placement on the page and in the way they are combined. As one soon perceives, each word borrows phonemes from two of its neighbors. Each is related to the word opposite and to one of the words above or below it. At this level, the composition consists of a four-term homology: the gulls are to the boats as the bulls are to the goats. Or alternatively, pushing the equation to its limits, we may say that the gulls are to the bulls as the boats are to the goats. Whether the equation refers to size, color, or some other physical characteristic is left to the reader/viewer to decide.

Pierre Garnier, who founded the Spatialist movement in France, employs a similar technique in a poem entitled "Grains de pollen" (EW, n. p.).

                            SOLEIL

                SOLEIL

                                    SOLEIL

          SOLEIL

SOLEIL

            SOLEIL   SOLEIL

       SOLEIL   SOLEIL

            SOLEIL

As one might expect, in view of the movement's name, the composition is highly spatialized. Like the previous work, it consists of a few words disposed in such a way as to suggest a group of corresponding objects. Despite (or perhaps because of) its minimalist aesthetic, it is marvelously evocative. At the same time, it differs from Houédard's poem in several important respects. In the first place, it is basically a portrait rather than a landscape (or seascape). This means that one views the scene from close up instead of from far away. The focus as well as the perspective are markedly different. Besides offering a more intimate experience, the composition possesses an organic unity that increases its cohesiveness. In the second place, the verbal components are all identical. Whereas Houédard utilizes phonetic transposition, Garnier resorts to repetition. The poem's natural unity is reinforced by its linguistic homogeneity. In the third place, the link between word and image is not tautological but metaphoric. Each grain of pollen is represented not by its verbal equivalent but by the French word for "sun." Despite the words' rectangular shape, we have no difficulty visualizing a swarm of tiny, orange spheres. Indeed, we can even tell which way the breeze is blowing. In the last analysis, the poem is essentially a concrete haiku. With a little effort it could be translated into verses such as these:

        Miniature suns drifting in the air,
        Grains of pollen brighten the day.

Another type of concrete poetry derives its effect from absence rather than from presence. Instead of indicating the position of an object or of several objects with verbal markers, the poet interrupts the linguistic flow. This device is especially useful for evoking concepts that are difficult to visualize. More precisely, it illustrates the network of relations associated with a particular concept. In contrast to the previous works, the three poems that follow are concerned primarily with concepts. Rather than pictographic exercises they present, in Claus Clüver's words, "structural parallels to the objective realities to which they refer."[12] The first poem, by the former futurist Carlo Belloli, employs a device that was destined to enjoy a certain popularity. Like its companions, it exemplifies the poetics of absence.

> cerchio cerchio cerchio cerchio
> cerchio cerchio cerchio cerchio
> cerchio cerchio cerchio cerchio
> cerchio cer   chio
> cerchio cerchio sfera   cerchio
> cerchio cerchio cerchio cerchio
> cerchio cerchio cerchio cerchio
>   (EW, n. p.).

Like many concrete poems, Belloli's composition relies heavily on repetition. With two exceptions the text consists of the Italian word for "circle," which is repeated some twenty-five times. Upon inspection the work turns out to comprise a double variation on this single typographical theme. The first variation occurs at the visual level and illustrates the principle of subtraction. The second takes place at the verbal level and involves the principle of substitution. That a work devoted to circular form should be cast in a rectangular shape is ironic, to say the least. Against all odds the poet has finally succeeded in squaring the circle. And yet his subject is not mathematics, or even geometry, but aesthetic form. As much as anything, the composition is concerned with rupture and metamorphosis. The question that arises at this point, one that is impossible to answer, is whether it is composed of multiple circles or of a single circle. Are the various elements meant to be apprehended simultaneously, one wonders, or sequentially? The problem with graphic

---

12 Claus Clüver, "Reflections on Verbivocovisual Ideograms," *Poetics Today*, Vol. III, No. 3 (1982), 138.

repetition is that it appeals to visual and to verbal conventions at the same time. Depending on whether one chooses to read the poem, to view it, or to recite it, the answer to these questions will vary. On the one hand, the poem could conceivably depict a chain link fence. On the other, it could represent successive views of a circle opening and closing. With a little ingenuity one could explain the gap and the "sphere" according to either scenario. The problem – if that's the right word – with Belloli's poem is that his vocabulary is not only limited but hopelessly concrete. It is all too easy to visualize the object(s) to which the words refer. The degree of undecidability is substantially reduced in the two remaining works, which are surprisingly similar but which employ a more abstract vocabulary.

>   ich gehe nicht allein
>   ich gehe nicht allein
>   ich gehe nicht allein
>   ich gehe nicht allein
>   ich gehe nicht allein
>   ich gehe nicht allein
>   ich gehe nicht allein
>   ich gehe nicht allein
>   ich gehe   allein
>   ich gehe nicht allein
>   ich gehe nicht allein
>   ich gehe nicht allein
>   ich gehe nicht allein
>   (SB, p. 62).

By choosing to replicate an entire sentence, Rühm de-emphasizes the individual words and directs the reader to proceed sequentially. Like its rectilinear companions, his poem deftly balances multiplication and subtraction. The initial phrase "ich gehe nicht allein" ("I go not alone") is repeated again and again with one crucial exception. Two thirds of the way through the composition, the poet deletes the negative particle and transforms the sentence into a positive statement. Whereas he seems to value companionship, all of a sudden he finds himself alone. Despite the conspicuous lack of details one fact stands out: the brevity of this experience. Judging from the haste with which he rectifies the situation, Rühm does not enjoy being abandoned. Like a tourist running after his tour group, he hurries to rejoin his companions before they disappear from sight. The solitary life clearly has no attraction for him.

>   silencio silencio silencio
>   silencio silencio silencio
>   silencio   silencio
>   silencio silencio silencio
>   silencio silencio silencio

Despite its humble appearance, Gomringer's contribution to rectangular poetry (MES, p. 91) is a masterpiece. Among other things, it illustrates his superiority as a concrete poet. Dismissing the syntactic approach favored by Rühm, he adopts a single, uniform building block consisting of the word "silencio." "Owing to the symmetrical, mirroring composition," Mary Lewis Shaw observes, "the graphic image of 'silence' appears to extend in all directions."[13] At the same time, the viewer's attention is drawn to the composition's vacant center, which serves as its focal point. As Solt points out, the message conveyed by the text emerges from the white space in the middle of the design (MES, p. 10). In other words, Webster adds, "the space presents iconically the meaning of the word."[14] Once again, the function of the visual elements is analogous to that of the verbal elements. Each is defined in terms of the other. In contrast to the verbal definition, which is purely denotative, the visual definition is essentially structural. As before, the missing piece of the puzzle turns out to be tremendously important. The subject of all three poems is precisely their lack of continuity. Like Belloli, who defines a gap as the absence of connection, and Rühm, who equates isolation with the absence of companions, Gomringer defines silence as the absence of sound.

Is this all there is to Gomringer's poem, one wonders, or can his basic definition be expanded to encompass other areas? Stephen Bann suggests that the work embodies Jean (Hans) Arp's vision of an art of silence, representing "the transition from the 'visible world' to 'silence, the inner being, reality'" (SB, p. 8). However, Solt believes that this describes the condition of poetry in general. What the poet is really saying, she maintains, is that "all true poems ... aspire to silence, the silence of the spirit at their center" (MES, p. 60). To a considerable extent, David Seaman

---

13 Mary Lewis Shaw, "Concrete and Abstract Poetry: the World as Text and the Text as World," *Visible Language*, Vol. XXIII, NO. 1 (Winter 1989), 33.
14 Webster, *Reading Visual Poetry After Futurism*, 141.

notes, how one interprets the composition depends on the function one ascribes to it: "The philosopher may find ... a reference to the ineffability of the divine, while a politician might see in it a comment on the futility of discussion."[15] Like all concrete poems, which disdain any form of closure, it invites the reader to complete its meaning.

The problem with Gomringer's poem, one comes to realize, is that silence is defined both as absence and as presence. In retrospect the two semiotic systems, visual and verbal, can be seen to contradict each other. Like a drawing by Martin Escher, the work embodies two mutually incompatible perspectives. On the one hand, since the color of silence is white, the color of sound must be black. The composition appears to depict a silent center surrounded by a wall of noise. On the other hand, judging from the verbal labels, it portrays a wall of silence surrounding a noisy center. From this point of view silence appears to be black, and sound turns out to be white. Thus each silent area is created at the expense of the other. The same principle governs the displacement of noise from the outside to the inside and back again. Mary Ann Caws draws an analogy to the role of figure and ground in art, which may undergo a similar reversal.[16]

In this case, at least, heteromorphism proves to be more interesting than isomorphism. Whether this is true of concrete poetry in general, which revolves about structural analogy, is difficult to say. Upon reflection, the fact that the reversals are symmetrical suggests that the poem may not be as atypical as it looks. Despite obvious areas of disagreement, it includes a significant isomorphic component. What this means, I think, is that we are dealing with a special kind of concrete poetry that exploits difference as well as similarity. More precisely, the work is constructed around the principle of isomorphic paradox. Readers of Gomringer's poem are exposed to this principle wherever they turn. They can choose either to alternate perspectives indefinitely or, tiring of the continual flip flop, to explore the inconsistencies associated with a single perspective. Ironically, the silence that exists at the poem's center, according to one interpretation, is obtained by deleting the word "silencio." A similar irony permeates the periphery, where a series of silent operations culminates in a burst of noise. "By its use of the word

---

15 David W. Seaman, *Concrete Poetry in France* (Ann Arbor: UMI Research Press, 1981), 231.
16 Mary Ann Caws, *The Art of Interference: Stressed Readings in Verbal and Visual Texts* (Princeton: Princeton University Press, 1989), 162.
17 Shaw, "Concrete and Abstract Poetry," 34.

'silence' to express its contrary," Shaw comments, "the poem makes a forceful statement about the nature of silence, about the fact that silence, as the saying goes, is always heard."[17] In the present instance, the amount of repetition suggests that the silence is positively deafening.

At the other end of the concrete spectrum one finds works that, for lack of a better word, can be classified as abstract. Although they are composed of recognizable (or in some cases unrecognizable) letters and words, neither the text nor the design is particularly informative. While each continues to exploit the isomorphic properties of the other, they are entirely self-sufficient. Relieved of its referential burden, the composition delights in the play of its visual and verbal signifiers. Like their ideographic companions, many abstract works can be viewed as metapoems, that is, as "signs about signmaking and the process of iconization."[18] However, as Webster implies, they retain their insular quality since they focus inward upon themselves. Breaking with the mimetic order, they transcend mere physiognomy, as the Pilot Plan directs, to arrive at a more advanced stage. Unlike the initial phase, which strives to reinterpret physical reality, the second rejects representation in favor of direct presentation. Whereas the one mediates between the reader and the phenomenal world, the other exposes the reader to the phenomenon in question.

In general, Shaw remarks, concrete poetry can be described as "a kind of thickening or reification of the poetic sign."[19] This is particularly true of the non-representational poems – especially those that are static. Deprived of the opportunity to interact with other letters or words, the verbal components lose much of their semantic force. Insofar as concrete poetry succumbs to this temptation, Shaw is undoubtedly right that it tends to "reduce and finally delete its very foundation: the verbal text."[20] And yet I would argue that this operation is not as threatening as it may seem. It would be more correct to regard the poems as examples of self-mortification rather than self-destruction. Conceived as ascetic exercises, they demand the utmost discipline on the part of the poet if they are to succeed. In order to achieve the desired result, the paucity of verbal effects must be offset at the visual level. The design must be strong enough not only to support the additional burden but to respond to the viewer's increased expectations.

18 Webster, *Reading Visual Poetry After Futurism*, 151.
19 Shaw, "Concrete and Abstract Poetry," 29.
20 Ibid., 30.

This program is exemplified by Aram Saroyan's monolithic poster poem depicting a gigantic "m" printed in boldface type (EW, n.p.). What makes the composition so intriguing is not the letter's size so much as the discovery that it contains an extra segment. In contrast to the original model, it consists of four vertical strokes linked by three curved lines at the top. Like Marcel Duchamp's portrait of a hirsute Mona Lisa, therefore, the poem constitutes an assisted readymade. Although the letter retains something of its original identity, it has been modified in keeping with its new role. Since the initial form persists, it is recognizable and unrecognizable, familiar and unfamiliar, natural and unnatural at the same time. One of the work's attractions stems from the fact that it mediates between two different worlds. Another is provided by its modular construction, where the same basic shape occurs again and again. Indeed, like a continuous hum, it seems possible to prolong the poem indefinitely. Nor should one neglect to mention its visual appeal, which is evident at first glance. While it is tempting to compare the design to an alchemical symbol, it functions above all as a monumental artefact. More than anything, it invites the viewer to contemplate its symmetrical form, which is essentially architectural. Translated into marble, it could serve as a cathedral, a mosque, or an Oriental palace.

Other works that belong to the same category include Jirí Valoch's experiments with optical poetry, which resemble paintings by artists such as Victor Vasarely and Bridget Riley. Instead of concentrating on a single isolated letter, the poet multiplies the letter dozens of times until he has enough to construct a grid, which he subsequently distorts according to one procedure or another. In "Homage o Ladislav Novák" (MES, p. 147), composed entirely of lowercase "l's", he creates the illusion of a spherical shape by cleverly manipulating the lines. Another, untitled poem consists of two grids of lowercase "i's" that have been superimposed and rotated slightly in opposite directions (MES, p. 148). Both compositions invite us to admire the interesting patterns that result from the optical phenomenon known as interference. Valoch's preoccupation with geometric form, which conforms to the program outlined in the Pilot Plan, is shared by numerous concrete poets. Many authors prefer to replicate individual words rather than letters because they are easier to work with. Thus Ilse and Pierre Garnier created a rectangular poem with a diamond-shaped cut-out by repeating the name "marie" (EW, n. p.). And Maurizio Nannucci has composed a series of works based on the word "nero" ("black"), one of which is reproduced below.

Concrete Poetry at the Crossroads

nero ner ne n ne ner nero
nero ner ne n ne ner nero
nero ner ne n ne ner nero
nero ner ne n ne ner nero
nero ner ne n ne ner nero
nero ner ne n ne ner nero
nero ner ne n ne ner nero
nero ner ne n ne ner nero
nero ner ne n ne ner nero
nero ner ne n ne ner nero
nero ner ne n ne ner nero
nero ner ne n ne ner nero
nero ner ne n ne ner nero
nero ner ne n ne ner nero
nero ner ne n ne ner nero
nero ner ne n ne ner nero
nero ner ne n ne ner nero
nero ner ne n ne ner nero
nero ner ne n ne ner nero
nero ner ne n ne ner nero
nero ner ne n ne ner nero
nero ner ne n ne ner nero
nero ner ne n ne ner nero
nero ner ne n ne ner nero
nero ner ne n ne ner nero
nero ner ne n ne ner nero
nero ner ne n ne ner nero
nero ner ne n ne ner nero
nero ner ne n ne ner nero
nero ner ne n ne ner nero
nero ner ne n ne ner nero
nero ner ne n ne ner nero
nero ner ne n ne ner nero
nero ner ne n ne ner nero
nero ner ne n ne ner nero
nero ner ne n ne ner nero
nero ner ne n ne ner nero
nero ner ne n ne ner nero
nero ner ne n ne ner nero
nero ner ne n ne ner nero

nero ner ne n ne ner nero
nero ner ne n ne ner nero
nero ner ne n ne ner nero
nero ner ne n ne ner nero
nero ner ne n ne ner nero
nero ner ne n ne ner nero
nero ner ne n ne ner nero
nero ner ne n ne ner nero
nero ner ne n ne ner nero
nero ner ne n ne ner nero
nero ner ne n ne ner nero
nero ner ne n ne ner nero
nero ner ne n ne ner nero
nero ner ne n ne ner nero
nero ner ne n ne ner nero
nero ner ne n ne ner nero
nero ner ne n ne ner nero
(EW, n. p.).

As these examples demonstrate, works in this group tend to gravitate to one of two poles. The vast majority is conceived either as monolithic or as distributional exercises. Interestingly, a number of poets move freely from one pole to the other as the inspiration strikes them. In all the compositions, Bann reminds us, the insistence on the materiality of letters and words challenges our deeply entrenched habits of interpretation (SB, p. 11).

This challenge yields to concerns of a different order when one examines the Pilot Plan's fourth category. Unlike the preceding examples, dynamic non-representational poetry is predominately verbal. To be sure, the bulk of the compositions conform to some sort of pattern, and a few – mostly those that employ special typography – can even be called monolithic. Since the drama is situated primarily on the verbal plane, however, the visual elements are much less important. The poetry's dynamic character derives not from its iconic properties so much as from the interaction of the words and letters. What sets these poems apart according to the Pilot Plan is their concern with pure structural movement. As this expression implies, they are preoccupied not simply with change but with systematic development. Although the poets indulge in considerable wordplay, there is nothing gratuitous about the way in which the elements are combined. Each poem is governed by a single unifying principle that determines where each word will be placed. Every step in the process is carefully regulated, leading the authors of the Pilot Plan to speak of "a matemática da composição" ("the mathematics of composition"). The following work by Claus Bremer typifies this methodical progression.

```
              abcdefghijklmnopqrstuvwxyz
              abcdefghijklmnopqrstuvwxy
              abcdefghijklmnopqrstuvwx
              abcdefghijklmnopqrstuvw
              abcdefghijklmnopqrstuv
              abcdefghijklmnopqrstu
              abcdefghijklmnopqrst
              abcdefghijklmnopqrs
              abcdefghijklmnopqr
              abcdefghijklmnopq
              abcdefghijklmnop
              abcdefghijklmno
              abcdefghijklmn
              abcdefghijklm
              abcdefghijkl
              abcdefghijk
              abcdefghij
              abcdefghi
              abcdefgh
              abcdefh
              abcdef
              abcde
              abcd
              abc
              a b
              a
```

(SB, p. 52).

Despite the absence of recognizable words, Bremer's composition manages to convey a surprising amount of information. Or rather, since it adopts a non-discursive posture, it depicts various stages of an ongoing process. In this case, Bann notes, the alphabet serves as a paradigm of linguistic activity, and a final, overprinted figure represents its cessation (SB, p. 11). Thus we witness the gradual disintegration of language as legibility yields inexorably to illegibility and meaning is slowly obliterated. The vision of existence that remains is of a world immersed in silence and totally devoid of meaning. Even if we could decipher its garbled signs, we would not know how to interpret them. Our faith in a rational universe and in the perfectibility of language proves to be illusory.

Whereas Bremer's poem is governed by repetition and subtraction, other works employ addition or a combination of the two operations. That these simple devices can be extraordinarily effective is demonstrated by Augusto de Campos's elegant poem protesting the condition of the Brazilian peasant (MES, p. 95). Angered at the appalling poverty of a large portion of the population, and at the government's lack of concern, the poet crafted an eloquent response.

sem um numero
    um numero
        numero
          zero
            um
              o
                  nu
                      mero
                        numero
                          um numero
                            um sem numero

According to the first line, much of the peasant's predicament stems from the fact that he is "sem um numero" ("Without a number"). He has never received any of the numerical forms of recognition invented by modern civilization. He has no idea what a draft card is, for example, nor has he ever visited a Social Security office. And since he has no money, he obviously pays no taxes. Due to his itinerant lifestyle, he has probably never even encountered a census taker. Thus the peasant's continued neglect is related to his anonymous position in society. Since he has never exchanged his name for a number, the government is not officially aware of his existence.

At first glance, the second and third lines appear to contradict this impression. By subtracting the preposition "sem" they manage to assign the peasant a number after all. Unexpectedly, we learn from the next three lines that both statements are actually true. So far as the politicians and bureaucrats are concerned, he is simply a big fat "zero." Translated into mathematical terms, this judgement is rendered a second time as "um o" ("a 0"). How rapidly the peasant's fortune has deteriorated can be seen from the text's tapering silhouette. By the time he reaches the center his social, political, and economic marginalization is complete. Stripped bare ("nu") by forces beyond his control, he retains his dignity and basic simplicity ("mero"). Despite the calamities that have befallen him, his fundamental purity ("mero" again) is unaffected.

If the first half of the poem charts the peasant's decline, the second half seems to predict his resurgence. Little by little his luck appears to change as he succeeds in regaining his original position. Judging from the work's appearance, the two operations are perfectly symmetrical. And yet when he arrives at what looks like his point of departure, we discover the reversal is not complete. Unaccountably, two of the words in the final line have been transposed. The upward journey turns out to lead not back to the beginning but in the opposite direction. The unfortunate peasant, who still has no number, has become "um sem número" – one of "innumerable" individuals exactly like him. Instead of a gradual resurgence there has been a population explosion. The first and last lines constitute the twin poles of the peasant's existence. Although he and his fellows *do not count* from the government's perspective, they exist in *countless* numbers. According to de Campos, the peasantry is plagued by two symmetrical evils: invisibility and a burgeoning population, whose relation to each other is doubly tragic. On the one hand, despite their decreasing resources, there are more and more peasants every day. On the other, despite their steadily increasing numbers, the peasants' plight has failed to attract any attention.

In addition to the techniques identified above, most of the poetry in the fourth category employs permutation and/or combination. Because this is primarily a linguistic phenomenon, it may or may not be recorded at the visual level. This describes one of Gomringer's poems, for instance, in which he juggles a tree, a child, a dog, and a house. Comprising four stanzas and a conclusion, it is organized according to the formula a(ab) + b(bc) + c(cd) + d(da) = abcd.

>baum
>baum kind
>
>kind
>kind hund
>
>hund
>hund haus
>
>baum kind hund haus
>(SB, p. 46).

The absence of a visual component is even more pronounced in a "Statistical Text" by Max Bense (MES, p. 122). Beginning with six words: "es" ("it"), "ist" ("is"), "wenn" ("if"), "aber" ("but"), "doch" ("still"), and "nicht" ("not"), he weaves them together in multiple combinations to form a seemingly endless catalogue.

es, ist, wenn, aber, doch, nicht; es ist, es doch,
es aber, wenn es, wenn ist, es nicht, aber ist,
doch ist, wenn doch, wenn aber, nicht ist, aber
doch, doch nicht, wenn nicht, aber nicht; wenn
es ist, es aber ist, ist es doch, wenn es aber, wenn
es doch, es aber doch, es nicht ist, es doch
nicht, wenn doch ist, wenn aber ist, aber doch
ist, es aber nicht, wenn es nicht, doch nicht ist,
wenn aber doch, wenn nicht ist, ist aber nicht,
wenn doch nicht, wenn aber nicht, aber doch
nicht; wenn es aber ist, es aber doch ist, wenn
es doch ist, wenn es aber doch, es doch nicht ist,
wenn es nicht ist, es aber nicht ist, wenn es
aber nicht, wenn aber doch ist, es aber doch
nicht, wenn es doch nicht, wenn doch nicht ist,
aber doch nicht ist, wenn aber nicht ist, wenn
aber doch nicht; wenn es aber doch ist, wenn
es aber nicht ist, wenn es doch nicht ist, es aber
doch nicht ist, wenn es aber doch nicht, wenn
aber doch nicht ist; wenn es aber doch nicht ist.

Concrete Poetry at the Crossroads

If it is hard to conceive of a visual design that would complement Bense's poem, it is equally difficult to imagine most of the Brazilian works without one. Since examples are plentiful, let us examine another, related genre instead which, like permutational poetry, tends to be highly verbal. Rather than variations on a theme, these works seek to effect some kind of metamorphosis. By adding, deleting, or transposing certain letters the poet succeeds in transforming one verbal manifestation into another. And since whatever affects the signifiers tends to affect the signifieds, a conceptual metamorphosis occurs as well. The best-known example, by the American poet Emmett Williams, manages to transform the words "SENSE SOUND" into "SOUND SENSE" in only four operations (EW, n. p.). Nevertheless, insofar as its appearance is concerned the poem is unremarkable. The final work, by Haroldo de Campos, demonstrates how visual and verbal elements may enter into collusion to produce a striking composition.[21]

```
                    voir
                    voir le
        entre
                    voir le
                    voir le vert
        entre
                    verts
                    ver s
                      le
                    vio le  t
        entrouvert
```

Although the poem glories in its fundamental indeterminacy, its structure is crystal clear. The poet has taken great care to divide the verbal elements into parallel groups in order to stress their similarity and their relation to each other. Each word, each group of words contributes to the work's organic development and leads to its conclusion. In contrast to the prefix "entre," which survives relatively unscathed, the infinitive "voir" ("to see") is transformed into the past participle of another verb entirely: *ouvrir* ("to open"). If the left-hand column invites the reader to "*enter*" the poem at three junctures, the metamorphosis is

---

21 Haroldo de Campos, untitled poem, *Texte Buchstabe Bild*, ed. by Felix Andreas Baumann (Zurich: Zürcher Kunstgesellschaft, 1970), plate 36.

restricted to the column on the right. The composition itself is divided into three movements followed by a coda. The first stanza consists of an invitation to gaze at an unspecified object that has not yet entered our field of vision. While the article "le" testifies to its proximity, not until the second stanza do we glimpse ("entrevoir"), the object in question. Unexpectedly, we discover we are looking at the color green ("vert") rather than a concrete artefact. Indeed, the third stanza suggests there may be several different shades by making the adjective plural.

The addition of an ambiguous homonym at this point introduces a whole new range of possibilities. For if the original green is situated "entre verts," it is also positioned "entre ver s" – between two lines of poetry or, conceivably, between two earthworms. At the same time, since *"ver s"* may also be a preposition (*"toward"*), it introduces an additional color: violet. Whether the single green or the multiple greens are juxtaposed with this color is impossible to say. The syntax offers no clue as to the "correct" reading. And yet it presumably makes a difference whether the violet is enclosed by the multiple greens or is located outside them. Synthesizing the preceding developments, the final term is subject to the same undecidability. While "entrouvert" ("gaping") seems to describe the violet hue, it could also refer to the green evoked initially. More than anything, perhaps, the shifting patterns and colors express the author's kaleidoscopic vision. In addition, they recall his brother's attempts to wed polychromatic poetry to music early in his career.[22] Like concrete poetry in general, as Finlay reminds us, the composition is "a model of order, even if set in a space which is full of doubt" (cited in SB, p. 9). As Clüver remarks in another context, "there is nothing arbitrary here, and yet everything rests on chance."[23]

---

22 See Claus Clüver, "Klangfarbenmelodie in Polychromatic Poems: A. von Webern and A. de Campos," *Comparative Literature Studies*, vol. XVIII, no. 3 (September 1981), 386–98.
23 Clüver, "Reflections on Verbivocovisual Ideograms," 139.

Semiotic Conditions of Originality in Concrete Poetry

Elizabeth Walther

ARISTOTLE HAD ALREADY designed a theory of signs, whereby he distinguished the signs, their objects and their meanings, and particularly the signmaker or *semiotikós*. The signmaker is not only someone who creates signs but also one who frames signs in a new way for better understanding, or representing things or events, and informing someone about something.

There are many sign-systems: visual, vocal, tactile, olfactory, and verbal, and also gestures, play of features, and the so-called body language. The highest, mightiest signs mankind possesses are languages, that is: repertoires of words, grammars, and syntaxes. Words, syntax and grammar are different in all languages; their rules depend upon speech communities and history, that is, they may change continuously.

Universal repertories may be divided into special smaller repertories, namely into the repertories of everyday language, of scientific languages, military language, etc., but also into repertories of restricted groups like families, children, students, craftsmen, etc., and in individual repertories of writers of any kind. There are words belonging to greater or smaller repertories depending on purposes or ends. The given words of the repertories are often used by persons without thinking about them, just as they learned and imitated them.

But there are also domains constructed by words and graphic signs, photographs, mathematical formulas, etc. depending on certain goals in science, design, arts, architecture, music, advertising and many other domains, and the systems of verbal signs constructed with them are, for instance, scientific books, articles, radio plays, posters, and information of all kinds such as letters, telegrams, phone calls, newsletters, reviews, journals, radio, television, and internet.

In addition, literary books, novels, poems, dramas, biographies, etc.

are verbal sign-systems. Their repertoires of words may be combined to build expressions, images, metaphors, comparisons, statements, assertions, conclusions, etc. In any case, they are the material of literary works. Poets use the learned words to make a work of art; that is something not yet known, an originality, a novelty. It is always surprising that the poet creates some new text or poem out of the "heap of old, used up words" as Francis Ponge, the French poet, said, or out of so many former texts of all kinds; but this is the whole intention of poets.

Words are nothing but the basis upon which the writer is creating his literary work. In addition, he must possess an idea (that is the background), and he must shape the words into an original form by certain general or special rules. There are traditional forms, known for a long time, but also new forms created by the respective writers. In literature, for instance in prose, we have words following one another, successively or one-dimensionally arranged words, but in poetry, we look upon words arranged in the plane, two-dimensionally shaped. Texts in prose do not need two-dimensional arrangements. But poems of all kinds, and not just in concrete poetry, were always carefully placed upon the page. Its total visual appearance is an iconical representation; it is the model of all similar forms. The reader may grasp immediately the poem's figure as a whole.

In the 1950s, Haroldo de Campos, Augusto de Campos and Décio Pignatari, known as the "Group Noigandres," founded the concrete movement in Brazil. Haroldo in his article in "Minima poética" (1999), thinks that the cycle of concrete poetry has only been interrupted, but nowadays we should better speak of "post-utopian poetry" to express our engagement. A new avant-garde should utilize all the new techniques like holography, laser, computer, television and so on, which could bring us to a new iconic, figurative language.

Obviously, also in concrete poetry the goal was to create a new poem, a new text, but with very few words from small repertoires, and to arrange them in a new way, to bring them in a new order never brought before. The play on words, the construction of words, the distortion of words, every action upon words was allowed. To show the words in all their facets, to bring them to light, that was the starting point of all concrete poets. The arrangement, the order, of these few words will direct the reader's attention particularly to the words themselves with all their different meanings, comprising different associations, allusions, and also their figurative sense. Objects, people, and events are represented by words, that is true, but this is not the main intention of poets. The goal is to present these chosen words for this particular text or poem, and this particular arrangement of words for some intellectual, political or sensible purpose. But besides, they also represent the author himself and his expressiveness.

We must not forget that words, also in concrete poetry, depend on their contexts and their arrangements. To work on words or with words, to create new constellations, new orders, new views is our friend Haroldo de Campos's goal too, but in a particular meaning. Creating a literary work, Haroldo uses words of different repertories, general repertories, restricted repertories of literature, painting, music, philosophy, natural sciences, medicine, sociology, plays, sports, etc. In this way, he chooses, first of all, his own repertory. By his repertory he is recognizable.

Another remark besides: It is known that Haroldo de Campos is not only interested in creating poems or texts in his own language, but in translating texts from other languages, in mediating between the others and his own language, and in "recreating" a literary text.

But not only words constitute a text. There are, of course, intellectual, even political, purposes or ideas, too. And a text considered as a sign-system also needs special relationships between the words, then by these relationships are made phrases, sentences, paragraphs, chapters, verses, strophes, and, finally, the whole text or poem. Isolated words as they appear in dictionaries are what Charles Peirce termed "legisigns," but brought into any context by an author they are realized, individual or singular signs, "sinsigns" as the American semiotician called them.

To give an example of the semiotical approach to a literary text, I would analyze semiotically one of Haroldo's poems. I must emphasize beforehand that this analysis is only a first step and can never be a complete illumination of its semiotical complexity.

I have chosen the following poem, and I quote first the original, and second the German translation.

Anatomia do Gol

jogar um
jogo
é como
jogar o jogo

Elizabeth Walther

da pintura ou
do poema

jogar o jogo
do poema
(ou da pintura)
é como
jogar qualquer
jogo

as mãos jogam
cartas ou
basquete
na
mesa ou na
quadra
os pés jogam
bola
no
campo ou na
praia

mas quem joga
mesmo é o
cérebro
suas bossas e
cerebelo
seus lobos:
um jogo de luz
sem peso
que faz passar por
um triz
por um cabelo
ou acertar
em cheio:
mão de baralho
plena
ou pé no tiro
certeiro

antonio
lizárraga joga
um jogo de
cartas marcadas
um jogo onde tudo joga
e tudo faz jogada

um futbol de papel
com peças de diamante
triângulos
setas
arestas
acuando o círculo
migrante

retranca aberta
dábliu-eme
pelo meio
ferrolho suíço
casados contra solteiros
pona reduado
overlapping
pelas pontas
triangulagem
carrossel holandês
quadrado mágico

chegados neste qua-
drado
a gente pára e medita:
se o círculo9 ficou acuado
se pensa como o estagi-
rita
ou se ainda foge →
evasivo →
perseguido por sagi-
tas →

o que se vê é o centro:
um triângulo   uma

tríade
(como charles sanders
peirce
gostava de ver com a
mente)
todo de branco o habita
é o uno posto no trino?
É o primeiro
Concluso no seu
Terceiro?
São as de pitágoras
Últimas categorias
Primevas?

Não se não sabe-
Mos
Por mais
Que e gente dê tratos
À bola
Ninguém atinge essa
Meta (sol)
Onde se exaura a pintura
E o poema:
Sede secreta
(gol)

Anatomie des Tors

ein spiel
spielen
ist wie
das spiel
der malerei oder
des gedichtes spielen

das spiel
des gedichtes
(oder der malerei) spielen
ist wie

irgendein spiel
spielen

die hände spielen
karten oder
basketball
auf dem
tisch oder auf dem
platz
die füße spielen
ball
auf dem
fußballfeld oder am
strand

aber was
wirklich spielt ist das
gehirn

seine talente und
das kleinhirn
seine lappen:
ein lichtspiel
ohne gewicht
das knapp
um ein haar
passen
oder ins schwarze
treffen lässt:
hand voller spielkarten
oder fuß beim
treffsicheren schuss

antonio
lizárraga spielt
ein spiel mit
gezinkten karten
ein spiel wo alles spielt
und alles gespielt wird

Elizabeth Walther

ein fußball aus papier
mit diamantstücken
dreiecke
pfeile
kanten
den beweglichen kreis
verlassend

offene defensive
we - em
durch die mitte
schweizer riegel

verheiratete gegen ledige
zurückweichende spitze
overlapping
an den spitzen
dreiecksbildung
holländisches karussell
magisches quadrat

angekommen an diesem
quadrat
hält man inne und überlegt:
wenn der kreis zurückgewichen ist
denkt man wie der stagirit
oder wenn er noch flieht →
ausweichend →
verfolgt von pfeilen →

was man sieht ist die mitte:
ein dreieck   eine
triade
(wie charles sanders
peirce
sie gern im geiste
sah)
ganz in weiß gekleidet
ist es die eins im dreifachen?
ist es die erstheit

> eingeschlossen in ihrer
> drittheit?
> sind es die pythagoreischen
> letzten ursprünglichen
> kategorien?
>
> ich weiss nicht   wir wissen
> nicht
> so gut
> man auch
> den ball behandelt
> niemand erreicht dieses
> ziel (Sonne)
>
> wo die malerei sich erschöpft
> und das gedicht
> geheimes verlangen
> (tor)
>
> (Translator: Elisabeth Walther, assisted by Rosa Carreira.)

For a better understanding of this poem, and understanding means *interpreting*, the best way, I thought, was to translate it into my own language. But I must admit that this way involves many other difficulties: the translated or interpreted text is in any case other than the original. But only by translating Haroldo's poem into German did I discover this poem's manifold meanings. For instance, I found that Haroldo uses different repertories of the Portuguese language: repertories of medicine, play in general, card-playing, poetry and painting, sports, the semiotics of Charles Peirce and the philosophy of Aristotle and Pythagoras, and so on. In literature, connections of repertories are not very surprising, but in Haroldo's poem they are made in an elegant, subtle manner.

This poem, semiotically speaking, is a complex sign, a supersign, a sign system, built up in two parts: the *title* and the following *text*. The title is an index of the whole poem that follows. It says: something will follow, namely the poem as such, and what is *expressed* in the title will be *explained* in the following text. The title "Anatomy of the Goal" is built on two nouns from two different repertories: the first is a medical term, meaning also the inner structure of something, the second belongs to the domain of sports, but it means also: aim, end, target. Unfortunately, in German this second meaning does not exist, so that the title's translation into German becomes too poor. "Anatomy" and "goal" are related by "of the" (do), the genitive of the article. The two nouns, considered separately, are "rhematic legisigns," following Peirce, and they represent general objects, that is, they represent "symbolically" or by "symbols." Here they build the phrase "anatomy of the goal." Its possible interpretation is "rhematic," it is an "open connex," as Max Bense explained the Peircean "rhema." There is no possibility of maintaining or judging this phrase, because phrases are never true or false. But every word suggests some meaning, and put together, they could be considered as a surprising, unusual, enigmatic, singular metaphor, more precisely, semiotically speaking, they are a "rhematic iconic sinsign."

The following *text* is divided in fourteen strophes of different verses without rhymes, and of different lengths. The first strophe is the comparison: "playing a play is like playing painting or poetry." The second strophe is a comparison, too: "playing the play of poetry or painting is like playing a play whatsoever." I do not know, if Haroldo remembered the aesthetics of Schiller, in which the concept of "play" is the most important aesthetical conception. Schiller considers all the arts as plays, and, obviously, Haroldo does the same. But there are not only comparisons in his poem. We observe also sentences, statements, descriptions, assertions, associations, questions, narrations, allusions, and plays on words. The combination of all these verbal possibilities shows Haroldo's capacity to handle these different forms and to bring them together in a unique manner.

From the play in general and that of the arts in the third strophe he turns, in the main, to details: first to hands and feet that are playing cards, basketball or football. He does not speak of men or women who are playing with something, but of hands and feet, and in the fourth strophe in particular of the brain, the cerebellum and the lobes which are playing and which may be considered as the inner structure of the player, the footballer or the artist. In this way, he reaches the "anatomy," not yet of the goal, but maybe of someone who is playing.

Translating this poem, I observed the very elaborated transitions from one idea to the next, from card playing to football playing, to "playing" the arts and to all the plays whatsoever. Only one proper name besides Pythagoras, Aristotle and Peirce is mentioned in the sixth strophe:

Antonio Lizárraga. I had to ask Haroldo to inform me about him. Antonio Lizárraga, I was told, is an Argentine painter who made a book with Haroldo about playing football. There is no quality given, no attribute to him, it is only said that "he is playing a play of marked cards." I confess that I did not completely understand the meaning of this sentence. At such a point arises a very important question for the context of the people, objects and events mentioned in this poem, and likewise for the whole poem's context. For the whole poem represents another semiotic level other than the contexts of the mentioned objects or events. Only the strophes all together, in toto, are representing the poet's intention.

In particular, it is the football match that is described by comparing it with something totally different, namely with the arts, with the Peircean triad of signs, and with the ultimate categories of Aristotle and Pythagoras. Only at the end of the poem appears an "I," the author's I, and an "Us," probably the author's and the reader's Us. Both, author and reader, do not know anything. All the efforts at playing ball do not lead to the goal (*meta*), and where painting and poem come to an end, there rests the secret thirst (*sede*) for the goal, the aim that never will be realized. All activities in sport and arts come only to a temporary stop. All plays and all works of art are fragments and will never come to perfection. They belong to the open system of arts or of sport which has no limits. But it is evident too, that *this* poem (or any other literary text) has come to its end: it is achieved; nothing could be changed without destroying it. It is no longer an "open" sign system.

Obviously, poems or paintings finished or broken off are bounded parts, small systems of the greater system of the possible author's works, belonging to the unlimited general system of literature. Here arise more interesting semiotic problems which I cannot handle now. We are capable of perceiving the author through the relationships in his works. They show some qualities by which the work is recognizable as the work of a certain author. Even if he does not express his feelings, he already expresses his own repertory through the chosen words. Choosing a repertory is an intellectual activity, which depends upon exact thinking on the one side and great sensitivity to their vocal qualities on the other side. Each word possesses a richness of possible meanings, a great semantic richness, as Francis Ponge emphasized so often. So, it is highly important to choose the "right" word, in every respect.

Through a published poem or literary text the author seeks to communicate with a reader, who recognizes the informational or communicational capacity of signs. Max Bense forced attention to this important point in his informational and semiotic aesthetics. In this way, each reader is an interpreter, a translator of the written text, even if he or she is not capable of translating immediately the aesthetic information received. Obviously, a reader is restricted by their interpretative capacity, knowledge, the intensity of their feelings, in short, by their interpretation field. I do not think that, in future, iconic signs will play an eminent role in literature, as Haroldo seems to maintain. The verbal expression is richer, more flexible, more precise than all images. Silent films need more activities and movements than sound films. Images without verbal explanations are ambiguous; they give only superficial information. If one does not already know the represented thing, a photograph gives only an image of some person, some landscape. Iconic signs must be explained by indexical signs (a proper name for instance) or by some symbolic signs. So, particularly in literature it seems impossible to give up indexical and symbolic signs.

But I must admit that Haroldo is right in considering iconic signs as the *structure*, the *form* of the literary work that immediately may be perceived. The form, the figure, the Gestalt, the well-shaped material, that is the iconic aspect not alone in logic (the conclusion figure), but also in literature. On the other hand, we must consider the *semiotic state* or the *aesthetic state* of any work of art, for these are really the same, as Max Bense emphasized in his semiotic aesthetics. Both can be characterized by the same sign class, namely the sign class of the sign itself, which Charles Peirce set in the great triangle's centre of his ten sign classes, and upon which all the others sign classes depend. So, the basis of poetry, or of any work of art, is this semiotic-aesthetical sign class, which is also the semiotic basis of any intellectual or artistic activity.

The Last Voyage[1]

Piero Boitani

READERS WILL HAVE to forgive me for beginning on a personal note. I first came across *Finismundo* in the second half of 1996, just after an international conference on Ulysses that I organized in Rome.[2] In 1992, without knowing anything about *Finismundo*[3] – which had appeared just two years previously – I published *L'ombra di Ulisse. Figure di un mito*,[4] which dealt with the reincarnations of this most polymorphous hero in European literature and history and which began with the famous ambiguity of Tiresias' prophecy to Odysseus in Book XI of the *Odyssey*.[5]

After predicting his return home, Tiresias tells Odysseus he shall have to embark on a last voyage directed towards a land where the sea, ships and salted food are not known. When he meets another traveller who takes his oar for a winnowing fan, Odysseus will know that he has reached his destination. He shall then make sacrifices to Poseidon and go

---

1 This is a slightly modified version of the address with which I concluded the conference *On Transcreation: Literary Invention, Translation and Culture (in honour of Haroldo de Campos)* in Oxford on 14 October, 1999. I am grateful to Else Vieira for having invited me, and feel privileged to have met there, and been heard by, Haroldo de Campos himself. I have deliberately kept changes in this printed version to a minimum. One could write an entire book on *Finismundo*, but this is only a short essay.
2 "Ulisse: Archeologia dell'Uomo Moderno," Rome, Palazzo delle Esposizioni, 29–31 May, 1996. The conference was accompanied by a superb exhibition organized by Bernard Andreae, the catalogue of which was published as *Ulisse: il mito e la memoria*, edited by B. Andreae and C. Parisi Presicce (Rome: Progetti Museali, 1996).
3 First published by Tipografia do Fundo de Ouro Preto. The edition from which I quote is *Sobre Finismundo: A Última Viagem* (Rio de Janeiro, Sette Letras, 1996), the first copy of which I owe to the courtesy of Ettore Finazzi Agrò and Maria Caterina Pincherle. This poem is also reprinted in *Crisantempo* (São Paulo: Editora Perspectiva, 1998), 53–9.
4 *L'ombra di Ulisse. Figure di un mito* (Bologna: Il Mulino, 1992, 2nd edn, 1999). In English, *The Shadow of Ulysses. Figures of a Myth*, translated by Anita Weston (Oxford University Press, 1994). The English edition is a slightly expanded version of the Italian original.
5 *Odyssey* XI, 119–37.

back to Ithaca. Finally, death will come to him *ex halos*: far away, or out of, the sea.

It seemed to me that all the adventures of Ulysses in subsequent literature arose out of the ambiguous meaning of Homer's expression, *ex halos*, and that each literary reincarnation of Ulysses foreshadowed – as if it were in a figural or typological manner – the next one, at the same time projecting both an existential and an historical halo. Thus, for instance, Dante's Ulysses "fulfills" Tiresias' prophecy by journeying westwards beyond the Pillars of Hercules and being shipwrecked by the "altrui," the supreme, unnamed Other representing the Christian God, the moment he sights the dark mountain of Purgatory, on the top of which lies Earthly Paradise.[6] In old age, "at this so short vigil of our senses," he embarks on a last voyage inevitably, and I think deep down intentionally, directed towards death. His journey is like the life of each human, from being to non-being. Yet the fact is that in *Inferno* XXVI, when Ulysses sights the other world, this is called "*nova* terra" – the *new* land. And Dante interpreters as well as poets like Tasso and fifteenth-century European explorers such as Amerigo Vespucci take the new land of Dante's Ulysses to be the New World, the Americas.[7]

One can therefore imagine how I felt when I read *Finismundo*. Here was a poet from the New World writing a poem on the Last Voyage which said, before me, much more briefly and much better than I could ever do, what I had been trying to say in my book and what, as I then wrote in a sequel to *The Shadow of Ulysses*,[8] I had been trying to live and conceive for the last forty years! Needless to say, we had an essay on *Finismundo* in the proceedings of the Rome conference,[9] which I sent, with a letter, to Haroldo de Campos.[10]

It may well be that one – the least important, of course – of Haroldo de Campos's destinies is that of anticipating Italian critics. He did so in

---

6 The text of the *Comedy* used here is that edited by A. M. Chiavacci Leonardi, *La Divina Commedia*, 3 vols. (Milan: Mondadori, 1991–7).
7 See *The Shadow of Ulysses*, *cit.*, 44–68, and references therein.
8 *Sulle Orme di Ulisse* (Bologna: Il Mulino, 1998).
9 *Ulisse: archeologia dell'uomo moderno*, ed. by P. Boitani and R. Ambrosini (Rome: Bulzoni, 1998). I am especially indebted to Maria Caterina Pincherle's essay in that volume (pp. 347–59), "Una Lettura di *Finismundo: a última viagem*, di Haroldo de Campos (1996)."
10 A wonderful correspondence then started, for which I would like to thank Helio Povoas, Jr., himself a passionate reader (and poet) of Ulysses.

1954 with Umberto Eco's later *Opera aperta*;[11] he has done it again with me in 1990 with *Finismundo*. But things in poetry, history and life are always slightly more complicated than mere coincidence or *Zeitgeist* seem to imply. Ulysses is ubiquitous in Western literature, and particularly in the twentieth century. Haroldo de Campos himself recalls (a-propos of *Galáxias*), an intertext which extends from Homer to Pound, Odorico Mendes, Father Vieira and Shakespeare.[12] He also mentions Joyce and T. S. Eliot.[13] But one could enlist in the Odyssean army of our century people like Conrad, D'Annunzio, Kafka, Bloch, Horkheimer, Adorno, Levinas, Derrida, Giono, Valery, Gide, Seferis, Kazantzakis, Fondane, Chagall, Canetti, Wallace Stevens, Primo Levi, Dallapiccola, Brodskij, Berio, and dozens of other philosophers, poets, novelists, musicians, painters and sculptors from all over Europe (particularly from Ireland) and the United States as well as from India and the Arab world.[14] Slowly, but with growingly significant results, the shadow of Ulysses moves to the Caribbeans and Latin America: Borges, Darío, Harris, Walcott, Carpentier, García Márquez, and many others.[15] There also exists – and it is obviously fundamental in the case of a Brazilian poet – a specifically Portuguese tradition. This begins in classical antiquity and makes Ulysses the founder of Lisbon (Ulixabona).[16] In due course, he becomes the ancestor of Vasco da Gama and Magellan. The names here include none less than Camões, Gabriel Pereira de Castro and Pessoa.[17]

It is, I believe, within this wider *imaginaire* that we have to place

---

11   See Eco's preface to the Brazilian edition of *Opera Aperta* (São Paulo: Perspectiva, 1968).
12   *Sobre Finismundo*, 26–7.
13   Ibid., 23.
14   See *The Oxford Guide to Classical Mythology in the Arts, 1300–1990s*, ed. by J. Reid (New York–Oxford: Oxford University Press, 1993), s.v. "Odysseus," 724–54. For further references to critical material, see *Ulisse: Archeologia*, 16, n. 14. For fuller discussion of some of these authors, see *The Shadow of Ulisses* and *Sulle Orme di Ulisse*, *passim*; and my "The Shadow of Ulysses Beyond 2001," *Comparative Criticism* 21 (1999), 3–19.
15   For Spanish-speaking Latin American writers, see N. Bottiglieri, "Ulisse Criollo," in *Ulisse: Archeologia*, 319–45. For English-speaking Caribbean poets, see "The Shadow of Ulysses Beyond 2001," p. 18, n. 40–6.
16   For references to Strabo, Solinus and others, see *The Shadow of Ulisses*, 18–19 and n. 10.
17   The *locus classicus* in Camões is *Os Lusíadas* VIII, 5, but see also V, 86–9. Gabriel Pereira de Castro's *Ulisséa, ou, Lisboa edificada* was published posthumously in Lisbon (Crasbeek) in 1636. See also Antonio de Sousa de Macedo, *Usillipo* (Lisbon: Alvarez, 1640). I have all too briefly examined Pessoa's *Mensagem* in *The Shadow of Ulisses*, 125–7; see also E. Finazzi Agrò's *"Per non essere esistendo: l'Ulisse di Fernando Pessoa,"* in *Ulisse: archeologia*, 303–17.

Finismundo, which therefore appears as part of an almost global intertext and as one of the latest of the shadows of Ulysses. In this respect, the genesis of the poem, which Haroldo de Campos already described in a note to the 1990 edition and on which he has expanded in the 1996 *Sobre Finismundo*,[18] is particularly interesting. For once, instead of anticipating an Italian critic, he actually followed one – D'Arco Silvio Avalle, who in an essay entitled "L'ultimo viaggio di Ulisse," had pointed out the "semiological models" that underlie the story of *Inferno* XXVI.[19] From Avalle's piece Haroldo de Campos moved on to Boccaccio's *Amorosa Visione*, where a clearly Dantean Ulysses is said to have transgressed, going beyond the sign in order to see: "per voler veder trapassò il segno."[20] This indeed became the epigraph to *Finismundo*'s first section.

In other words, the poet started from the interpretation (Avalle's) of an interpretation (Boccaccio's). *Finismundo* appears at first sight not so much as transcreation but as transexegesis, transmidrash. The primary text, Dante's own, surfaces only halfway through section 1 with "il folle volo"[21] and then stares into our eyes in the heading of section 2 with Virgil's peremptory order to the flame which envelops Ulysses and Diomedes, "ma l'un di voi dica / dove per lui perduto a morir gissi" (let one of you say where, being lost, he went to die).[22] In between these two moments, transcreation brews like faraway thunder coming nearer and

18 The 1990 note is reproduced in *Crisantempo*, 352–3. The genesis of the poem is described at length in *Sobre Finismundo*, 13–27. In an ideal essay on *Finismundo*, one would have to devote many pages to *Galáxias* (São Paulo, Ex-Libris, 1984), where many of *Finismundo*'s themes incubate in a fairly different stylistic register. I could sum up my personal view of the similarities and differences between the two by saying that *Galáxias* is a baroque, *Finnegans Wake*-version of both Homeric poems while *Finismundo* sounds like a *Ulysses*-rewriting of the *Odyssey*, Dante, and…Joyce's *Ulysses*.
19 D'Arco Silvio Avalle, "L'ultimo viaggio di Ulisse," in his *Modelli Semiologici nella Commedia di Dante* (Milan: Bompiani, 1975), 33–63. Haroldo de Campos's devotion to semiotics is well known. On this path, he has also encountered, among the Italians, Umberto Eco and, particularly as regards medieval texts and Dante, Cesare Segre. One should at least refer to his critical and theoretical work: *Metalinguagem* (Petrópolis: Vozes, 1967); *Metalinguagem e Outras Metas* (São Paulo: Perspectiva, 1992); *A Operação do Texto* (São Paulo: Perspectiva, 1976).
20 G. Boccaccio, *Amorosa Visione*, A XXVII, 85-8, in *Tutte le opere di G. Boccaccio*, ed. by V. Branca, vol. III (Milan: Mondadori, 1974), 92. The hybris of Boccaccio's Dantean Ulysses is accepted by Petrarch, too (*Triumphus Fame* II, 18, in F. Petrarca, *Opere italiane*, vol. II, gen. ed. M. Santagata [Milan: Mondadori, 1996], 398), in spite of his identifying with Ulysses in the *Familiares*. See *The Shadow of Ulysses*, 45–8.
21 *Inferno* XXVI, 125.
22 *Inferno* XXVI, 83–4.

nearer.

Yet things are far more complex. The epic hero of the poem's first part is in fact called Odysseus, following Homer rather than Dante, while the second part does not look Dantean at all, but rather like an upside down, post-modern version of Joyce's Ulysses. Furthermore, in the first section we get, quoted in the original, both Dante's *folle volo* and Homer's *thanatos ex halos*. In sum, the poem's epigraphs and lines force us to one somersault after another and to a continuous displacement in time and tradition, simultaneously constructing a sort of Chinese-box system of transmyth, staging a – literal, as one might appropriately say in this case – *mise en abyme* of its own theme.

This is no small feat. Brazilians like to think of themselves and their culture as being "on the margins." But it seems to me that if a culture is capable of expressing a writer who tackles (shall I dare say, given his Brazilian provenance, "cannibalizes") Homer, Dante and Joyce in one poem, then it is placing itself in the living center of Western tradition. The game – a great "agon" with the Canon itself[23] – is dangerous and could become fatal, Lucifer-like indeed. But Haroldo de Campos is as cunning as Ulysses and survives the whirlpool.[24] Let me point to just one detail to show how brave and *bravo* he is. In the epigraph to section 1, we find Boccaccio using two key words to describe the enterprise of Dante's Ulysses, "trapassò" and "segno." The former contains the root "passo," which alludes to Dante's own *Inferno* XXVI. In recounting his story there, Ulysses calls the sailing beyond Gibraltar "alto passo," the great "pass" or "journey beyond."[25] And this is a clear echo of Dante the pilgrim's own experience as described at the very beginning of the *Inferno*, when, likening himself to one who has survived shipwreck (precisely like Homer's Odysseus), he says he then looked back to contemplate "lo passo / che non lasciò già mai persona viva," the pass which never yet let any go alive.[26] The second and third stanzas of

---

23 Both "agon" and "canon" as used here are Harold Bloom's concepts. See his *Agon* (New York: Oxford University Press, 1982) and *The Western Canon* (New York: Riverhead Books, 1994). Discussing Haroldo de Campos's work (especially *Galáxias*) in the light of T. S. Eliot's idea of "Tradition and Individual Talent" and H. Bloom's view of the "struggle with the Father(s)" could be fruitful.

24 By "cunning" I also mean, according to the word's etymology, "knowing," "experienced," very able at making things with his hands and words, hence formally astute.

25 *Inferno* XXVI, 132: "passo" also alludes to imminent dying, "passing" (away); "alto passo" is the supreme "step" and "passing."

26 *Inferno* I, 26–7: this "passo" is, in Dante's allegorical view, that of mortal sin.

Finismundo 1 obsessively return to this: "vedando mais / um *passo* – onde *passar avante* quer / dizer trans-/ gredir a medida," "trans-/*passar o passo*." The last voyage is both Ulysses's and Dante's journey: transgressing, trespassing.

Let me introduce a further complication. The Italian "trapassare" also means to pierce through, to penetrate. Haroldo de Campos picks up this, too, for the last voyage of his Odysseus is defined as an attempt at "breaking the seal of the forbidden," a pretty strong "deflowering" – "des-/virginar" – of the veil.[27] Finally, the Italian "segno" indicates a "mark" in all its physical as well as metaphorical meanings. In *Inferno* XXVI, Hercules is said to have set up his marks at Gibraltar ("segnò li suoi riguardi") so that man should not pass beyond.[28] In *Paradiso* XXVI (the heavenly parallel of *Inferno* XXVI) Adam and Eve's original sin is called "il trapassar del segno."[29] *Finismundo* plays on these as well as other forms of the word. In part 1 Hercules's "watching pillars warn the wave: forbidding another step – where to proceed further means to trans-gress measure, the seal-ing signs [or marks: *si-gilosas siglas*] of No." Towards the end of section 1, when Odysseus, having lost his companions, sights the "longed for island," the "reachable Eden" almost at hand, the sky – or heaven, all that is left of Dante's ambiguous "altrui" appropriately transcreated as "céu"[30] – "prompts the leaps of the arcane" and the deep. Thrown back, the ship, like Melville's *Pequod*,[31] sinks into

27 In a thorough examination of *Finismundo*, I would speculate on the possible meaning(s) of this "véu," which is clearly tied to the "lacre" and the "proibido" of the preceding line.

28 *Inferno* XXVI, 108–9. Dante's lines are clear, yet deeply ambiguous. See my "Dall'ombra di Ulisse all'ombra d'Argo," in *Dante: mito e poesia*, M. Picone and T. Crivelli, eds. (Florence: Cesati, 1999), 207–26 (at p. 217).

29 *Paradiso* XXVI, 117. Haroldo de Campos refers to this line in his "elucidação" to the 1990 edition of *Finismundo* (now in *Crisantempo*, 353). Another critical Canto of the *Comedy* is *Purgatorio* XXVI, where Dante encounters his "fathers" in vernacular poetry, Guido Guinizzelli and Arnaut Daniel – a passage which would certainly appeal to a poet who, with his brother, has translated the latter as well as Pound, "il miglior fabbro" – for T. S. Eliot in *The Waste Land* – of *Purgatorio* XXVI, 117. And see Augusto and Haroldo de Campos, *Traduzir & Trovar* (São Paulo: Papyrus, 1968), 27–8 (Augusto); and, with D. Pignatari, *Antologia Poética de Ezra Pound* (Lisboa: Ulisséia, 1968; orig. edn, *Cantares de Ezra Pound*, Rio de Janeiro: MEC/Serviço de Documentação, 1960, expanded in 1983 and 1985).

30 The Italian "altrui" (the dative: "to another") is unnamed and could be impersonal (God, fate, fortune): "céu," meaning both "sky" and "heaven" or "Heaven," is a perfect rendering of this ambiguity.

31 H. Melville, *Moby Dick*, ed. H. Beaver (Harmondsworth: Penguin, 1972), 684–5: "And now, concentric circles seized the lone boat itself [...]carried the smallest chip of the Pequod out of sight." This is the "closing vortex" of the last page (687).

the abyss gulped down by destiny. What it leaves for a moment, precisely like the *Pequod*,[32] are bare signs, "passing traces in the whirlpool" (*efêmeros sinais no torvelinho*). They float on, yet also founder in an instant. Then, water only and "rasuras," the minimal leftovers of erasure. Dante's signs are becoming Mallarmé's;[33] the shipwreck, writing's ultimate fate. In the ironical version of part 2, the signs appear again as "the minimal trace digited and soon cancelled in the liquid green-flowing crystal" (the limited but potentially infinite, ever moving computer screen), and as automatic traffic lights, intermittently bringing almost meaningless[34] signs ("sema-foros").

At this point one should perhaps ask what exactly is the last voyage of *Finismundo*. Is it the traditional, Dantean one which it transcreates by joining *Odyssey* XI to *Inferno* XXVI? If so, then for this particular reader Haroldo de Campos's last voyage leads from Gibraltar to the West, to the Southwest and the "altro polo": in sum, following the traditional *imaginaire*, to South America, which Columbus and the first explorers thought of as a Garden of Eden. One could even imagine that this "reversed Ithaca" is Brazil, the medieval and sixteenth-century "island,"[35] and that the city which, in the poem's second section, is ironically called "penúltima...Tule," is in fact São Paulo.

This would give *Finismundo* a splendid, and doubly ironical, *Odyssey*-like, circular structure, somewhat akin to Joyce's *Ulysses*, which begins and ends in Leopold Bloom's house though Bloom himself dreams, in the novel's last but one section, of a last journey on which, for fear of incipient senescence, he would embark towards the ends of the Earth and then "to the extreme limit of his cometary orbit, beyond the fixed stars and variable suns and telescopic planets, astronomical waifs and strays, to the extreme boundaries of space, passing from land to land, among

---

32 *Moby Dick*, 685 and 687. Ishmael survives his "wheeling circle" floating on Queequeg's coffin to tell the story, i.e., to narrate *Moby Dick* (the epigraph to the last page is from the Book of Job: "And I only am escaped alone to tell thee").
33 Mentioned by Haroldo de Campos himself, *Sobre Finismundo*, 22. See also Mallarmé's "Salut," "Brise marine," and "Un coup de dés." Haroldo and Augusto de Campos, with Décio Pignatari, translated *Mallarmé* (São Paulo, Perspectiva, 1974).
34 I am told that, as in Naples, traffic lights do not mean much in São Paulo.
35 See Luciana Stegagno Picchio, *La letteratura brasiliana* (Turin: Einaudi, 1997), 31 and 43–5.
36 James Joyce, *Ulysses* (New York, Random House, 1961), 727–8. Note that Leopold Bloom is afraid of incipient senescence, which brings him close to Dante's Ulysses. I have analysed the passage in "The Shadow of Ulysses Beyond 2001," 3–5.

peoples, amid events."[36] In other words, Haroldo de Campos's last voyage would appear not just divided into two sections, the second parodically mirroring and teasing the first, but also as sequential narrative.[37] After the sea closes in over Odysseus, his next shadow, the urban Ulysses, "outliving" myth ("sobrevivido ao mito"), gets lost and, according to the Dantean epigraph, "goes to die" in our time and in our space.

Finismundo, then, becomes a parable. But why, a reader might ask, "finismundo"? Is this the *finis terrae* of ancient maps, the end of the world in spatial terms? Or is it, as for João Cabral,[38] the world at the end, the world of the ending in temporal, eschatological terms? The poem offers us no explicit answer. Towards the end, Ulysses' "ancient flame" is reduced to a flame-bringing "trifle," his Promethean fire to the "portable Lucifer" of a match's head. In the last lines piercing, incited sirens are said to cut now through Ulysses', and our, "daily heart" (which replaces the earlier and broader "heart of the Ocean sea"), and these quotidian ambulances, police cars, fire engines, the present versions of the archaic singers, could well be read as the shadows of the sirens announcing nuclear alarm and the end of the world as if they were Doomsday's trumpets.

In short, *Finismundo*'s contemporary legend "varies deviating," as the author says of the ancient one. It "unends the ending."[39] It makes a foolhardy, idiosyncratic reader like myself build up his own *opera aperta*. I therefore propose to call it not simply a triple transcreation or rewriting[40] of Homer, Dante and, say, Joyce, but also a fourth power "semiological model." Of, that is, at least four kinds of last journey.

One: a voyage through time, both forwards and backwards. I have already examined the movement towards the present and the end of the world. But in the course of the poem we are also swept towards the beginning, the "caos pelaginoso," "o mar / atrás do mar," in short to the *tohu wabohu*, the welter and waste and darkness ("ínvio obscuro"), the deep (the *tehinnom*) over which the *ruah elohim* of Genesis 1 hovered before Creation.[41] Haroldo de Campos is a passionate reader, and of

---

37 See the question by Ivan Teixeira and the answer by Haroldo de Campos in *Sobre Finismundo*, 29–30.
38 João Cabral, "O Fim do Mundo," in *O Engenheiro*.
39 The original is of course more complex: "desvaira variando: infinda o fim."
40 "Ri-Scrittura" is the word I would use in Italian: see n. 42 below.
41 Genesis 1, 1–2.

course a transcreator, of *Bereshit*, and indeed discusses Genesis at length in *Sobre Finismundo*.[42] In the poem's intertext, the face of the deep, the *arcano*, fuses the Bible with Homer, who calls the Ocean "genesis of the gods."[43]

Two: a journey to being and non-being, or paraphrasing Oswald de Andrade to both "tupy" *and* "not tupy": not to a place, but to an *outopos*, a utopia, the "aventuroso *deslugar.*" To a *locus contradictionis*: earthly and/but Paradise, "umbráculo" and/but "lucarna." There lies access to the "céu terrestre," a heaven which, however, is terrestrial. The daring ("ousar") that launches Odysseus further than return and beyond what is afterwards brings him to a great pre-Aristotelian and post-Einsteinian dimension: not to the finite, nor to the infinite, but to the trans-finite, the borderline between the universe and whatever might lie beyond, before or after it. The hybris that prompts him to "trans-pass the pass" leads him to a nice pre-Parmenidean and post-modern ontological cul-de-sac: the "*impasse*-to-be," an "enigma." The destination and destiny and erring folly of Odysseus' last voyage will then be the "non-mapped" end of the world (*finismundo*), where "the inviolate frontier"[44] of what has now become *extracéu* – out of the sky, outside and more than, heaven, *hyperspace* – begins. "Unredeemed and inevitable whirlpool-like mission"[45] indeed, the aim of which shifts all the time, unbalancing the reader until he ends up with a mere "postcard from Eden."

Three. This is of course a voyage of and towards poetry as well. Haroldo de Campos himself says as much in *Sobre Finismundo*.[46] It is a journey which begins with its own genesis, develops as a "hybris-prompted" cleaving of Poseidon's angry mirror, grows as a sailing on

---

42 Haroldo de Campos, *Bere'shith* (São Paulo: Perspectiva, 1994). His introduction to *Finismundo* in *Sobre Finismundo* significantly begins with a most interesting discussion of the poem's genesis, of Genesis and *toledoth* (pages 10–13). On the personal level on which I opened the present essay, may I mention the fact that Haroldo de Campos also anticipated me in this field. In 1997 I published a book entitled *Ri-Scritture* (Bologna: Il Mulino), now in English as *The Bible and its Rewritings* (Oxford: Oxford University Press, 1999). The elective affinities between us are indeed many.
43 *Iliad* XIV, 201.
44 In the original, "destino," "desatino," "não-mapeado / Finismundo," "infranqueada / fronteira."
45 "Irremissa / missão voraginosa": the whirlpool of *Inferno* XXVI and the abyss of Hell may both be present here.
46 *Sobre Finismundo*, 13–16: he sees his work as facing "o risco da criação pensado como um problema de viagem e como un problema de enfrentamento com o impossível, uma empresa que, se por um lado é punida com um naufrágio, por outro é recompensada com os destroços do naufrágio que constituem o próprio poema."

"the winedark heart of the Ocean sea" as if it were Dante's "gran mar de l'essere,"[47] and ends in shipwreck. The writer uses the ancient topos of the poet's enterprise as seafaring,[48] giving it a nice Mallarmean twist.[49] Once more, however, he complicates matters by not only identifying actual fragments of poetry as "passing traces in the vortex," as "rasuras" or, later, as the "minimal trace" digited and soon cancelled on the computer screen, but also by inviting us to stare at the furrow healing in Poseidon's breast, at the closing in of the sea, and to listen to the Ocean's resounding silence, to the calmed down cry of the Sirens.

The first move recalls Dante, who in *Paradiso* II presents himself as the pilot of a ship which "cantando varca" – singing goes beyond (transpasses) unknown seas – and who addresses his readers as the passengers of another boat, which holds his furrow before the water returns smooth again: "servando mio *solco* / dinanzi a l'acqua che ritorna equale."[50] The passage of *Paradiso* II – which of course Haroldo de Campos has translated elsewhere[51] – is filled with echoes and counterpoints of *Inferno* XXVI.[52] Thus, *Finismundo* joins the "sulco" to "clausurou-se o ponto," the reading to the writing, Heaven to Hell.

Tennyson had Ulysses point out to his sailors that "the deep / Moans round with many voices."[53] The round Ocean of Haroldo de Campos's *Finismundo* "resounds silently": it is a powerful oxymoron[54] for poetry and indeed for the reading of poetry, which becomes even more poignant in the following lines, the last ones of section 1, where the "convulsive song" of the Sirens, their "bittersweet cry," is presented as an "ultrasound *unperceived* by human ear."[55]

If this is what all poetry ends up as, where, ultimately, does the Last

---

47 The text is an original rewriting of the Homeric epithet, "o cor-de-vinho / coração do maroceano." The reference in Dante is to *Paradiso* I, 113. The translation by Haroldo de Campos in *Pedra e Luz na Poesia de Dante* (Rio de Janeiro: Imago, 1998, page 95) is "o imenso mar do ser."
48 See E. R. Curtius, *European Literature and the Latin Middle Ages*, translated by W. R. Trask (London: Routledge, 1953), 128–30.
49 See notes 33 and 45 above, and *Sobre Finismundo*, 22.
50 *Paradiso* II, 1–18. And cp. T. S. Eliot, *Four Quartets, The Dry Salvages*, III, 19-20.
51 See the beautiful translation in *Pedra e Luz*, 99.
52 I have examined the passage at length in *The Tragic and the Sublime in Medieval Literature* (Cambridge: Cambridge University Press, 1989), 250–78, at 262–7.
53 A. Tennyson, "Ulysses," 55–7. Tennyson, too, joins Tiresias' prophecy in *Odyssey* XI to *Inferno* XXVI.
54 Particularly powerful in the original: "O redondo / oceano ressona taciturno."
55 Italics mine. For parallels with the "silence" of the Sirens in Pascoli, Kafka, Benjamin, Blanchot, etc., see *The Shadow of Ulysses*, 129, 183–8; *Sulle orme di Ulisse*, 119–25.

Voyage of *Finismundo* lead? The answer is in a sense obvious: on the one hand, back to the Last War, which of course is also and always the First, the Trojan one – in short to the *Iliad*, in a transcreation of which the poet has been engaged for some time now; but, above all, *four*, to *Crisantempo* – a time of crisis, but also a blooming flower in and of time, a crystal of poetry.[56]

Perhaps I may be allowed to read the collection's title also as a "chrysalis" – the growing butterfly *in potentia*, hanging still on a silk thread, suspended between something and something else, between the earth and the sky, between creation and generation, sailing and foundering, writing and reading. I may perhaps be allowed to do this simply because I am, like most of us, a hypochondriac reader.[57] Because, following Walter Benjamin's and Haroldo de Campos's interpretation of Baudelaire,[58] I was the chosen, predestined *Leser*. Was I not, ever since I encountered, and worked on, Ulysses, Haroldo's *der Erwählte*?[59] I did not, of course, exist in the memory of God,[60] but I certainly am an *Hypocrit*, a sub-critic.

Yet I do feel I am Haroldo's *Freund* as well. It is as *semblable* and *frère* that I finally wish him happy birthday. Dante proclaimed that he had embarked on his last but one voyage, the *Comedy*'s, in the middle of the journey of our life, at thirty-five. At twice that, Haroldo de Campos has completed his last but one journey. Perhaps he will remember what T. S. Eliot, recalling Dante's Ulysses, wrote: "old men ought to be explorers."[61] So: not farewell, but fare forward, voyager.[62]

56   *Menis: A Ira de Aquiles* (*Iliad* I) appeared in 1994 (São Paulo: Nova Alexandria). It is interesting to note that already in 1996, while writing *Sobre Finismundo*, the poet should have changed the title of his forthcoming anthology from *Finismundo* to *Crisantempo*: see page 23.
57   "(Eu e Você meu hipo- / côndrico crítico / leitor)".
58   *Sobre Finismundo*, 33-6.
59   In Benjamin's translation of Baudelaire, and in Haroldo de Campos's quotation, *mein Erwählter*; but the Brazilian author also refers (*Sobre Finismundo*, 34) to Thomas Mann's *Der Erwählte*, to which, by yet another coincidence, I had devoted pages 131 to 134 of *The Tragic and the Sublime*.
60   *Sobre Finismundo*, 34 and 36.
61   T. S. Eliot, *Four Quartets, East Coker* V, 31.
62   *Four Quartets, The Dry Salvages* III, 19, 31, 44, 50–1. Haroldo de Campos seems to have taken this invitation literally: see his most recent poem, *A máquina do mundo repensada*, Granja Viana-Cotia-SP, Ateliê Editorial 2000, 1.1, 5.2, etc. The new poem "involves," the author writes, "a dialogue between (above all) three texts, Dante's *Inferno* I, *Purgatorio* XXIX, *Paradiso* XXXIII; Camões' *Os Lusíadas* V and X; and Drummond's 'A máquina do mundo'," with the addition of the cosmological theme from modern science and Genesis. The journey goes on indeed until Haroldo de Campos's death in the summer of 2003: the last voyage.

PART V

Haroldo de Campos: a Selected Anthology

Galáxias (1963–76)

'rounded by flowers / circuladô de fulô (21/24.02.65)

'rounded by flowers under god's under the devil's mercy god shall guide you for I myself can't guide godbless those who give me 'rounded by flowers and those who are still to give sounding like a shamisen made of a tensed wire a stick and an old tin can at the end of the partyfair at highnoonhigh but for many that music did not exist it could not because it could not popplay if not sung that music is not popular if not in tune it does not atone nor tarantina and yet struck in the gut of misery in the tensed gut of the meagerest physical misery aching aching like a nail in the handpalm a rusty blind nail in the palm clasping palm of the handheart exposed as a tensed nerve retensed a renigrated blind nail everlasting in the palmpulp of the hand in the sun while selling for meager cruzeiros gourds in which the good form is fine meagerness of matter morphing famineform of halfbaked clay in the rottenroot of distress until others vomit their plastic plates of embroidered borders empirestyle for mistress misery for this is popular for the patrons of the people but people create and people engender and people wonder people are the languageinventor in the malice of the mastery in the smartness of marveling in the vein to improvise stuttertrying to traverse oiling the sun's axis for people know no servitude pure or quasi metaphor people are il miglior fabro in the hammering gait aiming the impossible in view of the nonviable in the crux of the incredible oiled hammergait and the sunaxis but the wire that wire bladewire painpained like a demented plangent wire hammering its widowed dischord in blazing brasses of howling hunger 'rounded by flowers 'rounded by flowers 'rounded by flooowers for I myself cant guide check this book this object of consumption this undergodunderthedevilsmercybook which I arrange and disarrange which I unite and disunite voyages of a vagamonde in the vagaries of vague moons god shall guide the devil shall guide you then for I can't don't dare or care don't trick nor touch or trade but only for my change my pennies my pains my rings my fingers my minuses my nadas in the antennas in the galenas in these nests in these rests as we'll verify in the verbenas in the sugary açucenas or minor circumstances I know all this don't count all this disappoints I'm not sure but listen how it sings value how it tells savor how it dances and don't propose that I guide

Haroldo de Campos

don't pose dispose that I guide unguided that I pray for promise that I trust you leave me forget me let me go untie me so that at the end I stand erect at the end I revert at the end I concert and for the end I reserve myself as it will be seen that I am correct it will be seen that there is a way it will be seen that it's been done and that through wrongs I made it right that from a scent I made a cent and if I do not guide I do not lament for the master who taught me does not teach any longer baggage of mirrormoon in the mirage of the second that through inversion I was dexterous being inverted by the sinistrous I do not guide because I do not guide because I can not guide and don't ask me for mementos just dwell on this moment and demand my commandment and do not fly just defy do not confide defile for between yes and no I for one prefer the no in the knowing of yes place the no in the ee of me place the no the no will be yours to know
translated from Portuguese by a. s. bessa

circuladô de fulô ao deus ao demodará que deus te guie porque eu não
posso guiá eviva quem já me deu circuladô de fulô e ainda quem falta me
dá soando como um shamisen e feito apenas com um arame tenso um cabo e
uma lata velha num fim de festafeira no pino do sol a pino mas para
outros não existia aquela música não podia porque não podia popular
aquela música se não canta não é popular se não afina não tintina não
tarantina e no entanto puxada na tripa da miséria na tripa tensa da mais
megera miséria física e doendo doendo como um prego na palma da mão um
ferrugem prego cego na palma espalma da mão coração exposto como um nervo
tenso retenso um renegro prego cego durando na palma polpa da mão ao sol
enquanto vendem por magros cruzeiros aquelas cuias onde a boa forma é
magreza fina da matéria mofina forma de fome o barro malcozido no choco
do desgôsto até que os outros vomitem os seus pratos plásticos de bordados
rebordos estilo império para a megera miséria pois isto é popular para
os patronos do povo mas o povo cria mas o povo engenha mas o povo cavila
o povo é o inventalínguas na malícia da maestria no matreiro da maravilha
no visgo do improviso tenteando a travessia azeitava o eixo do sol
pois não tinha serventia metáfora pura ou quase o povo é o melhor artífice
no seu martelo galopado no crivo do impossível no vivo do inviável
no crisol do incrível do seu galope martelado e azeite e eixo do sol
mas aquele fio aquele fio aquele gumefio azucrinado dentredoendo como

um fio demente plangendo seu viúvo desacorde num ruivo brasa de uivo
esfaima circuladô de fulô circuladô de fulô circuladô de fulôôô
porque eu não posso guiá veja este livro material de consumo este aodeus
aodemodarálivro que eu arrumo e desarrumo que eu uno e desuno vagagem
de vagamundo na virada do mundo que deus que demo te guie então porque eu
não posso não ouso não pouso não troço não toco não troco senão nos meus
miúdos nos meus réis nos meus anéis nos meus dez nos meus menos nos meus
nadas nas minhas penas nas antenas nas galenas nessas ninhas mais pequenas
chamadas de ninharias como veremos vergbenas açúcares açucenas ou
circunstâncias somenas tudo isso eu sei não conta tudo isso desaponta não
sei mas ouça como canta louve como conta prove como dança e não peça que
eu te guie não peça despeça que eu te guie desguie que eu te peça promessa
que eu te fie me deixe me esqueça me largue me desamargue que no fim eu
acerto que no fim eu reverto que no fim eu conserto e para o fim me reservo
e se verá que estou certo e se verá que tem jeito e se verá que está feito
que pelo torto fiz direito que quem faz cesto faz cento se não guio
não lamento pois o mestre que me ensinou já não dá ensinamento bagagem de
miramundo na miragem do segundo que pelo avesso fui dextro sendo avesso
pelo sestro não guio porque não guio porque não posso guiá e não me peça
memento mas more no meu momento desmande meu mandamento e não fie desafie
e não confie desfie que pelo sim pelo não para mim perfiro o não
no senão do sim ponha o não no im de mim ponha o não o não será

Haroldo de Campos

passtimes and killtimes / passatempos e matatempos (Jul.–Aug. 1972)

passatempos e matatempos eu mentoscuro pervago por este minuscoleante
instante de minutos instando alguém e instado além para contecontear uma
estória scherezada minha fada quantos fados há em cada nada nuga meada
noves fora fada scherezada scherezada uma estória milnoitescontada
então o miniminino adentrou turlumbando a noitrévia forresta e um drago
dragoneou-lhe a turgimano com setifauces furnávidas e grotantro cavurnoso
meuminino quer-saber o desfio da formesta o desvio da furnesta só dragão
dragoneante sabe a chave da festa e o dragão dorme a sesta entãoquão
meuminino começou sua gesta cirandejo no bosque deu com a bela endormida
belabela me diga uma estória de vida mas a bela endormida de silêncio
endormia e ninguém lhe contava essa estória se havia meuminino disparte
para um reino entrefosco que o rei morto era posto e o rei posto era morto
mas ninguém lhe contava essa estória desvinda meuminino é soposto a uma
prova de fogo devadear pelo bosque forestear pelo rio trás da testa-de-osso
que há no fundo do poço no fundo catafundo catafalco desse poço uma testa-
de-morto meuminino transfunda adeus no calabouço mas a testa não conta
a estória do seu poço se houve ou se não houve se foi moça ou foi moço
um cisne de outravez lhe aparece no sonho e pro cisnepaís o leva num revôo
meuminino pergunta ao cisne pelo conto este canta seu canto de cisne
e cisnencanta-se dona sol no-que-espera sua chuva de ouro deslumbra
meuminino fechada em sua torre dânae princesa súcuba coroada de garoa
me conta esse teu conto pluvial de como o ouro num flúvio de poeira
irrigou teu tesouro mas a de ouro princesa fechou-se auriconfusa
e o menino seguiu no empós de contoconto seguiu de ceca a meca e de
musa a medusa todo de ponto em branco todo de branco em ponto
scherezada minha fada isto não leva a nada princesa-minha-princesa
que estória malencontrada quanto veio quanta volta quanta voluta volada
me busque este verossímil que faz o vero da fala e em fado transforma a
fada este símil sibilino bicho-azougue serpilino machofêmea do destino
e em fala transforma o fado esse bicho malinmaligno vermicego peixepalavra
onde o canto conta o canto onde o porquê não diz como onde o ovo busca
no ovo o seu oval rebrilhoso onde o fogo virou água a água em corpo
gazoso onde o nu desfaz seu nó e a noz se neva de nada uma fada conta um
conto que é seu canto de finada mas ninguém nemnuncaunzinho pode saber
de tal fada seu conto onde começa nesse mesmo onde acaba sua alma não tem

palma sua palma é uma água encantada vai minino meuminino desmaginar essa
maga é um trabalho fatigoso uma pena celerada você cava milhas adentro e
sai no poço onde cava você trabalha trezentos e recolhe um trecentavo troca
diamantes milheiros por um carvão mascavado quem sabe nesse carvão esteja
o pó-diamantário a madre-dos-diamantes morgana do lapidário e o menino
foi e a lenda não conta do seu fadário se voltou ou não voltou se desse ir
não se volta a lenda fechada em copas não-diz desdiz só dá voltas

passtimes and killtimes i wendaway darkling for mindamends through
this minimeandering instant of minutes instancing somebody and
instanced beyond to telltale a scheherazade thistory my fairy how
many fates are there in each nullitywee thread discard nines leaving
nought scheherazade scheherazade a nightstory a thousandtimes
overtold then the sonnyboy soulumbering into this nightdark florest
came and a drago sevensnouted dragoned his swellhand into a fernavid
and cavernish grottohollow my boy wants knowhow to unpick this
threadform how to sideslip this cavern only the dragon all dragoning
knows the key to this festival and now the dragon at his siesta is
asnoozing then when myboy began his ringawinnow round a
rosaromanorum gesta in the bosk he stumbled on the sleepy beauty
bellabella tell me a life thistory but sleppy beauty in the silence
sleepeyed on and nobody told him if there was any forthgoes myboy to
a kingdom interlunar where the dead king was up and the upwas king
is dead but nobody told him the sidedlip thistory myboy is only so
posed now to suffer the firetrial to ford the bosk and florrage through
the river for the headbone that is there in the well's depth in the depth
of pickatomb and catafalque in this well is a caput mortuum myboy
doth to godbye suffer a seachange in the caboose but the head does not
tell the thistory of its well if there was or if there was not if it was a girl
or a boy a swan of anothertime appears to him in a dream and to the
swan country takes him swirling in a bird flock myboy asks the swan
about the thistory he sings his swan song and swanenchants himself
and now is Mrs Sun in the One-Who-Waits and her golden rain
illuminates myboy she is in her danaë tower incubus princess crowned
by a shower tell me your pluvial tale how it was the gold in a torrent of
dust made spawn your treasure but auriconfused the princess of gold
clammed up and for to find the taletale myboy wend on his way from
post to pillar from muse to medusa all dot in white and white in dot

scheherazade my fairy this is all going nowhere princess my princess what a thistory of maze-understanding how many more veins and volutes and volutions find me a verysimil that will make of speech the verity and transform in fate a fairy this sybilline simil of destiny's mercurianimal serpentine malefemale and in speech transforms the fate find me this wickedworking blindworm fishword where the song sings the tale of the song where the why does not tell how where the egg searches in the egg for its retribrilliant ovality where the fire became water the water a body of vapor where the nude unmakes its not and the nut snows itself with nothing a fairy tells a tale that is her deathsong but nobody not even a tiny one can know of this fairy her tale where it begins indeed where it finishes there is no soul to face for to be told it she is all enchanted water go boy my tinyboy to unimagine this fatamorgana is fatiguising a malefelonious sentence you dig miles downunder and come out in the well where you dig you work three hundred for three cent you change diamonds myriads for a crude coal who knows if this coal might be diamondiferous dust the mother-of-diamonds morgana of the charmstones and the boy went and the legend does not tell of his ongoing if he came back or did not if from his going one does not come back the legend pokerface does not say only unsays only keeps going around and around and around

Translated by Norman Potter and Christopher Middleton

nascemorre (1958)

                    se
                    nasce
                    morre nasce
                    morre nasce   morre
                                    renasce remorre renasce
                                             remorre renasce
                                                     remorre
                    re   re
                    desnasce
          desmorre desnasce
desmorredesnasce desmorre
                    nascemorrenasce
                    morrenasce
                    morre
                    se

Haroldo de Campos

Vision of Paradise

profoundblue
agate lines
a lighter blue
ruby   ray   radiant

highlands greening
in opaque ash   leads/shadows

another frieze: lacquer aflame

(cabin's – yellow
bird's breast
a window ogives the
setting sky)

                               rubies
                               lusters of lacquer
                               red lances

this – iris on iris
– would become
paradise

                               (in the cabin
                               futile flames – cubes
                               of ice in
                               whisky – trivia
                               and aura)
the phosphorus eye of dante)   (clouded in liquorous neon light

Translated by K. D. Jackson.

Visão do Paraíso

profoundoazul
listas de ágata
azul mais claro
raia de rubi   radiante

coxilhas esverdeiam
no cinza opaco   chumbos/sombras

outro friso: laca acesa

(da cabina – amarelo
peito-do-pássaro
uma janela ogiva o
pôr-de-céu)

                rubis
                lumes de laca
                lanças vermelhas

disso – íris no íris
– se faria o
paradiso

                (na cabina
                fogos fúteis – cubos
                de gelo no
                uísque – trívia
                & parasselene)

o olho fostóreo de dante)   (se enubla em licorosa luz neon

Braniff: New York – Austin
14 – IV – 78

PART VI

Postscript:
Homages to Haroldo de Campos
(1929–2003)

On the Death of Haroldo de Campos*

Andrés Sánchez Robayna

HAROLDO DE CAMPOS'S voice has just been diluted, extinguished in the midst of interminable news about war on the international plane and shapeless political and social expectations in the Brazilian context. An impossible dilution, an impossible extinction, however, in the example of Haroldo de Campos and the word. Considered by Emir Rodríguez Monegal to be "one of the greatest humanists of the modern age," the Brazilian poet has become a kind of symbol in contemporary literature. Symbol, in the first place, of a concept of culture not as merchandise but literally as inexhaustible knowledge. Symbol in the same way of liberty, of the rigorous intellectual adventure, of permanent creative risk.

The extraordinary work that Haroldo de Campos has developed in the field of poetry, critical essay and translation – an enterprise begun in the 1950s, with the creation of the concrete poetry movement – has given him the highest prestige in the panorama of contemporary literature. He always saw himself as "an ecumenical poet of the Portuguese language," and from *O Auto do Possesso* (1950) to *Crisantempo* (1998), his poetry has been a model of creative coherence and of irrenounceable spiritual exploration. In his criticism, books such as *Metalinguagem* (1967), *A Arte no Horizonte do Provável* (1969) or the more recent *O Arco-Íris Branco* (1977) constitute ineluctable references in present day critical thought. Creation and criticism are joined together, on the other hand, in his work as translator. The role of the authors he has translated (always following a long period of study of the respective languages) is astonishing: Pound, Joyce, Mayakovski, Mallarmé, Dante, Goethe, Provençal poets, Japanese, Hebrew. In 2002 the second and last volume of his translation of the *Iliad* came out. Some time ago his versions of the

---

* First published in *Diario ABC* (Madrid), 20 August 2003

noh theater (1994), Chinese classical poetry (19969), *Ecclesiastes* (1990), and *Genesis* (1993) also appeared. In all of contemporary literature, there is probably no such comparable ecumenical vocation.

With words both meaningful and well chosen Jacques Derrida recently wrote: "In the field of thought, writing, poetry, on the horizon of literature, and above all in the intimacy of language: in all these I know that Haroldo will have had the same access as I, but before me, better than me; that is to say, that he was waiting for me on the other side, where he arrived before me, the first, on the other shore." Haroldo's works deserved words of similar tenor by Roman Jakobson, Max Bense, Umberto Eco, Octavio Paz, among many others. All of them recognized, in effect, the unique breadth of the work of this poet-thinker, whose presence and international influence has done nothing but grow in the past few years.

An inexhaustible work, actually. Today the man of the "niebla de nadas" ("misty cloud of nothings," as he himself translated the beginning verses of *Ecclesiastes*) disappears, but not his words. Today I could not mention other memories. How could I speak in this extreme moment of a person who so honored me with his friendship, as well as his advice and his example, for a quarter of a century? That memory can only die someday with me.

Books by Haroldo de Campos translated into Spanish

Concretismo (Lima, 1978).
De Noigandres (Lima, 1978; 2nd ed., 1983).
Transideraciones (poetry anthology; México, 1987; 2nd ed., 2000).
La Educación de los Cinco Sentidos (Barcelona, 1990).
Finismundo: el Último viaje (Málaga, 1992).
Yugen. Cuaderno Japonés (La Laguna, 1993).
De la Razón Antropofágica (anthology of essays; México, 2000).
Crisantempo (Barcelona, in press).

The work of Haroldo de Campos has merited homages in the Spanish journals *Syntaxis* (1987) and *Espacio / Espaço Escrito* (2003).

Translated by K. D. Jackson.

The Death of a Poet*

Umberto Eco

FOR A WRITER it is never advisable to die during the August holiday period. The papers are concerned with other matters – the heat, crowded highways, forest fires. Still, some attention should have been paid to the death of Haroldo de Campos (in São Paulo, at 74), one of the great poets of our time. I can't claim to have checked every newspaper, but, as far as I know, I can only name Lello Voce, who devoted to the event a long and emotional article in *L'Unità*.

Among the August mishaps is also the fact that I, too, am away from home, where I have Haroldo de Campos's complete works, and so I have to talk about him without being able to quote anything, and also because Campos largely owes his fame to concrete poetry, which is of an eminently visual character and draws not only on the typographical composition, but also on colors. How can you show these things in a brief magazine column? Still, I must say something about this exceptional figure and dearest friend of forty years.

He always lived (whenever he was not traveling around the world) in São Paulo, a city poisoned by smog and crisscrossed by streets suspended among skyscrapers reminiscent of Flash Gordon's megalopolises, not as livable as Rio de Janeiro. But Campos loved it as if it were the world's umbilicus. In São Paulo Haroldo lived to the fullest his Brazil, a country in which the rituals of Candomblé, the memory of *cangaceiros,* and a great and modern literary and artistic translation coexist. In the early 1960s, when I was their guest, Campos and his friends used to meet at a João Sebastian Bar and were working on neo-avant-garde experiments (ten years ahead of the Italian and French poets), while celebrating, following the example of some of their great "modernist" writers such as Mário and Oswald de Andrade, "Brazilian anthropophagy."

---

* First published in the Italian newspaper *L'Expresso*, September 4, 2003.

Albeit by way of the German milieu of Max Bense, who understood Pierce little, they were among the first to revisit the semiotics of this great American philosopher, snubbed in those times even by the US academia, while in the process of being rediscovered in Italy and Germany. At the same time, with the journal *Noigandres*, Haroldo, his brother Augusto and Décio Pignatari were initiating experiments in concrete poetry that set the standard all over the world. Lello Voce in his article laments the fact that Haroldo's works, which have received a huge amount of attention in several countries, are little known in our country, where not a single volume of his poetry in translation is to be found. But for aficionados Haroldo was a master, and he visited Italy, where he had many friends, just as we went to Brazil to be introduced by this group of "ethnic men of the Enlightenment" to the most advanced literary experiences, as well as the mysteries of syncretistic rituals and the discovery of the new primitive painters who were breathing fresh life into the polytheism of that amazing country.

Haroldo was a majestically jovial man, with an infectious laugh, and he was an enthusiast of the word. His fame may have been due in large degree to his avant-garde experiments, but Haroldo had a profound knowledge of several literatures and – while keeping an eye on Joyce – he was a formidable translator of great poets, from Cavalcanti to Goethe, with a keen attention to Chinese poetry (following in the footsteps of that Pound whom he considered to be one of his teachers) and (I am not afraid of saying so) Dante's greatest modern translator. His *6 Cantos do Paraíso* were published in 1976 by the Istituto Italiano di Cultura of São Paulo, but they have had an almost clandestine circulation, at least here in Italy.

Translating Dante is a difficult undertaking because, as Douglas Hofstadter noted in *Le ton beau de marot*, usually translators do not know whether they should recreate archaic terms or go for modernization; they are often brought to a standstill by the difficulties of the endecasyllable and the constraints of rhyme, and, in any case, they fail to capture the deep structure of the Dantean tercet where, if you move just one word from one line to the next, you lose the rhythm of Dante's poetry. Haroldo managed to overcome all these limitations. The Paradiso is without doubt the most difficult of the three canticles, but Campos's cantos from the Paradiso sound medieval and very modern at the same time: he really succeeded in recreating images and sounds of the *Divine Comedy* in his Brazilian Portuguese.

One regrets giving the impression of advertising oneself at the expense of a deceased friend, but those who want to see at least one page of the translation of canto 31, the one about the White Rose, can find it in my book *Dire quasi la stessa cosa*. You do not have to buy it; all you have to do is go to a bookstore and open it to page 297. Even if you cannot speak Portuguese, try to whisper to yourself softly (so as not to arise the bookseller's suspicions) Campos's Dante ("A forma assim de uma cândida rosa..."). Maybe you will understand what I have been trying to say.

Translated by Adria Frizzi.

The Inexhaustible Astonishment of Haroldo de Campos*

Jorge Schwartz

> alguma coisa acontece no meu coração
> que só quando cruza a Ipiranga e a avenida São João
> é que quando cheguei por aqui eu nada entendi
> da dura poesia concreta de tuas esquinas
> (...)
> eu vejo surgir teus poetas de campos e espaços
> tuas oficinas de florestas teus deuses da chuva
> "Sampa" (Caetano Veloso)

MAY HEAVEN REALLY exist and Haroldo de Campos meet there with Joyce, Mallarmé, Dante, Goethe, Mayakovsky, Homer, Leopardi, Bashô, Kurt Schwitters, his permanent interlocutors, or with his old friends Roman Jakobson, Octavio Paz, Severo Sarduy, Néstor Perlongher, Emir Rodríguez Monegal and so many others. The Cyclopian personality of our teacher and friend Haroldo, whom I met at Yale in 1978, leaves a momumental legacy to Brazilian culture. His overwhelming creativity and generosity linked him to the best vanguards in Brazil and, with respect to the literary ones, together with his brother Augusto de Campos and Décio Pignatari (the Noigandres group), he was a founder of concrete poetry (1956). He developed friendships and shared works with plastic artists such as Hélio Oiticia, Alfredo Volpi, Mira Schendel, Tomie Othake, Maria Bonomi; filmmakers such as Júlio Bressane; playwrights such as Gerald Thomas, and with an infinity of collaborators in his translations from Greek, German, Hebrew, Chinese, Arabic, Italian, Japanese, and Russian. He made intense ties with people from the world of music, including Caetano Veloso, who sings his verse "Circuladô." I

---

* First published in Haroldo de Campos, *El ángel izquierdo de la Poesía* (Buenos Aires: Ediciones Eloísa Cartonera, 2003), 63–5.

remember Caetano sitting in the great hall of the Faculty of Philosophy during the defense of the doctoral thesis "Morfologia do Macunaíma" that Haroldo wrote, directed by and dedicated to Antonio Candido, a thesis that he needed to defend in order to dedicate himself to graduate teaching at the Catholic University of São Paulo.

In recent declarations to the press after his death, Candido recognizes that Haroldo de Campos "had the rare capacity to alter the course of Brazilian literature in his time." What is certain is that Haroldo, supported by the theory of the retroactive effect of literature postulated by Eliot, Borges and Jakobson, re-makes the Brazilian literary tradition to impose what today would be called a new canon, free of historicist linearity and of predictable mechanicisms. In this way, he restored the baroque through Gregório de Mattos, enthrones Sousândrade, Pedro Kilkerry, and Oswald de Andrade, among others. As part of his collosal work, his "transcreation" or "transhelenization" of almost one thousand pages of the *Iliad* by Homer has just been published, a bilingual edition in two volumes. He even translated Nahuatl poetry, to come out in Mexico. Among Brazilians, he is without a doubt the poet and critic with the most intense ties with Spanish America; he leaves his *Transblanco*, the translation of *Blanco* by Octavio Paz, with a large critical apparatus and a vast correspondence between them, with Cabrera Infante, with Cortázar and with Severo Sarduy. Years ago, I began a translation with Haroldo of *De donde son los Cantantes*, later joined by Josely Vianna Baptista; the coming publication of this splendid novel will be a true homage to Haroldo and, doubtless, to Severo.

Last year, Haroldo appeared in Rio de Janeiro with Juan Gelman, about whose poetry he had spoken with enthusiasn. He also left his splendid "transcreations" of poems by Huidobro, Sor Juana, César Vallejo and Girondo. In recent times, to my surprise, he spoke with great enthusiasm about Lugones's poetry and the need to re-discover it and, all of a sudden, I realized that among other things Haroldo had planned a conference in October in Montevideo (in the ICUB) on Herrera y Reissig and Cruz e Souza. He always spoke enthusiastically about Girondo and to his great surprise discovered that *En la masmédula*, his favorite book, was from 1954, that is, parallel to the Noigandres group. Doubtless, an encounter of the young concretists with a mature Girondo would have produced unsuspected results. In a recent video, one sees the *Obras Completas* of Girondo (by Losada, organized by Enrique Molina) occupying a place of honor in Haroldo's library. He was always proud of having theorized the "neobaroque" and for having anticipated the concept of "open work of art" in Umberto Eco, a fact recognized by the Italian himself.

Among the innumerable national and international prizes he received, he was very proud of having been the first Brazilian to receive the Fundación Paz prize in Mexico (1999), and that same year he shared the Roger Caillois prize in Paris with Juan José Saer. There is not space enough here to enumerate the official recognitions that he has received in Brazil and that, doubtless, will increase in number over time.

He leaves more than thirty published books, still much unpublished work, and the idea of creating a foundation with his own library and manuscripts as a free, democratic, and cosmopolitan space devoted to research, which has just become a reality. In December 2004 the "Casa das Rosas," one of the noble mansions that survived the verticalization of Avenida Paulista, re-opened with the name "Espaço Haroldo de Campos de Poesia e Literatura" enriched by the 35,000 volumes donated to the City of São Paulo, and thanks to the initiative of his life-long companion and closest collaborator, Carmen Arruda de Campos and his son Ivan.

It will be difficult to go forward in the silence of Haroldo, although his words will remain perpetuated in a monumental legacy.

Translated by K. D. Jackson.

Salutation from the Wise Poet*

Gonzalo Aguilar

A LITTLE MORE than a week ago Haroldo de Campos died (born in São Paulo in 1929), a capital figure in Brazilian literature. At the time of death, he was advancing in his studies of Arabic and ancient Egyptian.

On 17th August past a complete poet died. Because since *Auto do Possesso*, his first book of poetry (1950), to recent months in which he moved his readers with *A Máquina do Mundo Repensada*, Haroldo de Campos never stopped writing or living poetry. It is true that he also practiced literary criticism, translation, wrote a doctoral thesis on *Macunaíma*, by Mário de Andrade, collaborated with popular musicians, rescued from the past Brazilian writers like the brilliant Sousândrade, was a university professor and participated in politics in the Brazilian PT. But everything that he did was done under the sign of poetry. And he was so furious and obstinate in his mission that, with Haroldo, not only did one of the most fascinating personalities of Brazilian poetry of the twentieth century die, but someone who represented a unique kind of writer: the wise poet. He was someone who thought of the whole machine of the universe with the instruments given to him by the materiality of language, and with the knowledge that poetic tradition put at his disposition and that he used with a vanguardist temperament. Jacques Derrida called him "poet-thinker" in an homage in which he asked himself: "this man knows everything, What is the secret he holds?"

Haroldo de Campos practiced concretism together with the other two great poets: his brother Augusto and Décio Pignatari. Created in 1956, this vanguardist movement had the virtue of re-activating ties of poetry with music and with contemporary plastic arts and of investigating spatiality and the specificity of poetic language. In the mid 1960s,

---

* First published in *Cearía.com. Periodismo por internet*, 30 August 2003

Haroldo followed his own path and serialized concrete minimalism in some prose texts that he baptized as *Galaxies*. Ever since then, his writing worked the tensions between narrativity and the poetic instant, following the model of the descent to Hell and epiphanic revelation, but all in the space of the page.

As a translator his predilection was for two tensions: to bring to Portuguese the Cantos of Dante's Paradiso and the Walpurgisnacht of Goethe's *Faust*; he took an interest in Homer's narrativity (his last publication was his translation of the *Iliad*) and the fragmentary language of Biblical texts. During his whole life, Haroldo followed the precepts of Ezra Pound (translate the form, consider translation as a creative act, choose authors from the past for their potential now), but was much more daring than his master, as much for his choices as for his permanent curiosity. In order to understand the central position that he gave to translation, he created a new term: transcreation. Of the Argentines, Haroldo translated Juan Gelman, Juanel e Ortiz and Oliverio Girondo. Perhaps in the passion that the latter two awakened in him, one may cite the fabulous task of his works: to find the passage that unites radicality of form with vital knowledge.

In the field of criticism, Haroldo was one of the most imaginative Latin American theoreticians, forging concepts and, if he was always up to date, he never failed to follow his own, original path. For literary history, he invented the concept of retrospective synchronic reading, whose purpose is to free the historian from inherited values and promote reading constellations from the past in terms of the present, without losing their historicity. He also kept up very active connections with the world of popular music, as his collaborations with Marisa Monte and Caetano Veloso demonstrate. With Haroldo, a whole lineage of Latin American writers begins to be extinguished that, having lived all their adolescence among books, suddenly discovers that that world can be prolonged in the mass media.

As a person, no one who has known him can forget his sacred enthusiasm and his generosity. Julio Cortázar, who was his friend and who visited him often in Brazil, made him into one of the characters in *Un tal Lucas*. And Néstor Perlongher translated various poems, among them the exceptional "Opúsculo Goetheano." In his last days, more than 70 years old, the Brazilian poet translated poems from Nahuatl (adding one more book to the thirty already published). Even in poor health, he never ceased studying, creating polemics, writing: Haroldo died, but the knowledge that he knew how to keep active during his whole lifetime still has much to reveal to us.

Translated by K. D. Jackson.

Galaxy of Thousands of Stars*

Guillermo Cabrera Infante

HAROLDO DE CAMPOS first arrived at my house on Gloucester Road and changed it into Glowster Road: the road kindled and rekindled in its splendor. At first sight he was tall, fat, bearded like some kind of southern Santa Claus. His language was Lusitanian, illustrious, ludibrious. We conversed. Or better, he conversed, with his perfect intoned Spanish, but with a certain accent, a certain Brazilian intonation that made him enchanting, an enchanter.

We spoke about other authors who lived more or less in London and also about another who lived in Barcelona. He said to me: "They don't interest me. A best-seller doesn't mean anything to me, if we're talking about literature. Neither Cervantes nor Joyce nor Machado were best-sellers, but they are literature. On the other hand, narrative literature doesn't interest me. That is something that should be left for the movies. Must I say that we agreed, an agreement that has lasted since? That was in 1968, we met several times after that: in London, in New York, in São Paulo.

On one occasion, Haroldo broke a leg and in a cast it looked as if Santa Claus had forgotten to clean the snow off one of his limbs. Some time later, he lived in Chelsea, the heart of "swinging London," in a house rented by Caetano and Gil with 40 other musicians. Haroldo, in the middle, told anecdotes, read poems, recited verses and all that "dawn patrol" (no one went to bed before three in the morning. How did they know the time? Very simple: Haroldo sang the waltz "Three O'Clock in the Morning", that no one knew) and they slept very late.

Haroldo changed himself into one of those late sleeping beauties and

---

* Text read in homage to Haroldo de Campos at PUC-São Paulo, October 4, 1996. Republished after his death as "Poeta Concebeu 'Galáxia' de Milhares de Estrelas" in *Folha de São Paulo*, August 18, 2003.

his monologue became a song. I never saw him so happy as he was among those boys: they sang, he spoke.

One time, in New York (or was it in Yale, a University for which he seemed to hold the key? New York, Manhattan, the Big Apple, what else?), I saw that Haroldo had gained so much weight without losing any of his joviality that Emir Monegal, his friend, my friend, our friend, was worried about his health. Not with his own, which should have worried him more, because soon afterwards he would die of colon cancer. While Haroldo, like Johnny Walker, continued so carefree.

To prove it, when I went to São Paulo, invited by the *Folha*, Haroldo organized a concert with Caetano and Gil singing their songs, while I read one or two fragments hardly legible but easily forgettable. More than 2,000 persons, almost all young, came to hear Gil and Caetano. Which proves Haroldo's power of invitation.

It's not for nothing that his name is Haroldo, which in Old Norse means "armed power." That is Borges's favorite name, bringing to mind the Saxon king who fought against William the Conqueror – to lose the battle of Hastings. "There, in a convent," I reminded Haroldo, "my daughters Ana and Carola studied." To learn a kind of English that is a mixture of Anglo and Saxon with a lot of French that King William brought with him on disembarking.

Haroldo knows all those languages, but, besides that, he knows language, as he proved in his poems, where not only the word but also the letter is poetry. His translations (of Joyce, Joyce of the "Mallarmé" poetry) allowed him to converse (and convert) with more abstruse authors in abstract verse. On the other hand (or better, side), I don't know any better stimulator of culture inside or outside of Brazil. Only his brother, Augusto, a Paulista gentleman, rises to his heights in South America, which is like saying America, which is like saying a new continent for literature.

Haroldo de Campos conceived of his "Galaxy" with thousands of stars. Now, in my kind of rhyme, I want him to be celebrated as one of them.

Translated by K. D. Jackson.

Usura Blunteth the Needle in the Maid's Hand and Stoppeth the Spinner's Cunning*

A usura embota a agulha nos dedos da donzela/ Tolhe a perícia da fianeira†

Regina Vater

WHEN I THINK of the Campos brothers, the first thing that comes to mind is: generosity. Immense intellectual generosity.

The quantity alone (of high quality) of translations of seminal texts of universal literature that they gave us as gifts, in the exile of our Portuguese language, would be enough to raise a monument in their honor of profound gratitude, in a country so lacking in communication with respect to the quality of information. They did everything possible in our culture to promote a continuous transfusion with the best blood circulating in the veins of world culture.

That, without mentioning the image of respect and admiration with which they projected Brazil in the circles of universal literature. I remember very well what happened to me at the beginning of the 1980s in New York, during the Reagan years, in an enormous protest march against the use of nuclear arms. I was part of a group of people trying to make a video about the event. We had a lot of energy and a funny old black-and-white camera from Downtown Cable Television. Without mentioning that the majority of our group was Latino, which gave us, especially because of that time, a tremendous seal of incompetence. Suddenly, I saw the great American poet Allen Ginsberg and his friend Peter Urloff (I think that was his name). With my impulsiveness and Brazilian spontaneity, I approached them and, following their quick pace, exclaimed: "Ginsberg, Ginsberg, please, would you give us an interview about what's happening here?" Without stopping, he looked us over with a sideways glance, continuing his forward progress in quick

---

* First published in Portuguese in the on-line journal PALAVRARTE, www.palavrarte.com, in the section "Poeta, lembrei de você."

† From "Canto 45" by Ezra Pound, via Haroldo and Augusto de Campos and Décio Pignatari.

steps. Without giving up, I rapidly insisted, almost shouting: "Please, I'm Brazilian and a friend of the Campos brothers from São Paulo." I remember very well that upon hearing "Campos brothers" he and his companion came to a stop and began to speak with me. The rest of that little incident, which was so interesting, can be told another day. By no means was that an isolated incident that happened to me and that I constantly experienced outside of Brazil, where respect and curiosity about the work of the Campos brothers frequently shows up with ardor and vehemence. Such was the case, almost two years ago, of an homage paid to them by some North American intellectuals (among them the notable critic of art and literature, Marjorie Perloff, and the poet, Charles Bernstein) at the Guggenheim Museum in New York, organized by Antonio Sergio Bessa.

As for me, since I am not a literary critic and don't dare to call myself a poet, what could I say about Haroldo and his brother Augusto? What could I communicate besides my enormous gratitude?

– Gratitude for the passport to all the great minds captured thanks to their translations.

– Gratitude for the experience and amazement with the verb, through the woven magic of the precise but delirious structures of their discourse.

– Gratitude for the shining poetry, full of signs, signifiers and inventions, always carrying us towards an ocean of discoveries and new experiences.

– Gratitude for the sensual way in which they invited us to experience our language in their texts, appealing to a main facet of our physical natures.

– Gratitude for all the stories of stories that they remembered for us or brought out of their vast culture and sharp erudition.

– And finally, gratitude for the metaphysical immanence that exudes from their texts in such a dense way, such as comes out of the great classics with which I have come into contact. From Haroldo all this will always remain with me, plus the memory of the rotund, reciting poet with whom I shared some evenings in São Paulo and in New York. Of a simple, gregarious person, good humored, constantly enthusiastic about creative power. Of a passion for ideas that I witnessed one night at a small dinner at John Cage's house, impregnating grand moments with his vibrant speech, paying homage to the composer host.

Taking a longer view, we can make out Haroldo's profile at ever more distant positions: in the music of Caetano (CIRCULADÔ); in the work and correspondence with Hélio Oiticica; in the impact on creative Brazilian minds such as Arnaldo Antunes, Lenora de Barros, Tadeu Jungle, Julinho Bressane, André Vallias, Paulo Miranda, Omar Khouri, to reduce the long list to a minimum of minimums.

But who am I to introduce Haroldo? Haroldo, who has claimed the reverence of such great intelligences as (to cite only a few) Umberto Eco, John Cage, Nicanor Parra, Octavio Paz, etc. Who am I to take on such a task when I think that, really, a person of the stature of Marjorie Perloff (another of his brilliant admirers) could do it much better? What is left for me is to give the personal and emotional testimony of an affectionate admirer, in the hope that some others, who are still worried about their success and the level of inventive intelligence in their poetry, will open up to a greater curiosity about understanding the great contribution that Haroldo has left us. And finally agree that without his existence as a writer and poet, our presence in the universal cultural arena would be much poorer.

Translated by K. D. Jackson.

Haroldo de Campos, a Great Brazilian Poet*

Lello Voce

It was a rather cold night of a now long gone 1988, when I got on a train, which gave me the opportunity to see the sun rising over Lake Geneva. I was going to Geneva because I could not resist the temptation to hear Haroldo de Campos, the great Brazilian poet, the father of concrete poetry and brilliant experimenter of any artistic form having something to do with the word, who had been invited by the cantonal university.

At the end of the lecture, I stepped up to the podium and slipped into his hands one of my first collections of poetry and a note with my address. That is how a friendship that lasted nearly fifteen years was born, almost by accident. A friendship that for me was one of "long fidelity," my personal, very intimate and decisive "long fidelity." And now that Haroldo has passed away, in São Paulo, on the night of August 16, almost as if he were the last meteor of the night of the shooting stars, I have trouble keeping personal grief and literary memories apart.

Born in 1929 in São Paulo, Brazil, Haroldo de Campos had been one of the leaders of the international neo-avant-garde since 1952, when together with his brother Augusto and Décio Pignatari he founded the journal *Noigandres*, definitively opening the season of the neo-avant-gardes, which groups of German, Italian and French poets would soon join. A linear neo-baroque and highly "expressive" poet, and at the same time the leader of concrete poetry, the poetics which turns verse into visual signs inhabiting the space of the eye, the "locomotive of São Paulo," as his friend and teacher Max Bense defined him, was also a semiologist (he was a student of Pierce's) and a fantastic translator of many languages, ancient and modern alike (from Arnaut Daniel to Joyce, from Goethe to Dante, all the way to ancient Chinese poetry and Homer)

---

* First published in the Italian newspaper *L'Unità*, August 30, 2003.

as well as the inventor of the theory of trans-creation. He was also a political polemicist and performer who collaborated with many of the Brazilian musicians, from the Bossa Nova era to our days (I'm thinking of Caetano Veloso, who named a CD after de Campos's "Circuladó de Filó," perhaps remembering the days when Haroldo's and Augusto's voices were the only ones to rise in defense of the man the Brazilian cultural establishment of the time was fond of calling "that faggot Veloso"); from the younger Marisa Monte and Cid Campos, to the poet-musician Arnaldo Antunes, to the guitarist Madan, lending them his texts and often his wonderful, unmistakable voice. And it was first of all thanks to him that the Brazilian culture of those years renewed itself and became what it is today: one of the liveliest, most creative and interesting laboratories in the world.

Haroldo had a particularly close bond with Italy. His, too, was a "long fidelity" which began early on, thanks to the friendship of and association with Ungaretti, who was then teaching at the university of São Paulo. Later it continued through his splendid translations of the *Divine Comedy* and Cavalcanti and was renewed with frequent visits to Italy and especially Venice, to visit the grave of his beloved Pound, and thanks to very close relationships with many of the poets and theorists of the Italian neo-avant-garde (Umberto Eco and Nanni Balestrini above all), as well as with some of the younger representatives of the generation of the fifties and sixties. A love that the official Italian culture certainly did not return, considering that an anthology of his and the *Noigandres* has been languishing in the drawer of some editor of Einaudi [a major Italian publisher] for years. Haroldo talked often about this project, which had been ready to go for a long time, except for the courage of those who should have given him the green light, evidently too busy following the latest fads, the irresistible fascination with mediocrity that always enthralls the functionaries of major Italian publishing houses. What is certain is that, to this day, no translations of Haroldo are available in Italy. Nor of any of the *Noigandres*. The only collection of essays devoted to him was published by the review *Baldus* in 1999. It is, I believe, an unenviable record, not shared by any of the major world cultures, since Haroldo has been translated not only in all the Western languages, but also in Chinese and Japanese.

Indeed, Italian misfortunes aside, his was a career rich in recognition and friendships: when, in 1995, Yale University devoted to him an entire conference (Symphosophia), there were poets from every continent to celebrate him, and among the authors of the introductory lectures for the farewell ceremony at the Catholic University of São Paulo were intellectuals of the caliber of Jacques Derrida. Later the Octavio Paz literary award would come, named after one of his best friends, of whom he was an untiring translator and with whom he co-authored *Transblanco*, a collection of translations and correspondence of which the Paulista author would always remain very fond.

The reasons for such widespread recognition probably lie in his inimitable knack for wedding his avant-garde instincts with a relish for experimentation and making these interact with his love for and assiduous frequentation of all major literary translations, European as well as Eastern ones.

Those who might think that Haroldo de Campos was just a "man of letters" would be wrong, however; rather, to say it in his own words, he was an "ágil atleta da palavra nos trapézios da aventura," and a part of this adventure was political, "committed," in a Brazil which, following the painful experience of the military dictatorship, was taking the first unsteady steps toward democracy. As early as 1962, in a poem entitled "Servidão de Passagem," he takes a clear position and claims for art and poetry a "social" role as well. In K. David Jackson's words, "In a landscape of 'pouca poesia,' Haroldo creates a poem to serve a time of hunger in which the ritual of naming becomes the poet's denunciation of social injustice: 'nomeio a fome.'"

And from then on, Haroldo always, and above all in his most important collection, *Galáxias*, "named the hunger." Some of the most beautiful among his last poems are dedicated to the Sem Terra, the people of Landless movement, because still today, as yesterday, ours is a time of hunger. And therefore, as he was fond of saying, poetic invention must have the courage to "pensar o texto num espaço impensável."

It is precisely this that Haroldo has taught me: to imagine the poetic text in an "unthinkable space": perhaps that is why today it seems unthinkable to me to even imagine the space, the cosmos of poetry, without Haroldo and his flowing white beard, his *Galáxias*. Perhaps that is why today, after his death, I feel so definitively impoverished and it is so easy for me to think that all of literature is impoverished as well, and therefore – ultimately – each of us. And I like to imagine that the authors dearest to him – Arnaut Daniel and his troubadour friends, Dante,

Lello Voce

Cavalcanti, Pound, Joyce, João Cabral de Melo Neto– are welcoming him at the threshold of the great beyond with a friendly slap on the back. And that they are inviting him to write with them a beautiful "renga," a collective poem, that begins with a verse that reads: We welcome in our midst the Amazonian "miglior fabbro" of romance languages.

Translated by Adria Frizzi.

Bibliography

Transcreations

EDEN – UM TRÍPTICO BÍBLICO (São Paulo: Perspectiva, 2004).

ILÍADA DE HOMERO, vol. 1, trans. Haroldo de Campos, intro. and org. Trajano Vieira, (São Paulo: Editora Mandarim, 2002, 2nd ed. São Paulo: Ed.ARX, 2002, 3nd ed. 2002, 4th ed. 2003).

ILÍADA DE HOMERO, vol. 2, org. Trajano Vieira (São Paulo: Ed. ARX, 2002, 2nd. ed. 2003).

OS NOMES E OS NAVIOS, HOMERO, ILÍADA II, trans. and critical essay by Haroldo de Campos; trad. Odorico Mendes, commented by Trajano Vieira, org. Trajano Vieira (Rio de Janeiro: Ed. Sette Letras, 1999).

PEDRA E LUZ NA POESIA DE DANTE, bilingual edition (Rio de Janeiro: Imago,1998).

ESCRITO SOBRE JADE, bilingual edition of 22 classical Chinese poems (Tipografia do Fundo de Ouro Preto, 1996).

HAGOROMO DE ZEAMI, Japanese classical theater, bilingual text, with special participation of Darci Kusano and Elsa Taeko Doi (São Paulo: Ed. Estação Liberdade, 1994).

MÊNIS: A IRA DE AQUILES, Canto I da ILÍADA de HOMERO (with an essay by Trajano Vieira), bilingual text (São Paulo: Ed. Nova Alexandria, 1994).

BERE'SHITH (São Paulo: Perspectiva, 1993, 2nd ed., 2001).

QOHÉLET (ECLESIASTES) O-QUE-SABE (São Paulo: Perspectiva, 1990, 2nd ed., 1991).

TRANSBLANCO, com OCTAVIO PAZ (Rio de Janeiro: Ed. Guanabara 1985; 2nd ; enlarged ed., São Paulo: Ed. Siciliano, 1994).

DANTE: SEIS CANTOS do PARAÍSO (Limited edition (100 deluxe copies, illustrated by João Câmara), Gastão de Holanda, editor, 1976; regular ed., Rio de Janeiro: Fontana/ Istituto Italiano di Cultura, 1978).

MALLARMÉ, with A. de Campos and D. Pignatari (São Paulo: Perspectiva, 1974; in this volume H. de Campos transcreated the COUP DE DÉS, 3rd ed. enlarged, 2002).

POEMAS DE MAIAKÓVSKI, with A. de Campos and B. Schnaiderman (Rio de Janeiro: Ed. Tempo Brasileiro, 1967; numerous reeditions São Paulo: Perspectiva, 5th ed. 1992).

POESIA RUSSA MODERNA, with A. de Campos and B. Schnaiderman (Rio de Janeiro: Ed. Civilização Brasileira, 1968; since 1985, numerous reeditions São Paulo: Ed. Brasiliense; 6th ed., Perspectiva, 2001).

TRADUZIR E TROVAR, with A. de Campos; in this vol. H. de Campos transcreated the

Canzone ("Donna mi priegha..." by G. Cavalcanti and the "Petrose" by Dante (São Paulo: Ed. Papyrus, 1968).

PANAROMA DO FINNEGANS WAKE DE JAMES JOYCE, with A. de Campos (São Paulo: Conselho Estadual de Cultura, 1962; numerous reeditions Perspectiva, 1971; new enlarged ed., 2001).

CANTARES DE EZRA POUND, with A. de Campos and D.Pignatari (Rio de Janeiro: MEC/ Serviço de Documentação – collection directed by Simeão Leal, 1960; enlarged with works by Mário Faustino and J. L. Grunewald, São Paulo: Hucitec/Ed. da Univ. de Brasília, 1983; 2nd. ed.

1985, under the title EZRA POUND: POESIA; Portuguese ed., Lisbon: Ulisséia, 1968, the title ANTOLOGIA POÉTICA DE EZRA POUND.

Theory and Criticism

JUNIJORNADAS DO SENHOR DOM FLOR, coord. Haroldo de Campos, Munira Mutran and Marcelo Tápia (São Paulo: Olavobrás, 2002).

ULÍSSES: A TRAVESIA TEXTUAL, coord. Haroldo de Camos, Munira Mutran and Marcelo Tápia (São Paulo: Olavobrás/ABEL, 2002).

DE LA RAZÓN ANTROPOFÁGICA Y OTROS ENSAYOS, selection, trans. and prologue by Rodolfo Mata (México: Siglo Veintiuno Editores, 2000).

GALAXIA CONCRETA, collection "poesía y poética," org., Gonzalo Aguilar (México: Universidad Iberoamericana, 1999).

O ARCO-ÍRIS BRANCO, essays on literature and culture (Rio de Janeiro: Imago Ed., 1997).

OS SERTÕES DOS CAMPOS – DUAS VEZES EUCLÍDES, with A. de Campos (Rio de Janeiro: Sette Letras Ltda., 1997).

TRÊS (RE)INSCRIÇÕES PARA SEVERO SARDUY (São Paulo: Memorial da América Latina,1995; 2nd. ed., 1999).

SOBRE FINISMUNDO: A ÚLTIMA VIAGEM (Rio de Janeiro: Sette Letras, 1996).

LIVRO DE JÓ, (1st. ed., 1852), critical intro. and ed. by Elói Ottoni (São Paulo: Ed. Giordano/ Edições Loyola, 1993).

O SEQÜESTRO DO BARROCO NA FORMAÇÃO DA LITERATURA BRASILEIRA: O CASO GREGÓRIO DE MATTOS (Salvador: Fundação "Casa de Jorge Amado," 1989).

DEUS E O DIABO NO FAUSTO DE GOETHE (São Paulo: Perspectiva, 1981).

RUPTURA DOS GÊNEROS NA LITERATURA LATINO AMERICANA (São Paulo: Perspectiva, 1977).

IDEOGRAMA, org. and introductory essay (São Paulo: Ed. Cultrix, 1977; 3a. Ed. EDUSP, 1994).

A OPERAÇÃO DO TEXTO (São Paulo: Perspectiva, 1976).

MORFOLOGIA DO MACUNAÍMA (São Paulo: Perspectiva, 1973); Critical intro. to vols. 2 and 7 of the OBRAS COMPLETAS DE OSWALD. DE ANDRADE (Rio de Janeiro: Ed. Civilização Brasileira, 1971 and 1972) (*Poesia Reunida, Miramar,* first printed by Difusão Européia do Livro, continued by Ed. Civilização Brasileira).

GUIMARÃES ROSA EM TRÊS DIMENSÕES, with Pedro Xisto and A. de Campos (São Paulo: Comissão Estadual de Literatura, 1970).

A ARTE NO HORIZONTE DO PROVÁVEL (São Paulo: Perspectiva,1969; 4th ed. 1977).

METALINGUAGEM, essays of criticism and literary theory (Petrópolis: Vozes, 1967; 3a. Ed., São Paulo: Cultrix, 1976); enlarged reedition,

METALINGUAGEM E OUTRAS METAS (São Paulo: Perspectiva, 1992).

SOUSÂNDRADE - POESIA, with A. de Campos (Rio de Janeiro: "Nossos Clássicos" Agir, 1967; 3rd ed., revised and enlarged, 1995).

OSWALD DE ANDRADE, trechos escolhidos (Rio de Janeiro: "Nossos Clássicos," Agir, 1967).

TEORIA DA POESIA CONCRETA, with A. de Campos and D. Pignatari, (São Paulo: Ed. Invenção, 1965; 2nd. ed., Editora Duas Cidades, 1975; 3rd ed. Brasiliense, 1987).

REVISÃO DE SOUSÂNDRADE, with A. de Campos (São Paulo: Ed. Invenção, 1964; 2nd. enlarged ed. Nova Fronteira, 1982, 3rd enlarged edition, Perspectiva, col. SIGNOS, 2002).

Creative Texts

"JOAN BROSSA I LA POESIA CONCRETA," catalog of the exposition Juan Brossa o la revolta poètica, Manuel Guerreiro, org., (Barcelona: Fundació Joan Miró, 2001)

A MÁQUINA DO MUNDO REPENSADA, poem (São Paulo: Ateliê Editorial, 2000).

CRISANTEMPO, poems and transcreations (São Paulo: Perspectiva, 1998). Cover: Project of Carmen de Arruda Campos; carried out by the Publisher.

KONKRÉT VERSEK, trans. into Hungarian by Petöcz András and Pál Ferenc (Budapest: Íbisz, 1997).

GATIMANHAS E FELINURAS, poems about cats, with Guilherme Mansur (Tipografia do Fundo de Ouro Preto, 1994).

YÛGEN, Japanese Notebook, poems translated by Andrés Sánchez Robayna, Tenerife, Ed. da Revista SYNTAXIS, 1993; YUGEN: Cahier Japonais, trans. by Inês Oseki-Dépré (Paris: La Main Courante, 2000). Cover: Tomie Ohtake.

OS MELHORES POEMAS DE HAROLDO CAMPOS (São Paulo: Ed. Global, 1992; 2nd Ed. 1997). AUTO DO POSSESSO – poetry anthology (São Paulo: Clube de Poesia, Novíssimos, No. 3, 1950).

INISMUNDO: A ÚLTIMA VIAGEM (Tipografia do Fundo de Ouro, 1990; reprinted in 1997 by Editora Sette Letras). Trans. into Spanish (A. S. Robayna), to French (I.O. Dépré) and to Italian (*Revista Baldus*, Treviso, 1997).

GALÁXIAS, 1963–76 (São Paulo: Ed. Ex-Libris, 1984, 2nd ed. revised, org. Trajano Vieira, São Paulo, Editora 34, 2004). Complete trans. into French by Inês Oseki-Dépré (Paris: La Main Courante, 1998); Roger Caillois Prize, with Juan José Saer (Paris: Maison de l'Amérique Latine).

A EDUCAÇÃO DOS CINCO SENTIDOS (São Paulo: Ed. Brasiliense, 1985). Trans. into Spanish by Andrés Sánchez Robayna, bilingual ed. (Barcelona: AMBIT Editorials, 1990); cover: Volpi; L'EDUCATION DES CINQ SENS, partial trans. by L.C. Brito Rezende (Editions Plein Chant, 1989).

VISÃO DO PARADISO, Braniff: New York-Austin, 14–IV–78. Trans. into English by K. David Jackson. Limited edition of twenty copies, printed by Pablo Beltrán de Heredia, signed by the author and translator, in Taller de Artes Gráficas de Gonzalo Bedia, Santander, Spain, 23 August 1979.

Bibliography

SIGNANTIA: QUASI COELUM (São Paulo, Perspectiva, 1979).

XADREZ DE ESTRELAS, Percurso textual, 1949/1974 (São Paulo: Perspectiva, 1976). Partially trans. into Spanish in *Transideraciones*, org. Eduardo Milán and Manuel Ulacia (Mexico: Ed. Tucán de Virginia, 1987; 2nd ed., enlarged, Ed. Mexico: Tucán de Virginia / Fundación Octavio Paz, Consejo Nacional para la Cultura y las Artes, 1999). Cover from original edition: Hermelindo Fiaminghi.

SERVIDÃO de PASSAGEM, poema-livro (São Paulo: Ed. NOIGANDRES, 1962). Trans. into English (Edwin Morgan), into Japanese (Seiichi Niikuni and L.C.Vinholes), into Italian (*Revista Baldus*, Treviso, 1997) and into Spanish (Gonzalo Aguilar, unpublished).

NOIGANDRES/journal-book 1 (1952); 2 (1955); 3 (1956 / national exibition of concrete art); 4 (1958), portable-book-exposition, with "Pilot Plan" in Portuguese and English, and vocabulary key (English) for reading Brazilian poems, cover: Fiaminghi; 5 (1962), anthology of previous numbers, with added recent poems, cover: Volpi.

www.ingramcontent.com/pod-product-compliance
Ingram Content Group UK Ltd.
Pitfield, Milton Keynes, MK11 3LW, UK
UKHW041431180426
11947UKWH00007B/387